A CENTURY OF
FOREST RESOURCES EDUCATION
AT PENN STATE

A CENTURY OF
FOREST
RESOURCES
EDUCATION
AT PENN STATE

*Serving Our
Forests, Waters, Wildlife,
and
Wood Industries*

HENRY D. GERHOLD

Published for the
School of Forest Resources

*The Pennsylvania State University Press
University Park, Pennsylvania*

Library of Congress Cataloging-in-Publication Data

Gerhold, Henry D.
A century of forest resources education at Penn State : serving our forests, waters,
wildlife, and wood industries / by Henry D. Gerhold.
p. cm.
Includes bibliographical references and index.
ISBN-13: 987-0-271-02964-9 (cloth : alk. paper)
ISBN-10: 0-271-02964-1 (CLOTH : ALK. PAPER)
1. PENNSYLVANIA STATE UNIVERSITY. SCHOOL OF FOREST RESOURCES—HISTORY.
2. FORESTRY SCHOOLS AND EDUCATION—PENNSYLVANIA—HISTORY.
I. TITLE.

SD254.P42P464 2007
634.9071'174814—dc22
2006023215

CONTENTS

LIST OF TABLES

PREFACE

Soon after Charles H. Strauss became director of the School of Forest Resources in 2002, he harnessed the energies of the faculty to pursue the immediate goals of preparing a strategic plan for the School, planning for a new building, and assembling information for an outside evaluation of our academic programs in 2003. He also organized preparations for the hundredth anniversary celebration of the School in 2007.

The fiftieth anniversary had been marked by the publication of the book *Forestry Education in Pennsylvania* (Clepper 1957), which has been an invaluable source of historical information. The sixtieth and seventy-fifth anniversaries also were commemorated with celebrations and marked by articles in *Pennsylvania Forests* (spring 1967 and July–August 1982). Ninety years of forestry at Penn State were described in 1997 (in the spring and summer issues of *Pennsylvania Forests*), and also in the School's biennial report of 1995–96. Chuck thought a second book covering especially the past five decades would be desirable and feasible. Using information from these and other sources, the book would document progress and offer a means of evaluating what has been accomplished in building the School's reputation.

The School's reputation is based on the opinions of alumni and members of various interest groups, as well as judgments of colleagues at other institutions. They take into account the quality of the faculty and students, curricular contents, scholarly publications, physical resources, and the accomplishments of alumni. Opinions and judgments are of course seldom entirely free of bias, but they should be based mainly on factual information.

So we decided to review briefly the first five decades of our history, to describe the past fifty years of accomplishments by the School's faculty and administrators as objectively as possible, and to add human interest stories about some of our more prominent or interesting alumni and faculty. They were selected partly from our own knowledge and include several who were recognized through awards from the School and some who were nominated by their classmates and other friends in response to a request in our newsletter, *Resources*.

Space limitations make it impossible to give proper credit to the manifold accomplishments of all our alumni and faculty. Our alumnus and historian Henry Clepper once stated, "Indeed, any forester who over a period of years has efficiently managed a forest, who has kept abreast of new techniques in forestry practice, and who has applied those techniques to the best of his knowledge and ability, has made a useful contribution to the advancement of forestry." We realize that the cumulative contributions are most impressive, without being able to know their full extent or the richness of their character. So we express regret to alumni and faculty for omitting many other worthwhile contributions to the professions and society as a whole.

But here's a suggestion. If we have missed one of your favorite alumni or faculty, send us the same type of information used herein and we'll publish it in our newsletter, so that others can learn about that person's accomplishments. Send it to SFR Newsletter, Forest Resources Building, University Park, PA 16802, or email it to ForestResources@psu.edu. We also shall accumulate these submissions for inclusion in the next volume of our history.

This is the chronicle of a fine institution in its first hundred years. The factual account is enlivened by the stories of some of the people who have helped to build the reputation of Penn State's School of Forest Resources.

Henry D. Gerhold
Charles H. Strauss

ACKNOWLEDGMENTS

Four people reviewed the manuscript thoroughly at several stages and offered many valuable suggestions, for which I am most grateful. I particularly thank Russell Hutnik, Rex Melton, and Charles Strauss, who served on the faculty for many years and thus could add their personal insights. Hutnik and Strauss also are alumni, and therefore had recollections of their student days. Strauss's critique was especially thorough and meticulous. A fourth reviewer who offered several good ideas was an anonymous reader appointed by the Pennsylvania State University Press.

Many of the current faculty and staff reviewed various sections and provided information about their activities and alumni they have known, as well as historical recollections. Several helped in locating photographs, both historical and recent ones. Cathy Arney and Ellen Manno were especially helpful in assembling data for certain of the tables. Collectively, they made invaluable contributions to the accuracy and thoroughness of the historical information about the School of Forest Resources.

Alumni and faculty who were asked for biographical information responded enthusiastically and promptly in most cases, though some were very busy even in retirement. Their contributions have added substantially to the interesting stories of the diverse careers that were made possible by a comprehensive forestry education. I appreciate their cooperation, enduring memories, and thoughtfulness. In summary, heartfelt thanks are extended to all who contributed information and photos and who commented on the manuscript at the various stages of development. I, however, take full responsibility for its accuracy.

Finally, I want to express my appreciation to Charles Strauss, director of the School of Forest Resources, for enabling me to take the time to work on the history of the School and its people, many of whom have meant so much to me.

HDG

This book is dedicated to the more than eight thousand graduates of the School of Forest Resources, and especially to those who sacrificed so much in military service to our country.

1

INTRODUCTION

Forestry education in Pennsylvania has a long, proud tradition, having begun earlier than in most other states. In 1876, on the occasion of the founding of the American Forestry Association in Philadelphia, Burnett Landreth of the nursery firm Landreth and Sons read a paper recommending the start of forestry education. "I wish to start the inquiry," he said, "whether in our classification of agricultural instruction the time has not come to teach forestry as a science." He suggested that those landowners who wanted to develop their forests employ an "expert—a class of men in this branch of industry not readily available in this Country." Landreth later became president of the Pennsylvania Forestry Association.

An act of 1876 created the state Board of Agriculture. Its first annual report stated that the two most important subjects to be brought before the board were forestry and fertilizers. U.S. Commissioner of Forestry Dr. B. F. Hough recommended at the commission's first meeting in 1877 that the states promote forestry by establishing instruction in forestry and experiment stations for testing new species and showing best methods.

Joseph T. Rothrock, who has fittingly been called the "Father of Pennsylvania Forestry," delivered the first of his Michaux Forestry Lectures in 1877. Elsewhere, some of the first college lectures about technical forestry were delivered in 1881 at the University of Michigan and in 1894 by Bernhard Fernow in Massachusetts. By 1897 twenty land grant colleges, including Penn State, had introduced the subject of forestry, typically in botany courses.

Between 1878 and 1890 various reports, papers, lectures, and meetings brought forestry and forestry education to the attention of Pennsylvanians. Rothrock pointed out the lack of a means to study forestry in our country when the Pennsylvania Forestry Association was organized in 1886. The first issue of its journal, *Forest Leaves*, argued that forestry should become an important branch of a general collegiate course of study, and the March 1890 issue laid out a suggested curriculum. Efforts to implement a course of instruction in forestry met with some resistance and are described in the biography of J. T. Rothrock that appears in Chapter 2.

Professional forestry education in Pennsylvania began officially in 1903, when the Pennsylvania State Forest Academy was founded at Mont Alto, and was expanded in 1907 when the baccalaureate degree program started at the Pennsylvania State College. The U.S. Forest Service had just been created in 1905. Only three professional forestry curricula had been taught in America before 1903—at Cornell University and the Biltmore School in North Carolina, both initiated in 1898, and at Yale University beginning in 1900. These were soon followed by the Forest Academy at Mont Alto and forestry programs at the University of Maine, the University of Michigan, Michigan State College, and the University of Minnesota. By 1907 there were thirteen forestry education programs in existence in eleven states.

When Penn State's Department of Forestry was founded in 1907, what was the campus like in the small rural village of State College? There were few streets and no main highways (see Figs. 1 and 2), but a train did come to the end of the line at a railway station on the campus. Cars were a novelty among the still popular horse-drawn carriages and wagons. The Farmers' High School had been founded just five years earlier, and in 1861 became the Pennsylvania State College, the first American institution to confer baccalaureate degrees in agriculture. Old Botany, the second-oldest building now on campus, was built in 1887. The Nittany Lion, "the fiercest beast of them all," became Penn State's mascot in 1904. Edwin Erle Sparks was the new president of Pennsylvania State College in 1907, and he saw enrollment grow to more than three thousand during his thirteen-year tenure. A view from the original Forestry Building took in the Carnegie Building, the Armory, Schwab Auditorium, and an earlier Old Main. In 1929 Old Main was demolished and replaced by the current structure at the same location, and two years later the Nittany Lion Inn opened for business during the Great Depression. Near the Forestry Building was an orchard, a tree nursery, and a sawmill; Mt. Nittany was visible in the distance. All in all, the scene was rather tranquil compared to the hustle and bustle of today's campus.

In 1929 the Forest Academy at Mont Alto, which had been renamed the Pennsylvania State Forest School in 1920, became part of the Pennsylvania State College. Thus their histories are entwined. Mont Alto students

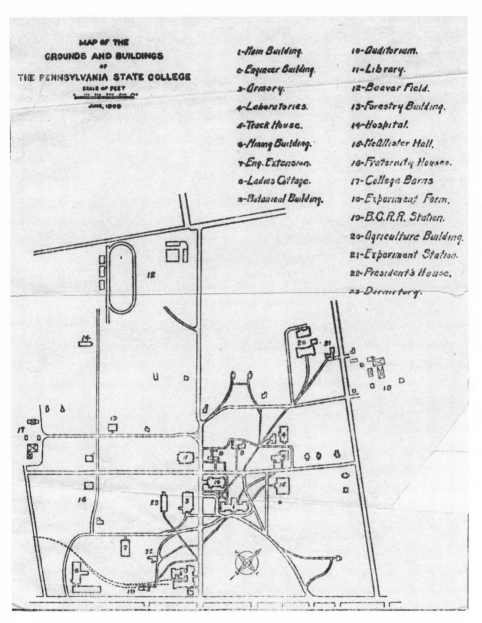

MAP OF THE
GROUNDS AND BUILDINGS
OF
THE PENNSYLVANIA STATE COLLEGE
SCALE OF FEET
JUNE, 1908

1-Main Building.
2-Engineer Building.
3-Armory.
4-Laboratories.
5-Track House.
6-Mining Building.
7-Eng. Extension.
8-Ladies Cottage.
9-Botanical Building.
10-Auditorium.
11-Library.
12-Beaver Field.
13-Forestry Building.
14-Hospital.
15-McAllister Hall.
16-Fraternity Houses.
17-College Barns
18-Experiment Farm.
19-B.C.R.R. Station.
20-Agriculture Building.
21-Experiment Station.
22-President's House.
23-Dormitory.

FIG. 1   1908 map of the Pennsylvania State College campus. The forestry building is number 13, to the left of map center and west of Main Building, number 1. Penn State University Archives, Pennsylvania State University Libraries.

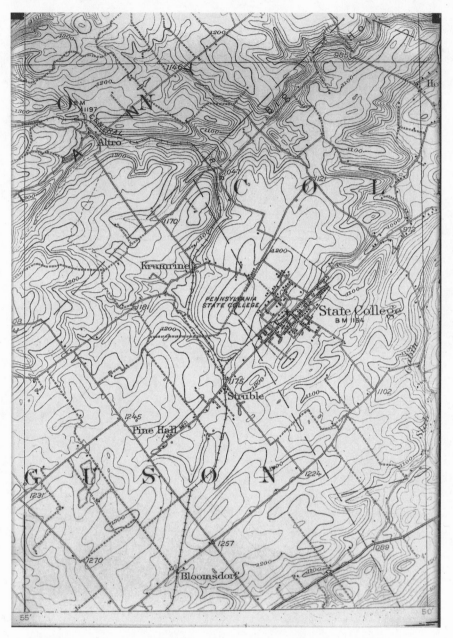

FIG. 2 Topographic map of State College and vicinity prior to 1920 showing buildings in town and on campus, railroad tracks, and absence of any main highways. School of Forest Resources negative #468, Penn State University Archives, Pennsylvania State University Libraries.

FIG. 3   View from "Fergie's Woodshed" of Old Main, Carnegie Library to the
left and Armory to the right. School of Forest Resources negative #190, Penn
State University Archives, Pennsylvania State University Libraries.

FIG. 4   Well-dressed forestry students at sawmill on campus, with Old Main in
the background. School of Forest Resources negative #827, Penn State University
Archives, Pennsylvania State University Libraries.

were adamantly opposed to the merger and in protest hanged two state officials in effigy. Many disgruntled students followed former professor Julius V. Hofmann to North Carolina State College, and a few transferred to other institutions. Over the years the hard feelings mellowed, and subsequent students who started as freshmen at Mont Alto and then completed their degree at State College/University Park feel a strong bond of loyalty to both campuses. Now together in the university, WE ARE PENN STATE!

More than 8,300 students will have received degrees from Penn State's School of Forest Resources in its first hundred years. Very few of the professional exploits of these graduates in forestry, wildlife, and wood products have been documented, and those only by scattered articles. Their cumulative effect on their professions and on our natural resources can never be known, though we have heard many of their stories. If you are one of our alumni, these biographies should be especially meaningful, add to your appreciation, and keep you "Penn State proud."

So, as the hundredth anniversary of the School of Forest Resources in 2007 approaches, it is timely to update *Forestry Education in Pennsylvania* (1957), the book that Henry Clepper edited for the fiftieth anniversary. Besides reviewing progress in the School's academic programs and facilities, we'll take a look at the accomplishments of some of our more interesting and prominent graduates and faculty. These took place at a time when dramatic changes were occurring in the United States. In the twentieth century, life expectancy climbed from forty-seven to seventy-seven years, agricultural workers fell from 35 to 2.5 percent of the workforce, and ownership of autos exploded from 1 percent to 91 percent of the population. Forestry also experienced revolutionary changes that are interrelated with our history. The very meaning of the word "forestry," which was very broad when the profession started in our country, has been amplified to "forest resources," to indicate the inclusion of wood products, water, wildlife, and other benefits associated with forests.

WHAT FOSTERED FORESTRY EDUCATION?

What exactly was it that sparked the interest in forestry education in Pennsylvania? In colonial times people undoubtedly had ambivalent feelings about forests—seemingly endless trees that presented obstacles yet were also utilitarian, beautiful, and inspirational. The European colonists were confronted nearly everywhere with vast forests that harbored wild animals and "savages," as they struggled to clear trees for agriculture. But these same forests provided fuel, timber for buildings and all sorts of wooden implements, pure water, and certain kinds of food and clothing derived from trees and wild game. These forest resources appeared to be inexhaustible. So there was no obvious reason to be concerned about protecting or managing forests until well into the nineteenth century, and therefore no need for educating professional foresters. To be sure, as early as 1681 William Penn advocated the planting of trees and the preservation of woodlands. But Penn's admonition was not widely heeded beyond Philadelphia. His desire and plans for trees in his "Greene Countrie Towne" did foreshadow the advent of forest stewardship, urban forestry, and open-space planning three centuries later.

During the 1800s and early 1900s timber barons cut over nearly all of Pennsylvania's forests, joined in this pursuit by the charcoal industry, which fueled iron making. The devastating effects of the chestnut blight, after it was discovered in 1904, were just beginning to be recognized when forestry education started. From 1900 to 1932 annual lumber production declined sharply, from 2,200 million board feet to 73 million board feet. Wildfires followed in the wake of logging, clogging waterways with sediment and ashes. Agricultural historian S. W. Fletcher wrote, "There is no more shocking example of greed and utter disregard of public welfare than the ruthless devastation of the forests of Pennsylvania by the lumber companies between 1840 and 1900" (1955, 11). And yet the lumber was needed by our rapidly expanding young nation.

On the national scene, forestry was in its infancy a century ago, as it was in Pennsylvania. In 1905 a group of people from all over the country gathered in Washington, D.C., for the first American Forest Congress, which led to the creation of the U.S. Forest Service. President Theodore Roosevelt addressed the first congress about daunting challenges that were not obvious to everyone. Roosevelt spoke of forests in trouble, of timber profiteers whose only idea was "to skin the country and go somewhere else." He spoke of a possible timber famine, but he also spoke of hope. He challenged the delegates to figure out how they could continue using the nation's resources without destroying them. The delegates in 1905 set the stage for generations of Americans from all walks of life to practice conservation, both in their professional careers and in their personal habits.

Within the past hundred years the forests of Pennsylvania have regenerated and matured remarkably well. In 2002 they contained approximately 86 billion board feet of lumber. The state had a $15 billion forest products industry that employed about one hundred thousand workers. The state's 17 million acres of restored forests now also protect watersheds, provide habitat for diverse flora and fauna, and offer recreational opportunities that are vital to the tourism industry. What happened to bring about this recovery?

A pronounced change in public attitudes toward forests became evident during the late 1800s and early 1900s, as people began to realize the destructive impact of widespread logging and its aftereffects. Logging in the United States peaked about 1906 at 46 billion board feet. By then half of the nation's original forest cover had been removed, and practically all of Pennsylvania's forests had been cut over at least once. The reaction against the extensive logging, followed by wildfires and soil erosion, resulted in the urgent realization that forests and watersheds ought to be protected and managed. But this awakening to the need for conservation did not arise spontaneously. Pioneers in forestry education had to convince the people, and also public officials, that a forestry crisis required prompt attention and action. There were hardly any trained forestry professionals at that time, so a means of educating them also was needed.

During the transition from deforestation to reforestation, forestry education was born in the Commonwealth and contributed to the recovery of forests in many ways.

HOW HAS FORESTRY EDUCATION INFLUENCED THE RELATED PROFESSIONS?

To comprehend how forestry education at Penn State has influenced the professions related to forestry and uses of the forest, in the state and in the nation, one must first understand the components and delivery of educational programs by the School of Forest Resources, and then examine accomplishments of alumni and faculty. This is the story that follows. But a thorough, quantitative evaluation of Penn State's role is beyond the scope of this book. Nor could an evaluation be unbiased unless it were to be done by a panel of impartial experts.

So our story is more limited in its purpose. To place in perspective the history of Penn State's School of Forest Resources, the events that led to its founding are described first. Several pioneering men and one woman deserve the most credit for this feat, and through their biographies we see how forestry education was started in the Commonwealth. Next, the principal developments of the subsequent years are reviewed through the biographies of the School's directors, followed by an account of the ensuing expansion in administrative organization, faculty, facilities, curricula, graduates, research, and outreach during the past five decades. Each of these topics is covered separately, to show how they developed over time. Fascinating little-known anecdotes, such as students hanging officials in effigy, an interloping bear in a classroom, administrative struggles, and the tale of the original Nittany Lion, are interwoven with descriptive factual data. Then come biographical sketches of several exemplary graduates and faculty that offer insights into what their experience at Penn State meant to them, and the ways in which they have contributed to their professions.

The final chapters review the story of Penn State's School of Forest Resources and sum up what it has meant to forestry and related professions, and to the people and agencies that take an interest in our forests. Plans for the future are outlined briefly. The educational, research, and outreach activities of the School are summarized and synthesized with the accomplishments of alumni and faculty, pointing to significant contributions to forestry. Readers can use this information to learn about the School of Forest Resources, or simply to reminisce about the past, understand what is going on currently, and imagine what may happen in the future.

2

PENNSYLVANIA'S PIONEERS IN
FORESTRY EDUCATION

Joseph T. Rothrock and Gifford Pinchot were the best known and most influential of the pioneers who promoted conservation and forestry education in Pennsylvania. Others involved in the movement and important to forestry at Penn State included Mira Lloyd Dock, a respected friend and fellow forestry commissioner of Rothrock; George H. Wirt, Edwin A. Ziegler, and Joseph S. Illick, directors and instructors at the Mont Alto Academy; Bernhard E. Fernow, the first federal forestry employee and the first forestry professor at Penn State; and the first two directors of the Forestry Department at Penn State, Hugh P. Baker and John A. Ferguson.

The roles of these pioneers followed a natural progression in founding and developing forestry education in Pennsylvania. Rothrock and Dock stirred up the citizenry about conservation, marshaled the political support and financial resources for forestry education, and even taught in the Academy they started at Mont Alto. Wirt and Ziegler, as directors and instructors, developed the practical curriculum of the Academy and supervised students, faculty, and facilities. Illick taught a variety of courses, filled in briefly as director, and wrote many publications. Baker and Ferguson built the professional forestry curriculum at Penn State, after Fernow had gotten it started. Governor Pinchot set into motion the amalgamation of the two programs, and Ferguson resolved the academic difficulties that arose from the merger, despite lingering animosities. Ferguson then nurtured the faculty and students as the program grew in size and stature through some challenging times.

Their personal stories are the first of many that are included in this book. They are arranged here in the sequence in which these pioneers influenced forestry education at Mont Alto and Penn State. Much of the information was drawn from Henry Clepper's book (1957), the history of the Academy at Mont Alto by Elizabeth Thomas (1985), and the Rothrock biography by Eleanor Maass (2003). These books contain many more details about the early years, which are summarized briefly through the contributions of the pioneers. We then proceed to a more thorough account of the second fifty years of forestry education at Penn State.

Joseph Trimble "JTR" Rothrock (1839–1922)

Renowned as the "Father of Pennsylvania Forestry," Rothrock studied botany under Professor Asa Gray at Harvard and earned the M.D. degree at the University of Pennsylvania. This multifaceted man was amazing! His studies were interspersed by fighting in the Civil War and recovering from his wounds, collecting natural history specimens in British Columbia and Alaska on a sixteen-hundred-mile trek, and later serving as a scientific explorer with the military in the West. There he discovered and named several plant species; his four-hundred-page report on 637 plant genera and fifty new species was a definitive work on the flora of the Southwest.

JTR practiced medicine for a time and then vacillated between careers in botany and medicine before engaging in his forestry exploits. He taught botany at the Pennsylvania Agricultural College in State College from 1868 to 1870. William A. Buckhout became his assistant and later a distinguished professor who gave the first forestry lectures at Penn State in 1889. JTR presented Michaux Forestry Lectures at the University of Pennsylvania from 1877 to 1894, supported by a bequest from the son and collaborator of the famous plant explorer André Michaux. Rothrock's lectures were known as "the forestry agitation," and he illustrated them by lantern slides showing extensive forest devastation.

He also traveled throughout Pennsylvania by horse and buggy to enlighten the populace about the need for forest conservation. Rothrock preached about what the forests meant to him personally—physical health, peace of mind, hunting and fishing, pure drinking water and flood control, cleansing the air near cities, and especially forests for timber, managed sustainably. His good friend Mira Lloyd Dock, a proponent of the City Beautiful movement, assisted him in promoting and implementing conservation measures and forestry education.

Rothrock was instrumental in organizing the Pennsylvania Forestry Association in 1886 and was elected its first president. At the first meeting he called attention "to the schools of forestry in foreign countries as contrasted with the lack of any means for the study of forestry in our country."

As Pennsylvania's first forest commissioner from 1893 to 1904, Rothrock created the Pennsylvania State Forest System and personally inspected many cutover lands for acquisition as Forest Reservations. More

FIG. 5   Joseph Trimble Rothrock, a romantic pose on Monaghan Rocks in South
Mountain Reserve in 1907. School of Forest Resources negative.

than a million acres were purchased between 1898 and 1927 at an average
cost of $2.29 per acre. He set in motion the training of foresters for state
service, the establishment of tree nurseries for reforestation, and the formation of a system of facilities and people to detect and extinguish forest
fires. The administrative burdens were exhausting, so he often took to the
woods to recuperate. Though a dedicated conservationist, Rothrock stated
in a 1901–2 report to the Department of Forestry, "The popular idea of
forestry is that no trees are to be cut. This is a delusion! Forestry has been
said to begin with the axe."

Rothrock recognized that trained foresters were needed to manage the

Forest Reservations and that an educational program in Pennsylvania was essential for this purpose. In 1896 he proposed a forestry program to the Pennsylvania State College but was told by the School of Agriculture dean, Henry Armsby, that forestry was just a passing fad that would disappear as quickly as it arose. Rothrock's overture to the University of Pennsylvania also was not successful. A scheme to obtain land for a forestry school at Eagles Mere never materialized, either.

In June 1900 the State Board of Agriculture approved a resolution requesting "the State Legislature to make a sufficient appropriation for the erection and maintenance at The Pennsylvania State College of a suitable building for the teaching of the different branches of agriculture, including dairying and forestry." Six months later Henry Armsby contacted Rothrock "to consult with you as to what would be necessary in the way of equipment and maintenance for a reasonable beginning of a School of Forestry at State College." Rothrock immediately replied, "I am glad to learn that State College at last has forestry on its mind. Four years ago it might have safely started this school of forestry without having had any opposition from other colleges. . . . I must nevertheless warn you in advance that you must count on this opposition [he was referring to Cornell, Biltmore, and Yale]. Nevertheless I believe that the State College should teach forestry to its pupils, and that it has certain advantages which other institutions do not have." Initially nothing came of this overture, though Armsby in 1902 did submit a resolution approved by the State Board of Agriculture requesting $25,000 from the legislature for instruction in forestry.

So, in 1901, disillusioned and frustrated by the lack of progress at State College, Rothrock requested funds from the legislature for a practical-training forestry school at Mont Alto, writing, "Clearly then, our first duty is to obtain competent, trained men, to direct and do our forestry work." State Forester George H. Wirt worked closely with Rothrock to get the school started, even before the legislature had approved it.

The Pennsylvania State Forest Academy was founded at Mont Alto in 1903 when the legislature finally appropriated funds. The enabling act called for "practical instruction in Forestry, to prepare forest wardens for the proper care of the State Forestry Reservation lands." At that time there were only about twenty U.S. citizens with forestry training, two of whom had obtained it in Europe. The name academy was carefully chosen to indicate a professional school, taking as models the medical and military academies and the Tharandt Forest Academy in Germany. JTR stated,

"Exactly the same high principles of truthfulness, honor and honesty which exist at West Point and Annapolis should be developed in those who are to care for the forestry interests of this Commonwealth."

Rothrock wrote in 1906 that he had become disillusioned with his initial view that "the logical place for a course of professional forestry was in the School of Agriculture at the State College," so "we reluctantly opened the Forest Academy at Mont Alto." He maintained his interest in the Academy for many years, and often lectured to the students. After his death his grandson, Joseph Trimble Rothrock II, graduated in 1926 from the Academy, which had been renamed the Pennsylvania State Forest School. He became engaged in landscape and nursery work.

In 1914, at eighty, Rothrock resigned from the State Forestry Commission because of ill health. He had laid the foundation of Pennsylvania state forestry and built it well. Rothrock was well respected by other founders of the American conservation movement, by Gifford Pinchot and other Pennsylvania governors, and by newspaper editors and many others interested in forestry. Memorials in various places honor him, and a state forest was named for him. Eleanor Maass (2003) has portrayed the life and personality of this remarkable man in a carefully researched book.

In 1924 Gifford Pinchot, at the dedication of a memorial plaque at McVeytown, spoke these words in a tribute to Rothrock: "As a forester Dr. Rothrock performed a task among the most difficult and ungrateful which any man can undertake, a task that of all his great services to the State he loved was perhaps the first and most enduring. Year in and year out, in season and out of season, Dr. Rothrock, at the cost of grinding labor to himself, carried to the people of Pennsylvania the message of forest destruction and of the need for a rebirth of the forests of this Commonwealth.

"In the face of public indifference, in the face of ridicule, of open opposition and secret distraction, he carried to every part of the Commonwealth the story which at last brought the people of Pennsylvania squarely behind his program of forest protection and rehabilitation. The task at which he worked was as long as it was difficult. When he began, public opinion in favor of the forest was practically negligible. Here and there an enlightened mind had grasped the significance of the problem, but for the most part public sentiment was wholly without appreciation of the conditions which he knew and the timber famine which he foresaw.

"With such unselfish labor as few men have given to any similar task, Dr. Rothrock earned the title of Father of Forestry in Pennsylvania. However numerous his other services, however great the admiration of those of us who knew him for his brilliant mind and his supremely unselfish character, this will be his enduring title to fame. For generations and generations the benefits which he has conferred upon his State will be reaped and the people will never forget that it was Dr. Joseph Trimble Rothrock who was the Father of Forestry in Pennsylvania." ·

Mira Lloyd Dock (1853–1945)

In an era when most women stayed home to rear their children, Miss Dock was promoting her message of environmental reform through writing, lectures to civic groups enlivened with slides, and advice to politicians and leading conservationists of her day. She has been described as tall with a formidable presence, yet as a person of great warmth, charm, enthusiasm, and sincerity who captivated audiences. She had been educated at schools for women in Harrisburg, Lancaster, and Media, and also enrolled in botany courses at the University of Michigan. Dock took a study-tour of German forests, as German foresters had long enjoyed an enviable reputation in forest management. Through her writings and lectures she developed a large acquaintance with landscape architects, conservationists, and foresters, including Gifford Pinchot.

Mira Dock often filled in for Rothrock on the lecture circuit after 1895. One of her lectures was titled "Forestry at Home and Abroad." An avid photographer, Dock illustrated her lectures with her own glass lantern slides, 4 × 4 inch negatives projected on a wall with a kerosene lantern. Her slides are now in the archives of Penn State's Pattee Library. She presented lectures on botany, forestry, and village improvement to women's clubs and professional organizations throughout Pennsylvania. Mira loved forestry and eagerly shared that love with city dwellers by introducing rural environments, properly tended and idealized, into urban settings.

She also was very active in the Pennsylvania Forestry Association. In *Forest Leaves*, later renamed *Pennsylvania Forests*, she advertised free "lectures on forestry and village improvements, with or without lantern slides." Her diary of a visit to England indicated that she was delighted to see that local improvement organizations had been more effective than government bodies in producing "garden cities."

Dock lobbied tirelessly to restore Pennsylvania's forests to their former glory. She assisted in the establishment of the Mont Alto Forest Academy, where she frequently lectured students on botany and forestry subjects until 1929. She was close to her teaching and her students. On Sundays

FIG. 6   Mira Lloyd Dock, a promoter of forests and gardens. Pennsylvania Historical and Museum Commission, Bureau of Archives and History, Harrisburg, Pennsylvania.

she would invite the forestry students to her home for milk and cookies, and to talk informally about forestry, something she had learned from Sir Dietrich Brandeis in Germany in 1899.

She was the first woman appointed by a governor to any commission in Pennsylvania, a distinction she gained when she took her seat on the Pennsylvania Forestry Commission in 1901. Rothrock and Dock both traveled extensively to acquire properties for Forest Reserves. Inspecting the parcels offered for sale meant traveling by train to the closest town, then renting a horse and buggy to take them to the sites, where they inspected the land on foot. Upon her retirement in 1913, J. T. Rothrock introduced a resolution that stated, in part, "Her voice was always for earnest, wise work. With a woman's instinct she saw the need of measures which escaped notice of other members of the Commission, and with a woman's tact she led to their adoption."

Botanist, environmentalist, crusader, and educator, she worked with Harrisburg civic leaders Vance C. McCormick and J. Horace McFarland. Together they contrived a scheme to transform Pennsylvania's state capital from a dingy, filthy industrial town into a model city. They encouraged the city to develop new sewerage and drainage systems, construct a sanitary dam, pave streets, build Riverfront Park and the river wall along the Susquehanna, and create the Greenbelt, an emerald necklace of parkland around the city. A state historical marker honoring Mira Dock stands in Riverfront Park.

George H. Wirt (1880–1961)

George Wirt was Pennsylvania's first technically trained forester. His interest in forestry had been awakened by Dr. J. T. Rothrock, a fellow native of McVeytown. He graduated from Juniata College and then from the Biltmore Forest School in 1901. Starting as the first state forester in the same year at age twenty-one, he was one of only three employees making up the entire Department of Forestry. Wirt arrived at Mont Alto in 1902 to take charge of the state Forest Reserve there.

Wirt became the first director of the State Forest Academy in 1903. At the time he was described as a small, lithe man of integrity, an earnest upright Christian gentleman. With two assistants he reconditioned buildings, started a tree nursery, and recruited students. He devised the first curriculum "with much prayer and meditation," having studied a U.S government bulletin describing European forestry schools and the forestry curricula of Biltmore, Cornell, and Yale. The year-round course of study

FIG. 7 First class at Mont Alto mounted on horses, which students were required to have in the early years (1903–1920s) of the Pennsylvania State Forest Academy. *Forest Leaves*, February 1904.

FIG. 8 Mont Alto students in 1918 on horseback in front of Wiestling Hall. Copy of photo on display at Penn State Mont Alto.

was two years at first, but soon was lengthened to three years to provide a more liberal education.

Wirt taught practically all of the technical courses in the first year, giving students a balance of practical and theoretical knowledge and practical skills through physical labor. Rothrock gave some lectures and his collaborator Mira Dock taught botany. In the early years students were actually paid to attend the Academy. They were required to wear uniforms, and until 1917 each had to supply his own horse. After graduation they were assigned to warden positions in the state's Forest Reserves, in keeping with an agreement they had signed when they enrolled in the Academy.

By 1910 the Academy was running smoothly and the state needed an administrator to take charge of the 900,000 acres of Forest Reserves and to coordinate the work of 41 foresters, 120 rangers, and their work crews. Wirt was appointed to this position and then became the chief forest fire warden in 1915 under a new law enacted that year. From that beginning he built an organization of about 4,000 wardens, 31,000 trained fire fighters, and spotters in 150 fire towers. His employment continued in the Department of Forestry, which was elevated to the Department of Forests and Waters in 1923, until his retirement in 1946. He also continued to teach at times in the Academy. In 1929 he was a member of the committee that attended to the consolidation of the Academy with Penn State.

Wirt received many honors and commendations for his professional accomplishments in building and protecting the state's forests and for starting the Academy at Mont Alto. He also served as chairman of the Allegheny Section of the Society of American Foresters, and as vice president of the Pennsylvania Forestry Association. Wirt and the second director, Edwin Ziegler, were present in 1957 at the fiftieth anniversary celebration of the School of Forestry at Penn State. A historical marker erected in 2005 at Mont Alto commemorates Wirt and his achievements.

Edwin A. Ziegler (1880–1967)

Edwin Ziegler was the second and last director of the Academy, serving from 1910 to 1929. In 1917–18 he was an artillery officer in the army in World War I. He had graduated from Franklin and Marshall College in 1902 and worked for the U.S. Forest Service until 1908. He had several field assignments, and then transferred to Washington, D.C., to compile all forest measurements made by the U.S. Forest Service. Zeigler co-authored the revised 1910 edition of *The Woodman's Handbook*, the definitive book on the subject, which gave rules and tables for measuring wood and timber.

In spring 1909 Zeigler lectured on forest mensuration at Penn State, and in the fall he transferred to Mont Alto to become professor of forest economics and mensuration. He also taught courses in forest statistics, forest finance, surveying, roads, general economics, and trigonometry.

Former students repeatedly described him as "highly respected" and "extremely fair," even though "he was quite prone to hand out small punishments for infractions of the rules," according to Henry Clepper. Demerits were given for violations of the rules that had been crafted by George Wirt. Violations included insubordination, tardiness, neglect of studies, telling an untruth, profanity, drinking intoxicating liquor, smoking in Wiestling Hall, indecent behavior or language, and abuse of horse. Any student whose demerits exceeded eight per term, twelve per year, or thirty in all was expelled.

Ziegler wanted the school to establish a national reputation for academic excellence. To that end he strengthened the curriculum, sought out well-qualified students, and selected rigorously among applicants, who were required to take two-day qualifying exams at Harrisburg. During his long academic career he published a respectable number of bulletins and articles in national periodicals.

After the merger of the Academy with Penn State, Ziegler returned to the U.S. Forest Service as senior forest economist at the Southern Experiment Station in New Orleans. In 1932 he returned to the Pennsylvania Forest Research Institute at Mont Alto, which had been formed in 1930. It was the first forest research institute inaugurated by a state government agency, offering opportunities for employment by faculty and postgraduate studies by students. After the institute closed in 1937, Ziegler became professor of forest economics and management at the University of Florida's School of Forestry at Gainesville until his retirement in 1951. Newins-Ziegler Hall there honors his memory and that of the school's first director, Harold S. Newins.

Joseph S. Illick (1884–1967)

Illick was one of the early forestry authorities in Pennsylvania. After earning a B.A. from Lafayette College in 1907 and intending to study medicine, he took what he thought would be a temporary appointment as biology instructor at the State Forest Academy at Mont Alto. After three years he decided to remain in the fledgling profession of forestry. He studied at the Biltmore School (B.F. 1911, Forest Engineer 1913) and specialized in forest pathology at the University of Munich. He returned to Mont Alto in 1912 and remained until 1919, advancing to professor of silviculture and serving as acting director during World War I.

His dendrology course was a favorite of the students, enlivened by his enthusiasm and engaging personality. Students even regarded their annual twenty-mile dendrology hike to Gettysburg as an interesting excursion, not an ordeal. A Pennsylvania Dutchman, Illick exhorted the students to show "wim, wigor, and witality." He had a habit of telling an anecdote about each tree, so that students could remember its features more easily. For example, "the blue spruce is feminine in nature. It is beautiful until it is twenty-five years old, then it wanes rapidly."

Pennsylvania Trees was his major work on tree identification, a Department of Forestry bulletin first published in 1914. By the time the plates of *Pennsylvania Trees* wore out in 1927 from a number of reprintings and revisions, forty-five thousand copies had been distributed. He wrote a total of twelve books, ten major bulletins, and more than 150 articles. His other books include *How to Know the Hardwoods, The State Forests of Pennsylvania,* and *Outline of General Forestry.*

Illick served as chief of the Bureau of Silviculture in Pennsylvania's Department of Forestry after leaving Mont Alto in 1919, and was state forester from 1927 to 1931. He then moved to Syracuse, New York, to become professor of forest management and then head of the Department of Forestry for twelve years. In 1945 he became dean of the New York State College of Forestry, retiring in 1951. He helped organize the executives of the nation's twenty-two forestry schools and colleges, and served as the organization's first chairman.

The year after he retired Illick visited Mont Alto and gave an inspirational talk to the freshmen. He referred to Mont Alto as "hallowed ground to me," the place where he began his teaching career, completed the historic *Pennsylvania Trees,* and dedicated himself to his lifelong career in forestry. He pointed out the vital importance in every human career of friendliness, cooperativeness, enthusiasm, and good habits of working hard, finishing tasks, thinking positively, living confidently, and looking ahead.

In an autobiographical article he wrote, "During my whole career in forestry education and administration . . . I have not found a more deeply and enduringly dedicated faculty and student body than at the Pennsylvania State Forest Academy during the formative period of its development.

I will always think of my associations and experiences at the Pennsylvania State Forest Academy among the richest of my whole teaching career. For these precious experiences, enriching memories, and especially the continuing personal friendships of former students and associates, I am deeply and everlastingly grateful. Mont Alto will ever be with me a blessed memory." Apparently he harbored no resentment about having been burned in effigy in 1929 by students protesting the Mont Alto–Penn State merger.

Bernhard E. Fernow (1851–1923)

Fernow was selected in 1906 to be the first professor of forestry at Penn State and taught there during the spring semester of 1907. Born in Prussia, Fernow graduated from the forest academy at Muenden, Germany. He was appointed in 1886 as the first chief of the Division of Forestry in the U.S. Department of Agriculture.

Fernow was dean of the New York State College of Forestry at Cornell University from 1898 to 1903, inaugurating the first professional forestry school in North America almost simultaneously with the start of the Biltmore School in North Carolina. He was a preeminent authority on forestry and gave twenty-five lectures on the subject at Yale in 1904. These he published as *A Brief History of Forestry in Europe, the United States, and Other Countries* in 1907 (subsequent editions in 1911 and 1913). Upon leaving Cornell he relocated to New York City and opened the first consulting forestry practice in the United States.

After teaching for just one semester at Penn State, Fernow left to organize the Faculty of Forestry at the University of Toronto. He had argued with J. T. Rothrock that Mont Alto should not have departed from its role as a ranger school to pursue higher aspirations, and he gave that as one of his reasons for leaving. His part in organizing the first forestry curriculum at Penn State is not entirely clear. Records are sketchy about his relationship with Hugh Baker, who became department head in 1907 and years later questioned the validity of a reference to Fernow as founder of the department.

Hugh P. Baker (1878–1950)

Hugh Baker was a graduate of Michigan State College (1901) and the Yale School of Forestry (1904). He organized and headed the forestry curriculum at Iowa State College from 1904 to 1907.

When Baker became professor of forestry at Penn State in 1907, he organized the new Department of Forestry and headed it until 1912. Botany professor William A. Buckhout, a helpful friend of Baker, had taught the first course in forestry at Penn State in 1889. Probably he had been inspired as a student in the classroom of J. T. Rothrock when he had taught botany there. Upon his arrival Baker found a two-story frame Forestry Building. This second Hemlock Hall (another Hemlock Hall had been built in 1895) had just been completed but was empty. In fact, he had to wait a few days for a desk and chair. It was built of hemlock because hemlock was the cheapest lumber. Later the building was popularly known as the Old Green Shack, the Pea-Green Shack, or Fergie's Woodshed, the last in reference to Baker's popular successor, John A. Ferguson.

The college catalog described the new curriculum in forestry organized by Dr. Baker as follows: "The course in Forestry is planned to give students a thorough and practical training in forestry so that on graduation they may take up professional forestry work. Several hours a week are spent in field work. The students are made thoroughly familiar with the tree, form, bark, leaves, flowers, buds and seeds. Measurements are made of the volume and growth of individual trees and forests as a whole. Forest production is studied. Excursions are made to nearby forest lands to study forest conditions and at the end of the junior year two weeks are spent in camp on some forest tract where a complete plan for the tract is made."

Baker wrote to Fernow in November 1908, "When I came here there were nine men who had more or less worked with you. During the past year this number was increased to thirty-one and this fall we have seventy-four men classified in the four year work in forestry. This, I believe, makes us the largest undergraduate school east of Michigan."

Upon leaving Penn State in 1912 Hugh Baker became the first dean of the New York State College of Forestry at Syracuse until 1920, and returned to serve as dean a second time (1930 to 1933). In 1920 be became executive secretary of the American Pulp and Paper Association. He was hired by the U.S. Chamber of Commerce in 1928 to be manager of the trade association department. After his second term as dean, Baker became president of the Massachusetts State College (1933–47).

John A. "Fergie" Ferguson (1873–1963)

Affectionately called "Fergie" by his students, John A. Ferguson was hired by Hugh Baker as instructor of forestry in 1908 upon graduation with an M.F. degree from Yale. He was briefly employed by the U.S. Forest Service on the Boise National Forest in Idaho. His B.A (1896) and M.A.

(1903) were from Hamilton College. Ferguson took part in the first conference on forestry education, in 1909, to help define what a minimum-standard curriculum in forestry should include. The conference in Washington, D.C., was hosted by Chief Forester Gifford Pinchot and was also attended by J. T. Rothrock and Dean Henry S. Graves of Yale. In 1911 Ferguson left Penn State to found the Department of Forestry at the University of Missouri.

Ferguson returned to Penn State as head of the Department of Forestry and served from 1913 until 1937, when he retired with emeritus status. Under his direction the department expanded to a faculty of fourteen and a student body of more than four hundred. His accomplishments included establishing an acclaimed undergraduate forestry program and a graduate curriculum, acquiring a modern building and a 6,300-acre research forest, and producing hundreds of successful alumni. His quarter-century of leadership far exceeded that of any of the other department heads or school directors.

Ferguson worked under trying difficulties in the Old Green Shack to improve the faculty, facilities, and equipment. Given only a severely limited budget, he economized by hiring new faculty on a temporary, short-term basis and then replacing them at the end of the term, no matter how good they were. He spent a summer installing wallboard for insulation, as the School of Agriculture refused to pay for the work. He purchased books for the library at his own expense at first, before he was finally given permission to use college funds. In 1914 he announced that more than sixty acres had been set aside permanently by the trustees for the gradual development of a forest arboretum, but "permanent" turned out to be only temporary. A century later this aspiration may finally become a reality.

Fergie gained a reputation as an inspiring, dynamic teacher. The students had great admiration for him, with his broad smile, deep philosophy, and sometimes a sprig of heather in his hat. A favorite saying was, "Bite off more than you can chew—and then chew it!" A large number of instructors who developed under Fergie's guidance became professors or deans at other institutions. A new Forestry Building, completed after he retired, was dedicated to him in 1967 at the sixtieth anniversary of the School of Forest Resources as a tribute to his accomplishments. His wife and daughter attended the ceremony.

A member of the class of 1910 wrote in the December 1949 *Journal of Forestry*, "John Arden Ferguson, affectionately known as Fergie by Penn State forestry graduates since 1909, has earned and enjoys an enviable rep-

FIG. 9   Professor John A. Ferguson at his desk in 1925.
School of Forest Resources photo.

utation among foresters as an educator, administrator, and builder of character. Devoting his life to education, he lacks some of the qualifications
which would entitle him to be classed with the dirt foresters, but he rates
high in the esteem of the many dirt and desk foresters who have had the
good fortune to learn their profession under his wise direction during the
nearly three decades he shaped and guided the destiny of forestry training
at the Pennsylvania State College."

This alumnus continued, "The history of forestry instruction at Penn
State is largely the story of aims, objectives, and policies, and of the hard-
won success which he and his associates achieved. Over the years he carried on the affairs of the department in the belief that better facilities,
equipment, and teaching staff would result in raising the quality, proficiency, and ethical standards of its alumni. For many years, he and his

associates carried on under the most trying difficulties—with cramped, substandard quarters, inadequate teaching staff, practically nonexistent equipment, and many other discouraging handicaps. But he aimed high, held tenaciously to the mark, and eventually scored. The Penn State forestry alumni and the forestry profession owe him a great debt of gratitude."

Gifford Pinchot (1865–1946)

Gifford Pinchot played a less direct yet crucial role, compared to the other pioneers of forestry education in Pennsylvania. A Pennsylvanian by birth, he was the first technically educated American forester, having studied in France and Germany. North American degrees conferred on him were the A.B (1889) and A.M. (1901) by Yale University, the Sc.D. (1907) by Michigan Agricultural College, and the LL.D. (1909) by McGill University. He joined the Pennsylvania Forestry Association in 1887, just after it had been founded. His first work in forestry began in 1892 as a forest surveyor at George Vanderbilt's mammoth Biltmore estate in the vicinity of Asheville, North Carolina. He was deeply religious, never drank or smoked, and called himself "a red-hot prohibitionist."

Pinchot became chief of the U.S. Forest Service, serving from 1898 to 1910. It was President Theodore Roosevelt and Pinchot who gave the name "conservation" to the movement for the preservation and wise use of all natural resources. They believed that unless forests were put under scientific management, America would fail to meet its future needs. Under Pinchot, the Forest Service added millions of acres to the national forests. The rank and file of foresters in the Forest Service practically revered the man. In 1909 Pinchot convened a conference of fifteen colleges and universities, including Penn State, to establish a minimum-standard curriculum in forestry.

Pinchot was appointed commissioner of the Division of Forestry in the Pennsylvania Department of Agriculture in 1920. At once he set out to reorganize the Division of Forestry and to instill a new spirit. Subsequently he became the secretary of the Department of Forests and Waters when the division was reorganized.

After being elected governor of Pennsylvania in 1922, Pinchot initiated discussions on a possible merger of the Pennsylvania State Forest School at Mont Alto with the Department of Forestry at Penn State. But the two institutions remained distinct during his tenure. He conferred with Penn State dean of agriculture Ralph L. Watts, Professor John A. Ferguson, and

Edwin A. Zeigler of the Mont Alto School about the proposed merger, but they were unable to reach an agreement. So Pinchot requested that the college confine instruction to farm forestry. Thereupon the college temporarily changed the department's name to Farm Forestry and retained the name while Pinchot was in his first term as governor.

These pioneers in forestry education established a defensible beachhead in academia. But their successors were destined to undertake several more decades of campaigning, facing the same severe challenges that confronted John Ferguson, before forestry education at Penn State would achieve the support and stature that it deserved. University administrators and entrenched agricultural interests first had to be convinced of the importance of forests, forest industries, watersheds, wildlife, and forestry-related recreation, and of their contribution to the economic, employment, and environmental interests of the Commonwealth.

3

ADMINISTRATIVE EVOLUTION OF THE
SCHOOL OF FOREST RESOURCES

Many organizational changes have occurred since the founding of the forestry programs at Mont Alto and State College (Table 1). Until 1929 the
two programs developed separately, in keeping with their different purposes. The aim of the Forest Academy was to train men for the practical
management of state forests. It was the only school in the nation established by a state expressly to train foresters for state service. In contrast,
the objective at Penn State was to prepare students more broadly for professional forestry careers in various types and places of employment.
Therefore the curriculum included both conceptual knowledge and some
practical experience. The Forest Academy at Mont Alto changed its name
to the Pennsylvania State Forest School in 1920 and lengthened the curriculum from three to four years. At Penn State the Department of Forestry was temporarily changed to the Department of Farm Forestry in
1922, to placate Governor Gifford Pinchot after an abortive attempt to
merge the two programs, as already mentioned in the previous chapter.
By then few of the Academy's graduates were needed by the state, as the
Pennsylvania forest system was fully staffed, and questions had been raised
about the propriety of using state funds to support two independent
schools of forestry.

There was little rivalry between the two institutions in the early days,
according to a 1952 report by John A. Ferguson. He had been intimately
acquainted with both schools since 1908. Mont Alto's change from a
three- to a four-year curriculum may have been made partly to facilitate a
possible consolidation. But the faculty and students at Mont Alto were
reluctant to give up their identity and traditions. Furthermore, both institutions recognized that difficulties would have to be overcome in reconcil-
ing entrance requirements and curricula, especially during a period of
transition. Competition intensified after Governor Pinchot presented a
plan for consolidation. Mont Alto director Edwin Ziegler resisted, and

Table 1   Chronology of Changes in Organization and Programs Related to
Forest Resources Education at Penn State

1889	Lecture course started in forestry by Professor of Botany William A. Buckhout
1903	Pennsylvania State Forestry Academy founded at Mont Alto
1907	Department of Forestry established in School of Agriculture, Pennsylvania State College
1920	State Forest Academy's name changed to Pennsylvania State Forest School
1922	Department of Forestry temporarily renamed Department of Farm Forestry
1929	Pennsylvania State Forest School at Mont Alto merged with Department of Forestry in the School of Agriculture
1938	Cooperative Wildlife Research Unit established
1942	Department of Forestry added curriculum in wood utilization
1953	Pennsylvania State College renamed Pennsylvania State University
1954	Department changed to School of Forestry, with Department of Forest Management and Department of Wood Utilization
1961	Forestry major changed to forest science, wood utilization changed to wood science
1963	Associate degree program in forest technology started at Mont Alto Campus
1965	Names changed to School of Forest Resources, Department of Forestry and Wildlife, Department of Wood Science and Technology
1966	School advisory committee established
1970	Associate degree program in wildlife technology started at DuBois Campus
1971	Departments eliminated, replaced by assistant director, administrative assistant, chairs of forest science and wood science majors, and chair of forestry and wildlife extension
1972	Forestry and wildlife extension specialists transferred officially to the School from the College of Agriculture
1972	Five planning groups established in the School of Forest Resources for forest management, forest biology, forest influences, forest products, and wildlife
1978	Executive committee established, including program chairs for majors, assistant director, chairman of graduate studies, and extension coordinator
1981	Ten (later twelve) standing committees established with defined roles
1982	Cooperative Fish and Wildlife Research Unit formed in the School; Cooperative Fisheries Research Unit transferred to the School from the Biology Department, College of Science
1984	Annual report of the School of Forest Resources initiated; became biennial report in 1995–96
1985	Assistant director named for research and graduate studies
1990	Urban and community forestry extension program established
1991	School of Forest Resources strategic plan for 1991–95 completed
1994	Assistant directors named for academic programs and for extension
1996	Natural resources extension strategic plan completed
1998	"Design for the Second Century," strategic plan for 1998–2008 completed
2002	"Gathering Our Forces," strategic plan for 2002–5 completed
2003	Assistant director for outreach established for liaison with the advisory board, alumni group, cooperative extension, and all stakeholders
2005	"The Centennial and Beyond," strategic plan for 2005–8 completed

Penn State's new president, John M. Thomas, took no action, not being conversant with the history of the proposed merger.

In 1929 the state legislature authorized the merger of the two schools, after a decade of consideration and discussion by academic and political principals. Penn State president Ralph Dorn Hetzel appointed an advisory committee, upon the request of Governor Fisher, to proceed with the consolidation. The committee included representatives of the Pennsylvania Department of Forests and Waters, the School of Agriculture, officials and alumni of both forestry programs, and several other people.

Students at Mont Alto angrily condemned the merger. They organized a demonstration attended by more than a thousand people from the vicinity, and hanged and burned in effigy Secretary of Forests and Waters Charles E. Dorworth and State Forester Joseph S. Illick. Mont Alto students were invited to transfer to Penn State with credit for their completed courses, but many felt betrayed and enrolled instead at North Carolina State College in the new School of Forestry established by former Mont Alto professor Julius V. Hofmann. A few transferred to other institutions.

Some Mont Alto graduates harbored resentment for years afterward, and several resorted to political intrigues. President Hetzel tried for at least six years to assuage the feelings of the merger's adversaries and to cope with their threats against state appropriations to the college, as shown by documents in Penn State's archives. In 1931 Miles Horst of the Penn State Alumni Association attended a meeting of Mont Alto alumni and reported, "Some of the alumni felt very bitter . . . some accused the men who helped to make the arrangements . . . as crooked and the transactions as illegal. . . . I sensed that the bitterness expressed was not so much against the College as it was against the past administration of the Forestry Department [i.e., Bureau of Forestry], particularly was the feeling intense against Mr. Illick, Deputy Forester in the Fisher administration. Professor Ferguson seemed to stand in well with the group." In 1935 President Hetzel learned about an attempt by George S. Perry, president of the Mont Alto Alumni Association, to have the legislature restore Mont Alto as the only professional forestry school in Pennsylvania. Perry resorted to political pressure and presented a questionable financial analysis, but did not succeed.

At about the same time, Professor H. H. Chapman of Yale wrote to the secretary of the Pennsylvania Forestry Association. He had learned about an attempt to restore the status quo of the two institutions before they had merged. He was chagrined that Gifford Pinchot had reversed his attitude about the basic principles of education in his endeavor to terminate the teaching of professional forestry at State College. Chapman believed that Pinchot's vacillation was extremely injurious and detrimental, leading to hostility and resentment by students and graduates.

After the dust had settled, men of good will promoted understanding and acceptance of the merger for more than two decades, and they largely succeeded. For example, Mont Alto graduate Henry Clepper, in his 1957 book *Forestry Education in Pennsylvania*, wrote, "aside from the affection and loyalty in the hearts of all alumni to the old Mont Alto school, the maintenance of high standards of professional education in Pennsylvania called for such support and good will by Mont Alto men as would be helpful to the College and welcomed by its officers."

The organization of the Department of Forestry at Penn State was simple at first, when Hugh Baker and John Ferguson were department heads. They handled the administration and presumably had little need for the kind of committee structure or assistants to the director that evolved after the department became a school. One may assume that the department heads consulted with faculty in delegating various duties and assignments, although no pertinent records appear to have survived.

The rather simple administrative relationships began to change after Victor Beede became director. He made several attempts to elevate the status of the Forestry Department. Beede proposed a School of Forestry separate from the School of Agriculture in 1939, and again in 1944, though without success. The Penn State–Mont Alto Alumni Association mounted an effort too, having voted in 1942 for a separate School of Forestry. Clepper described the situation in 1939 this way: "To put it bluntly, certain College administrators failed to perceive the realities of this growing profession. Weaknesses were allowed to exist because forestry had not yet been fully accepted as a viable component of an institution largely oriented to agricultural arts and sciences" (1969, 47–48). The association's recommendation of 1942 was reported to agriculture dean S. W. Fletcher by alumnus I. T. Haig, though he realized that reorganization was not appropriate in a time of war.

In 1945 the alumni arranged and paid for a study of professional forestry education in Pennsylvania, conducted by Samuel S. Spring, dean emeritus of the New York State College of Forestry. University president Hetzel and agriculture dean Lyman Jackson approved of the study. Spring's 1946 report documented that departmental budgets and salaries for forestry were depressed compared to other departments and in relation to teaching loads and enrollments. His recommendations included elevating the department to a School of Forestry and Forest Products, erecting a building for wood utilization, raising salaries, and adding five faculty positions. Henry Clepper requested a conference with President Hetzel to discuss the report, but Hetzel died in February 1948, and no action was taken on the recommendations. In 1949 a bill was introduced mysteriously in the legislature that would separate the Department of Forestry from the School of Agriculture, apparently without involvement of the forestry faculty or the forestry alumni association; the bill did not succeed.

The addition of the wood utilization program in 1942 led to the formation of two departments in 1954, when the department became the School of Forestry upon the recommendation of department head M. K. Goddard. The Department of Forest Management was headed by William C. Bramble, and later by Robert E. McDermott and then Ronald A. Bartoo. Newell A. Norton was named head of the Department of Wood Utilization in 1954, followed by Wayne K. Murphey in 1965, when it was renamed the Department of Wood Science and Technology.

Under the leadership of Peter W. Fletcher, in 1965 the names were changed to the School of Forest Resources, the Department of Forestry and Wildlife, and the Department of Wood Science and Technology. The new names reflected the broader scope of interests and greater emphasis on science and research that Fletcher and McDermott were promoting. The departments were replaced by a realignment of administrative responsibilities in 1971, however, as part of a reorganization under Wilber W. Ward.

It was a stressful time. Dean of agriculture Russell E. Larson had appointed Ward director of the School after ruthlessly deposing Fletcher. Dean Larson never gave his reasons to Fletcher or the faculty. But they believed that Larson did not tolerate Fletcher's open exploration of moving the School to another college so that it could grow more freely than it was permitted to within the College of Agriculture. Despite this insult to himself personally, Peter Fletcher worked constructively with Wib Ward and the faculty to weather the storm. That was the last attempt to separate the School from the college. The relationship since then has improved significantly and fostered mutual respect, as a succession of School directors gradually convinced the college deans of the importance of forest resources and the need for adequate financing. That enhanced the academic stature of the School and brought greater recognition of its contributions to the university in research, teaching, and outreach.

Various new administrative arrangements in the past fifty years resulted from a variety of leadership styles of the directors of the School (Table 2). Furthermore, the faculty became more involved in administration as new majors and degrees were added and as enrollments swelled. First wildlife (in 1981) and then fisheries (in 1988) gained recognition as additions to the School's undergraduate programs in forestry and forest products. Duties that had been assigned somewhat informally to certain faculty, such as course scheduling, handled by Orvel Schmidt and Rex Melton, evolved to more formal arrangements. Various faculty leadership positions were established for instructional programs and research; positions changed from department heads to chairs and assistant or associate directors. The positions culminated in chairs of the forest science, wood products, and wildlife and fisheries science majors and assistant or associate directors for resident instruction/academic programs, research and graduate studies, and outreach/extension. These faculty members have had administrative and advisory responsibilities in assisting the director, though without official recognition at higher levels of the university or commensurate compensation.

Table 2   Years When Department Heads or Directors Served the Department or School

1907–1912	Hugh P. Baker
1913–1937	John A. Ferguson
1937–1952	Victor A. Beede
1952–1955	Maurice K. Goddard
1955–1958	William C. Bramble
1958–1959	H. Norton Cope*
1959–1966	Peter W. Fletcher
1966–1977	Wilber W. Ward
1977	Rex E. Melton*
1977–1987	Robert S. Bond
1988	Henry D. Gerhold*
1988–1993	Alfred D. Sullivan
1993–1994	Kim C. Steiner*
1994–2001	Larry A. Nielsen
2001–2002	Charles H. Strauss*
2002–present	Charles H. Strauss

* Indicates interim director

4

SCHOOL DIRECTORS AND DEPARTMENT HEADS

Three directors presided at the Mont Alto Academy from its founding in 1903 until it became part of Penn State in 1929 (Table 3). Their stories have been told in Clepper's *Forestry Education in Pennsylvania* (1957). Since 1929 there have been nine executive officers of the Mont Alto Campus until the present time (Table 4), the first five of them foresters. After 1970 none of the executive officers at Mont Alto has had a degree in forestry or wildlife, nor have any at the DuBois Campus.

At State College/University Park seven men have provided leadership as department head or director of the School of Forest Resources during the past fifty years, and five during the first fifty (Table 2). Altogether there have been eleven, as William C. Bramble's term spanned the two periods. The longest terms of office were those of John A. Ferguson, twenty-five years, and Victor A. Beede, fourteen years. The others ranged from three to eleven years.

In addition, five interim heads or directors have served temporarily while searches for new directors were under way. Normally interim leaders are not expected to become director, and there has been only one exception. The school faculty and the dean of the College of Agricultural Sciences concluded that Charles Strauss had better qualifications than any of the other candidates who had been interviewed while he was interim director, so he was named director in 2002 after being evaluated through the same process as the other candidates.

Table 3 Directors of the Mont Alto Academy

1903–1910	George H. Wirt
1910–1917	Edwin Allen Ziegler
1917–1919	Joseph S. Illick
1919–1929	Edwin Allen Ziegler

Table 4   Executive Officers of the Penn State Mont
Alto Campus

1929–1942	H. Norton Cope
1943–1946	Campus closed during World War II
1946–1952	Maurice K. Goddard
1953–1959	Wilber W. Ward
1959–1963	Robert W. Lang
1963–1970	Henry H. Chisman
1970–1987	Vernon Shockley
1987–1997	Corrine Caldwell
1997–2001	David Goldenberg
2001–present	David C. Gnage

Biographical sketches of the first two department heads at State College, Hugh Baker (1907–12) and John Ferguson (1913–37) appear in
Chapter 2, with the other pioneers of forestry education. The following
biographies thus begin with that of Victor Beede, followed by that of
M. K. Goddard, confined to his academic career until he became secretary
of the Department of Forests and Waters, and continue sequentially with
the remaining directors. Each had a unique personality, as their former
students and colleagues will remember.

Victor A. "Vic" Beede, Director 1937–1952

Victor Beede had broad experience in forestry before coming to Penn
State. He earned his B.A. at Yale University in 1910 and his M.F. in 1912.
After graduation he worked for the Massachusetts Forestry Association; in
1914 he was appointed assistant state forester of New Hampshire; and in
1916 he became secretary for the New York Forestry Association. Beede
then was employed for twelve years as forester for the Brown Corporation
in Quebec; one of his assignments was to observe forest practices in Scan-
dinavian countries. He worked in Colorado with the U.S. Forest Service
before coming to Penn State in 1931.

Beede was appointed department head when John Ferguson retired in
1937. One of his first tasks was to serve on the committee that drew up
plans for a new forestry building, which later was named Ferguson Building. Other notable developments occurred while Beede was director, besides the new forestry building and attempts to change the department to
a school. A federal camp for transients near Marienville was acquired in
1939 from the U.S. Forest Service for a summer camp and named Blue
Jay Camp. Research was strengthened with several faculty appointments,

by the organization of the College Farm Woodlands in 1939 and the Stone Valley Experimental Forest in 1943, and by the approval of the Master of Forestry degree in 1943. A curriculum in wood utilization was established in 1942, but the program did not get under way until after World War II.

Several challenging problems confronted Beede during his tenure as director. As described earlier, he made several unsuccessful attempts to elevate the status of the Forestry Department, urged on by alumni and friends of the department. During World War II many of the faculty and students entered military service and served our country with distinction, including too many who made the ultimate sacrifice. The depleted ranks in the department swelled suddenly as the veterans returned, and occasionally someone expressed a belligerent attitude that required adjustments by the faculty or staff. Resources had to be found to accommodate the inflated enrollments, which was not an easy task.

At social gatherings of the faculty and students, such as annual dances and forestry banquets, Beede would lead the singing in a rousing rendition of "Allouette," reminiscent of his experiences in Quebec logging camps. He fostered a spirit of camaraderie, and all faculty were expected to participate in departmental events, including spouses at social affairs. Beede retired in 1952 and was succeeded by M. K. Goddard, who continued some of Beede's traditions and added his own.

Maurice K. "M. K.," "Gramps," or "Pop" Goddard, Director 1952–1955

"Maurice K. Goddard was a remarkable man living in a remarkable time," according to his biographer, Ernest Morrison (2000). His influence on education and state agencies has improved the lives of all Pennsylvanians in recent decades. Born in Massachusetts in 1912, Goddard grew up in Pretty Prairie, Kansas.

After graduating from the University of Maine in forestry in 1935, he was appointed instructor at the Mont Alto campus of The Pennsylvania State College. Goddard was reassigned in 1937 to the State College campus to teach silviculture. He was promoted to assistant professor after receiving the M.S. in forest management from the University of California in 1938. Goddard served as faculty advisor to the forestry fraternity Tau Phi Delta, and received a gift of twenty-five silver dollars from the brothers when he entered the U.S. Army in 1942. He dutifully gave twenty-four of them to his wife and carried the other one in his wallet until 1984, when he pulled it out and told the story to the brothers at the fraternity's sixtieth anniversary.

From 1942 to 1946 Goddard served in the U.S. Army, first in South Carolina and then in the Adjutant General's Corps in Massachusetts. He arrived in England at Supreme Headquarters, Allied Expeditionary Force (SHAEF) on the eve of the Normandy invasion. He kept track of personnel records and drafted letters for Generals Dwight Eisenhower, Walter Bedell Smith, and Thomas Jefferson Davis. After the war Goddard told Joe Ibberson, who had been his student at Mont Alto, that he had kept track of him while, as transport commander, Joe took twenty-two shiploads of men across the Atlantic. Goddard liked to keep tabs on most if not all of his former students. After Germany's surrender Goddard was moved to Versailles (he "lost" Ike's dog there one weekend), and later to Frankfurt. He was promoted repeatedly up to the rank of lieutenant colonel and was awarded the Bronze Star and the Legion of Merit.

In 1946 Goddard returned to Mont Alto as resident director. He had a special knack for handling the returning veterans, with his direct manner of speaking in his gruff voice. Once he was called upon to restore harmony at Blue Jay Camp when the camp director was unable to control a bunch of unruly ex-GIs. A favorite saying before fieldtrips on rainy days was, "Your skin doesn't leak—let's go." His weekly convocations with all the students inspired them by his enthusiasm for forestry, and he also instituted these gatherings of the faithful when he became head of the Forestry Department at Penn State.

In 1952 Goddard was named head of the Forestry Department at State College. Milton Eisenhower, brother of Ike, was president of Penn State at that time. By 1954 Goddard had persuaded administrators to change the department's name to the School of Forestry and to form the Departments of Forest Management and Wood Utilization. This took place after The Pennsylvania State College had been elevated to a university, and the School of Agriculture to the College of Agriculture. Goddard maintained good relationships with the Bureau of Forestry and the Pennsylvania Forestry Association, serving the latter on the board of directors and as president.

Goddard was appointed secretary of Pennsylvania's Department of Forests and Waters in 1955, having been recruited to that position without seeking it. He was granted a leave of absence from Penn State and continued a close relationship with the School of Forestry for some months, conferring often with William Bramble, who was helping with administrative matters. But eventually he realized that his full energies would be required in Harrisburg, so he stepped down as director of the School. His subsequent career with the state is described later among the biographical sketches of those who worked in parks and recreation, as the expansion of state parks was one of his principal achievements.

William C. "Bill" Bramble, Director 1955–1958

William C. Bramble earned a B.S. in forestry at Penn State in 1929 and a master's degree (1930) and Ph.D. (1932) at Yale. He was an instructor in the Botany Department at Carleton College in Minnesota from 1932 to 1936 and conducted postdoctoral studies in ecology for a year at Zurich, Switzerland, on a National Research Council fellowship. As a captain in the U.S. Army Air Corps in Africa and the Mediterranean theater from 1942 to 1945, he received seven battle stars and two presidential citations. Bramble was affiliated with Penn State's Department/School of Forestry from 1937 to 1958, first as a research professor and then as director from 1955 to 1958. He helped design Ferguson Building in 1937 and served as an officer of the Forestry Alumni Association in 1946.

Appointed head of forestry research at Penn State in 1945, he pioneered studies of Virginia pine ecology, coal spoils revegetation, Christmas tree production, and most notably right-of-way vegetation management and ecology as affected by herbicides. The research that he and his colleague, W. R. "Dick" Byrnes, conducted for more than fifty years forever changed the way vegetation managers maintain rights-of-way for electric transmission lines. A faculty office in the new Forest Resources Building has been named to commemorate Bramble and Byrnes.

Bramble taught several graduate courses and mentored many graduate students, giving them broad exposure to research topics and experimental methods. He insisted on educating and training his students thoroughly, which undoubtedly contributed to their professional success. They will remember his easygoing, pleasant demeanor and the beagle that he always took along on fieldtrips.

Bramble was recruited to be head of the Department of Forestry and Natural Resources at Purdue University in 1958. From 1962 to 1963 he was a member of President Kennedy's Committee on Forest Policy. He was on the forest policy advisory committee for the Indiana Department of Natural Resources from 1958 to 1963. Bramble was named professor emeritus when he retired from Purdue in 1973.

In 1972 Bramble helped found Environmental Consultants Inc. in

Southampton, Pennsylvania, and was on the board of governors until 1997. After his retirement from Purdue, he continued as a research consultant in forest ecology. He remained active in his research on vegetation management on utility rights-of-way for many years. After a long and very productive life, he died in 2003 at the age of ninety-five.

Dr. Bramble was a fellow and golden member in the Society of American Foresters and served on the SAF council from 1960 to 1966. He received the Outstanding Alumni Award from Penn State's School of Forest Resources in 2001. In the same year he was also awarded the Sigma Xi Certificate of Recognition for seventy years of distinguished service in the honorary research society. In 2003 he and his colleague William R. Byrnes jointly received the L. C. Chadwick Award for Arboriculture Research from the International Society of Arboriculture. Other awards include a Distinguished Service Award from the Pennsylvania Electric Association in 1988 for his ecological research, the Wildlife Conservation Award from the Pennsylvania Game Commission, also in 1988, and the Education Award from the Utility Arborists Association in 1996. He was active in his church, the Elks, and Rotary International.

H. Norton Cope, Interim Director 1958–1959

H. Norton Cope received the B.S. degree in Forestry from Penn State in 1915. He served for two years with the 10th Forestry Engineers Regiment of the U.S. Army in France during World War I. The 10th Regiment supplied huge quantities of wood needed by the troops—timbers, railroad ties, bridge trusses, firewood, and many other wood products. In 1918 there were eighty-one sawmills in operation, producing more than 2 million board feet daily. After returning, Cope was employed by the U.S. Forest Service in the Southwest.

Cope served as director of the Mont Alto branch from 1929 until 1943; then the campus was closed temporarily during World War II. He also taught some of the forestry courses and coached athletic teams. At Mont Alto he had the reputation of being a stern disciplinarian. He expected all students to attend a Sunday church service of their choice and required signed notes indicating their attendance. Students also remembered him for his method of instruction, which was modeled after Socrates: "If you can't answer the kid's question, ask him one." However, students who had difficulties in adjusting to college found him to be understanding and compassionate. He even made special arrangements for Albert Kligman, who had little money, to work for his education (see his biography under "Entrepreneurial Mavericks" in Chapter 14).

Cope transferred to State College in 1943 and continued on the faculty until he retired in 1959. He taught silviculture courses and also courses for forestry transfer students, drawing upon the wealth of knowledge and experience he had acquired over the years. He managed the Stone Valley Experimental Forest until 1955, when Rex Melton took over that responsibility. During 1958 and 1959 Cope was interim director of the School of Forestry. He was active in the Lutheran Church of State College and the Boy Scouts. He was the faculty advisor to the Alpha Phi Omega chapter of the Boy Scouts service fraternity.

Peter W. "Pete" Fletcher, Director 1959–1966

Peter Fletcher received his B.S. degree in forestry at Penn State in 1933, the M.F. degree from Yale University (1934) and the Ph.D. from the University of Missouri (1950). His father, Stevenson W. Fletcher, was dean of the College of Agriculture at Penn State from 1939 to 1946.

Pete held various positions with the U.S. Forest Service from 1934 to 1943 and 1946 to 1948 before applying his talents to forestry education. He served in the U.S. Navy in World War II. In 1948 he was appointed to the forestry faculty of the University of Missouri. His research there and with the Forest Service was concerned with forest soils, hydrology, and silvics.

After eleven years at the University of Missouri, Fletcher became director of the School of Forestry at Penn State in 1959. His tenure was marked by rapid growth in enrollments, modernization of the curriculum, and expansion of research. Professor Robert E. McDermott, his close friend and colleague, was a source of many of the concepts and strategies for implementing these developments. It was a time of stressful adjustment for the faculty, who were expected to increase support through grants for their research projects and still keep up with teaching larger classes and more course sections.

For seven years Pete tried hard to convince college administrators that forestry education was being shortchanged financially. During this period the School produced about one-third of the graduates from the College of Agriculture and carried about one-fourth of the teaching load, but received only about one-sixth of instructional funds and one-twelfth of research funds from state appropriations. Fletcher presented data to the dean of Agriculture showing that $1.00 of every $4.00 derived from farm and forest natural resources came from wood and fiber. By adding the values of water, wildlife, and recreation, Fletcher showed that forests contributed $1.00 of every $3.00. In 1966 the dean of Agriculture abruptly dismissed Fletcher without giving a reason either verbally or in writing, but apparently because he could not tolerate Pete's attempt to gain greater autonomy for the School of Forest Resources.

Pete continued to teach and conduct research as a senior professor of forest recreation. A true gentleman, he never openly complained about his mistreatment by the dean, but instead worked constructively with his successor, Wilber Ward. His "study retreats" to a family cabin along Pine Creek with graduate students and faculty were symbolic of his devotion to teaching and his enthusiasm for research. He maintained an active involvement in regional planning and complex environmental issues tied to growth. At his retirement in 1977 he told the faculty, "I've always been proud to be a forester, and especially a Penn State Forester."

He held many positions of leadership in professional societies and received awards from several honor societies. At a memorial service after his death in 1985, a friend described Peter Fletcher as "a man of nature and a man of God." He recalled also that Pete once said, "God is the Great Organizer, and as man is made in the image of God, so should man be."

Wilber W. "Wib" Ward, Director 1966–1977

Wib Ward's career, most of it at Penn State, can be characterized as scholarly, steadfast, and dependable. Wiry and small in stature (five-foot-six), he lettered in varsity gymnastics and became prominent in academics and leadership. He received his B.S. (1940) and M.F. (1952) degrees from Penn State, and the D.F. degree from Yale in 1962. Before starting as instructor at Mont Alto in 1948, he had been employed by the Pennsylvania Railroad Company, and also had operated a sawmill with his partners. From 1953 to 1959 he served as resident director of the Mont Alto campus. After completing his doctoral studies he returned to teaching and research at University Park, became professor of silviculture in 1965 and then director of the School of Forest Resources from 1966 to 1977. He retired in 1980 with emeritus rank.

Ward's teaching included courses in dendrology, mensuration, botany, farm forestry, and silviculture. He supervised eighteen M.S. students and one doctoral student. Together they extensively researched the silviculture of hardwoods, including site evaluation, regeneration, fertilization, flooding tolerance, and strip mine reclamation. He produced fifty-five publications, including twenty articles in refereed journals such as *Forest Science, Journal of Forestry, Ecology,* and *Botanical Gazette.*

When Ward was abruptly appointed director of the School in 1966, he exerted a calming, stabilizing influence on the faculty, who were greatly upset by the manner in which the dean of Agriculture had relieved Fletcher of his administrative responsibilities. Ward faced difficult circumstances. He was challenged with continuing the School's expanded role in research and coping with the burgeoning enrollments at a time when financial strains within the College of Agriculture made it very difficult to add faculty. Students were attracted by expanded employment opportunities for foresters, at a time when our nation was increasingly concerned about environmental issues. Courses that had typically enrolled thirty to forty students per semester were then exceeding a hundred. Multiple sections were added to certain courses, and larger lecture halls had to be found. Also, a new means of transporting students on fieldtrips became mandatory, as flatbed trucks with canvas tops no longer were considered safe. Ward negotiated solutions for these problems with the dean and found a way to convert temporary instructors to faculty positions gradually. He excelled as a mentor of these young faculty members.

Ward was active in various professional organizations, with leadership responsibilities especially in the Society of American Foresters and the Pennsylvania Forestry Association. He served as chairman of the Northeast Forest Research Advisory Council and was a member of the Governor's Council on Natural Resources. His article "Clearcutting in the Hardwood Forests of the Northeast" was included in a report to the U.S. President's Council on Environmental Quality and in the 1974 book by Horwitz, *Clearcutting: A View from the Top.* His achievements were recognized by the Outstanding Service to Forestry Award of the Society of American Foresters, Allegheny Section (1979); the Forestry Achievement Award of the School of Forest Resources (1982); the Penn State Mont Alto Alumni Centennial Award in 2004; and as fellow of the Society of American Foresters. The silviculture laboratory in the new Forest Resources Building has been named to commemorate Wib Ward.

Rex E. Melton, Interim Director in 1977

Rex Melton received the B.S. degree in agriculture at the University of Missouri in 1946. His education was interrupted by service in the U.S. Army Air Force as a B-24 pilot during World War II. He received the Air Medal with two oak leaf clusters, the Purple Heart, and the Distinguished

Flying Cross. He completed the B.S. degree and then earned the Master of Forestry in forest entomology at the University of Michigan in 1947.

Rex taught dendrology, surveying, mensuration, and forest practice at Mont Alto from 1947 to 1955, and also taught at Blue Jay Camp from 1948 to 1954. He served as director of the Stone Valley Experimental Forest from 1955 until 1978. He moved the School's sawmill there in 1962 and managed it as a profitable auxiliary enterprise until 1976. In 1966 he relocated to Ferguson Building to resume teaching and help with the administration of instructional programming. Besides his expert teaching of dendrology, advanced dendrology, silviculture, and logging, he and Todd Bowersox developed and taught the service course, "The Forest Environment and Man." For several years Melton assisted with the continuing education program, Administrative Management for Natural Resource Managers, offered jointly with the College of Business Administration. He served as editor of the alumni newsletter from 1974 until 1988, when he retired as professor emeritus.

FIG. 10 Former directors of the School of Forest Resources in 1982 *(left to right)* M. K. Goddard, Rex Melton, Wilber W. Ward, Robert S. Bond, Peter W. Fletcher. Photo by K. C. Steiner.

During his distinguished forty-one-year teaching career at Penn State, Rex also was recognized for his devotion to academic advising and personal counseling of students. Upon receiving the 1988 Excellence in Academic Advising Award from the College of Agriculture Alumni Society, he said, "It has been a privilege and a pleasure to have been associated with the fine young people who have been the students in the School of Forest Resources during the past forty years." Supporting letters from former students attested to his sincerity and wise counsel, which helped to guide them in pursuing their aspirations. Alumni also contributed funds to honor him by endowing a founder's tree in the Mont Alto Arboretum. Melton was elected fellow of the Society of American Foresters and became a golden member.

Robert S. "Bob" Bond, Director 1978–1988

Robert Bond received the B.S. degree in forestry from the University of Massachusetts in 1951, the Master of Forestry from Yale University in 1952, and the Ph.D. in forest economics from the College of Forestry, SUNY, at Syracuse University in 1966. From 1943 to 1946 he served in the U.S. Coast Guard. He was employed by the Fordyce Lumber Company in Arkansas (1952–54), and as a service forester by the Massachusetts Department of Natural Resources from 1955 to 1956. Then Bond was hired as instructor in the Department of Forestry at the University of Massachusetts and moved up through the professorial ranks (1956–77). His publications were on forest products marketing, forest labor, and forest recreation.

Bob served as director of the School of Forest Resources for a decade. True to his word from the start, he retired after ten years. His administrative skills helped to strengthen the faculty and staff, improve programs of education and research, and enhance the School's reputation. In a period of falling enrollments and financial difficulties nationwide, he recruited several new faculty members and upgraded facilities, including the School's first microcomputer laboratory. On his watch the M. K. Goddard Chair in Forestry and Environmental Resource Conservation was endowed, and Louis W. Schatz established student and faculty travel endowments. Southern forestry fieldtrips were organized, and a program of fisheries education and research was started. Bob initiated a faculty newsletter called the *Drumming Log*, and required each faculty member to submit "green sheets" that reported annually on accomplishments and plans for the next year. His format for the annual reports has been continued until the present time.

Throughout his career Bond has been involved in leadership positions in professional organizations, including chapters and sections of the Society of American Foresters, the Consortium of Environmental Forestry Studies, the Association of State College and University Forestry Research Organizations, and the National Association of Professional Forestry Schools and Colleges.

Since his retirement Bob and his wife, Barbara, have kept in touch with friends at Penn State and have returned for visits occasionally. He wrote, "Barbara and I fondly recall our ten years at the University and wish we could visit more frequently."

Henry D. "Slim" or "Hank" Gerhold, Interim Director, 1988

Henry Gerhold earned B.S. (1952) and M.F. (1954) degrees at Penn State, and the Ph.D. (1959) at Yale University. From 1951 to 1955 he was employed by the U.S. Forest Service in Montana, Idaho, Maine, and Pennsylvania. He became a faculty member at the School of Forest Resources in 1956 without even applying, and advanced through the ranks to professor of forest genetics. While still a graduate student at Yale and newly married, Gerhold was shocked by a letter from the dean informing him that his fellowship was to be terminated prematurely. Upon inquiring of Dean Garratt for the reason, Gerhold was relieved to learn about a job offer from Bill Bramble (his former advisor) at Penn State that had been arranged through the "old boys' network." The responsibilities at Penn State would enable him to complete his doctoral research, embark on an academic career, and be financially secure.

Gerhold served as the School's chairman of graduate studies from 1964 to 1985, as assistant director for research and graduate studies from 1985 to 1992, and as chairman of the intercollege graduate program in genetics from 1978 to 1982. He has conducted research and published widely on the genetic improvement of Christmas trees, landscape trees, and timber species, and has been a leader of the extension program in urban and community forestry that started in 1990. The improved varieties of Scotch pine and Douglas-fir that he developed have been planted by Christmas tree growers in several states. *Street Tree Factsheets* and *Landscape Tree Factsheets*, which he co-edited, and also the *Landscape Tree Factsheets CD*, have been very popular throughout North America as illustrated guides for selecting species and cultivars to be planted in towns and cities.

His awards include the 1992 Pennsylvania Forestry Association Award for Outstanding Achievement in Urban and Community Forestry, the National Arbor Day Foundation's 1995 Book Award for *Street Tree Factsheets*, the 1998 Education Award of the Utility Arborists Association, and the 2003 Dr. Joseph Trimble Rothrock Conservationist of the Year Award of the Pennsylvania Forestry Association. He was honored as an alumni centennial fellow of Penn State Mont Alto in 2004. He is the author of this book and a forthcoming biography of alumnus Joseph Ibberson, *A Forester's Legacy: The Life of Joseph E. Ibberson*.

Alfred D. "Al" Sullivan, Director 1988–1993

Al Sullivan received his B.S. in forestry (1964) and the M.S. in wildlife management (1964) from Louisiana State University. He specialized in biometrics for his Ph.D. in forestry, conferred by the University of Georgia in 1969. A native of New Orleans, he was known to be especially fond of Cajun food and music, yet his tastes were eclectic.

Sullivan's academic career began at the Virginia Polytechnic Institute and State University, serving as biometrics section leader in forestry until 1973. His next professorial position was in the Department of Forestry at Mississippi State University, where he was founder and director of the Forest Growth and Yield Research Cooperative. He also was a leader there in founding the University Faculty Development Center. In 1987 he became an American Council of Education fellow in the office of the chancellor at North Carolina State University.

In 1988 Al became director of Penn State's School of Forest Resources. He was active in several national professional groups, including the National Association of Professional Forestry Schools and Colleges, the National Association of University Fisheries and Wildlife Programs, and the National Association of State Universities and Land-Grant Colleges. Records show that his accomplishments were highly regarded by administrators of the College of Agricultural Sciences, and some faculty of the School agreed, but not all. He served in a period of "belt tightening" at the university, which made leadership more difficult. In 1993 Al moved on to be dean of the College of Natural Resources at the University of Minnesota, and in 2004 he was appointed executive associate vice president of the university.

Sullivan received several awards and honors. He served in 1972–73 as national forester of Xi Sigma Pi, the forestry honor society. In 1973 he was given the Faculty Award for Teaching Effectiveness, Division of Forestry and Wildlife Resources, Virginia Polytechnic Institute and State University. He was named a Danforth Foundation associate in 1981, and in the same year received the Outstanding Professor Award of the School of Forest Resources, Mississippi State University.

Kim C. Steiner, Interim Director 1993–1994

Kim Steiner, a native of Illinois, received his undergraduate education in forestry at Colorado State University, graduating with highest distinction in 1970. He was a founding member there of the first student chapter of the Society of American Foresters. He did his graduate work at Michigan State University, earning an M.S. (1971) and Ph.D. (1975) in forest genetics.

Steiner joined the Penn State faculty in 1974 as assistant professor of forest resources and advanced to professor of forest biology in 1987. His record of research includes more than 130 published papers on the genetics and ecology of forest trees. From 1983 to 1989 he chaired the forest science program faculty within the School. From 1994 to 2002 he was assistant and then associate director for academic programs. In 1999 he began a part-time appointment by the university provost as the first director of The Arboretum at Penn State, a project that he led almost from its inception in 1995. Steiner was chair-elect and chair of the university's faculty senate from 2003 to 2005, the only faculty member of the School who has served as chair of the senate. That body represents the more than five thousand faculty members of Penn State in the governance of the university.

Kim was active in forestry education issues for many years at the national level and served on the Society of American Foresters Committee on Accreditation beginning in 2002. In 2004 Steiner was elected chair of the Allegheny Society of American Foresters. He was particularly proud of founding the national Conference on University Education in Natural Resources, which had its inaugural meeting at Penn State in 1996; subsequent biennial meetings were held at Utah State University, the University of Missouri, North Carolina State University, and Northern Arizona University.

Larry A. Nielsen, Director 1994–2001

Larry Nielsen earned his master's degree in fisheries biology from the University of Missouri in 1974 and his doctoral degree in the same discipline from Cornell University in 1978. His 1970 undergraduate degree from the University of Illinois was in honors biology. He became an expert on sustainable resource management and natural resource education. Nielsen is a certified fisheries scientist, a fellow of the American Institute of Natural Fisheries Biologists, and an honorary member of the American Fisheries Society. His Danish extraction sometimes surfaced through a wry sense of humor and a unique way of running meetings, always with a bottle of water at hand.

While director of the Penn State School of Forest Resources from 1994 to 2001, Nielsen raised several million dollars in private funds and received authorization for the construction of a new forestry building. He helped create the Louis W. Schatz Center for Tree Molecular Genetics and a Center for Watershed Stewardship, established a professional development program for exceptional graduate students in natural resources, and initiated a student and faculty exchange program with the University of Freiburg, Germany. He conceived and led the "Day of Six Billion" event, which involved faculty, staff, and students.

Nielsen was named dean of North Carolina State University's College of Natural Resources in 2001. Four years later he became provost and executive vice chancellor of academic affairs at North Carolina State University. Previously he had been a faculty member at Virginia Polytechnic Institute and State University from 1977 to 1994, serving the last five years as head of the Department of Fisheries and Wildlife Sciences. He was recognized three times for teaching excellence at Virginia Tech. During his tenure there, he spent a one-year sabbatical as a special assistant to the Bureau of Fish Management in the Wisconsin Department of Natural Resources. Prior to his academic career he served in Vietnam as a military policeman and laboratory technician.

Nielsen has written more than a hundred scientific and popular articles, and has co-edited or co-written three textbooks on fisheries management. In 1998–99 he served on the U.S. Department of Agriculture's Committee of Scientists, which recommended new approaches to land and resource management planning in the U.S. Forest Service.

Charles H. "Chuck" Strauss, Director 2001 to the Present

Chuck received the B.S. degree in forest management from Penn State in 1958, then the M.S. degree in wood products marketing from Michigan State University in 1960. Following graduation he accepted a position with the California Redwood Association in San Francisco as a products and marketing specialist. Strauss was hired by the School of Forest Resources

48

in 1961 as an instructor and extension specialist in forest products, a new position providing education programs on lumber drying, timber marketing, and capital investments. Concurrently at Penn State he earned an M.A. in economics (1968) and a Ph.D. in agricultural economics (1974).

Strauss began his teaching career in 1966 when he joined the resident teaching staff as instructor in forest economics. He taught forest mensuration during the last summer camp ever held at Stone Valley, in 1966. He taught forest economics and finance for forty years, as well as other required courses such as forest resources inventory and forest management. He is a consummate raconteur of humorous tales. "I have always enjoyed teaching, and advising is a natural expansion of my interest in students, as a whole," he writes. "I find that teaching and advising complement each other, since both provide students with direction, purpose, and a sense of accomplishment."

His doctoral research produced a financial model of operating and capital costs for Pennsylvania's system of state parks. This led the Bureau of State Parks to establish a formal research program with Strauss and Penn State that lasted twenty years. He wrote or co-wrote more than 140 publications, many of them about the economics of recreation and tourism, short-rotation biomass production for energy, availability of timber supplies, and economics of wood products industries. He also surveyed the placement of the School's baccalaureate graduates annually, starting in 1973, and summarized twenty-five years of employment data in 2000. Before becoming director, he and his colleagues brought in more than $4.5 million in grants, and he guided nineteen graduate students to M.S. and Ph.D. degrees.

Strauss served on the university senate for twenty years. He was faculty advisor to the Penn State Forestry Society (1965–75), the Xi Sigma Pi forestry honorary society (1967–77), the Sylvan yearbook (1985–94), and the Tau Phi Delta forestry fraternity (1968–97). Internationally Strauss served as advisor to Philippine universities about biomass research (1976) and to the Republic of China about forest management and wood marketing (1985). He was a visiting professor at the University of Freiburg, Germany, in 2000.

When first appointed director in 2001 he worked on planning and financing a new $30 million building for the School, recruiting Harry Wiant as the first Joseph E. Ibberson Chair in Forest Resources Management, and adding another Ibberson chair, this one in Urban and Community Forestry. He also has encouraged greater collaboration among faculty

and adjusted the School's budget to financial constraints caused by reduced state appropriations. He had to manage changes in faculty assignments as several senior faculty retired, trying to maintain the integrity of
academic programs during a period of retrenchment within the College
of Agricultural Sciences. Furthermore, he saw to it that the School expanded its recruitment of students toward all three majors and established
closer ties with its DuBois, Mont Alto, and Williamsport faculties.

Strauss received honorary awards from Phi Eta Sigma (freshman), Phi
Epsilon Phi (botany), Gamma Sigma Delta (agriculture), Xi Sigma Pi (forestry), Pi Gamma Mu (social science), and Omicron Delta Epsilon (economics). His achievements have been recognized by awards from the
Pennsylvania Parks and Recreation Society (1982), the Pennsylvania Forestry Association (1992), and by students of the School of Forest Resources
as the outstanding faculty member in 2001. He received the Pennsylvania
Forestry Association's Dr. Joseph Trimble Rothrock Conservationist of
the Year Award in 2004, recognizing Strauss for his important long-term
work in forest economics and in particular his forty years of teaching in
forest economics, forest measurements, and forest management. Alumni
of Tau Phi Delta made a gift to name a faculty office for Strauss in the
new Forest Resources Building.

5

STAFF

Staff members provide vital services to assist the director, faculty, and students. Older records of staff employed by the Department of Forestry, which became the School of Forest Resources, are decidedly incomplete. A reference was found to a stenographer in the early days, and there have been many secretaries and various kinds of staff assistants. For example, twenty-two secretaries served the Cooperative Fish and Wildlife Research Unit between 1938 and 2005. The secretaries' tools of the trade have changed from typewriters, mimeograph machines, and telephone switchboards to computers, photocopiers, and fax machines. During the past fifty years Kathryn B. Johnson (1940–74), Sara J. "Sally" Clark (1966–85), and Cathy Arney (1985–2006) have served as administrative assistants to the department heads and directors and have supervised secretaries in several buildings. These accomplished ladies, through their technical skills and work ethic, occasionally have "pulled the fat out of the fire" for many a director and faculty member. Cathy Arney was recognized for her leadership and administrative skills in 2004, when she received the first Staff Laureate Leadership Award in the College of Agricultural Sciences.

Research and other technical assistants have worked with faculty on a wide variety of research, extension, and instructional projects. Stories about them are legion, and are best recounted by those who worked with them. Lester "Les" Rishel (1967–86) and Edgar H. "Ed" Palpant (1966–83) assisted with research and teaching after the Forest Resources Laboratory was completed in 1966. Les managed the sawmill and woodshop, and he also was an accomplished artist recognized for his woodcarvings and chainsaw sculptures. The Rishel family donated one of his wood sculptures, *Wind Song*, to be displayed in the new Forest Resources Building. Lee R. Stover has been assisting with wood products research and teaching since 1980. Ed Palpant took care of the greenhouses, assisting faculty with a wide variety of research projects that involved growing tree seedlings

FIG. II   Current administrative and staff assistants in 2006 *(seated left to right)* Andrea Lego, Barb Irwin, Kathy Kasubick, *(standing)* Cathy Arney, Stephanie Dalrymple, Emily Hill, Delores Breon, Carol Leitzell. Photo by H. D. Gerhold.

and other plants. Tree breeding and provenance testing were among his specialties, and Christmas tree growers especially appreciated his knowledge of western conifers.

For the most part faculty have relied on graduate students employed as research and teaching assistants for help in teaching courses and conducting research and extension projects. This relationship continues today, for it is also advantageous for the students to gain experience and learn from their mentors in this way.

The current secretarial and technical support of teaching, research, and extension activities is far better than it was through most of the School's history, but still is modest compared to other units of the College of Agricultural Sciences. There are thirty staff positions that have various titles reflecting their duties and sources of financing. Ten of these are designated as staff assistants who perform vital secretarial or accounting services. Another thirteen assist with research projects, with titles such as research assistant or research technician; in addition, several people are employed part-time on research projects. Other staff positions include extension associate, alumni coordinator, and arboretum program assistant. The Forest Lands Office has three foresters who are responsible for management activities on forest properties of the School and university.

Miss Junia Shambaugh was the first full-time librarian of the Forestry Department. Before her, John Ferguson had served as librarian of the forestry library, which he created from scratch. He assembled the first collection, for many years at his own expense because the School of Agriculture would not provide funds. Later, Agriculture dean Watts gave permission to purchase books from the forestry budget. Ferguson "pounded out the card catalog by the two-finger method," as he described it. When Dean S. T. Dana of Michigan admired the catalog during a visit, Ferguson granted permission to copy the card catalog for his school. The agriculture library had insufficient space for the forestry collection, so no attempts were made to combine the two collections until many years later. The forestry library moved temporarily to the basement of the Carnegie Library and then to the new Forestry Building when it was completed in 1940.

Lorraine Kapitanoff served as the last forestry librarian in Ferguson Building, starting in the 1940s and continuing until about 1962. At that time the forestry collection was combined with the agriculture library and moved, with it, first to the basement of a North Halls dormitory and then to the Paterno wing of Pattee Library. Lorraine had been studying Russian for some years while serving as forestry librarian. Afterward she went on to complete her Ph.D. degree in comparative literature at Penn State, started teaching Russian, and eventually became professor of Russian history, literature, and language. During all that time she and her irrepressible husband, Jack, hosted spirited Christmas parties at their home for the "old-timers" of the Forestry Department, continuing for some five decades.

6

FACULTY

The size of the forestry faculty at State College was small at first, just three to five men until 1929. After the merger with Mont Alto the faculty grew to about fourteen before World War II and remained at this level for ten years. In 1956 there were fifteen forestry faculty members at University Park and four at Mont Alto; in addition there were five secretaries, and two staff foresters at the Stone Valley Experimental Forest. Increases in faculty then came about as new curricula and graduate degrees were added, student enrollments increased (Appendix A), and employment opportunities grew in the natural resources professions.

In 2005 the School's personnel consisted of forty-six faculty members; four of these held joint appointments with the Penn State Institutes for the Environment and one faculty member had a joint appointment with the Life Sciences Consortium. There were twenty-five tenure-track faculty members at University Park and one each at Mont Alto and DuBois. Six instructors served in various capacities at University Park, Mont Alto, and DuBois. The adjunct members with the Pennsylvania Cooperative Fish and Wildlife Research Unit carry certain responsibilities similar to our faculty's; e.g., they are major professors for graduate students, teach graduate courses, and serve as principal investigators on research grants and contracts. The Goddard chair and the Ibberson chair professors are in endowed, non-tenure-track positions.

The expertise of faculty also broadened in scope over the past five decades, and this is reflected in a proliferation of their titles (Table 5). As the number of faculty gradually increased, so did the diversity of disciplines. They engaged in more sophisticated research as new specialties appeared in the natural resources professions. Before 1957 there had been thirteen different professorial titles. Most of the titles for the seventy-six professors, associate professors, assistant professors, and instructors hired before 1957 simply were designated as forestry. After that, thirty-six additional

Table 5 Professorial Titles of Faculty Who First Held Them, Listed Before and After the School's 50th Anniversary and Within the Three Baccalaureate Programs

Title	Faculty	Before 1957	After 1956
Forest Science			
Botany	Wallace E. White	1929	
Botany and Forestry	W. G. Edwards	1914	
Coordinator for Undergraduate Programs	Jamie A. Murphy		2006
Forest Biology	Kim C. Steiner		1993
Forest Biometrics	F. Yates Borden		1965
Forest Ecology	Russell J. Hutnik		1970
Forest Ecology and Physiology	Marc Abrams		1987
Forest Economics	Charles H. Strauss		1974
Forest Genetics	Henry D. Gerhold		1966
Forest Hydrology	William E. Sopper		1966
Forest Management	Victor Beede	1931	
Forest Mapping	Robert H. Carey	1936	
Forest Research	Arthur C. McIntyre	1927	
Forest Resource Management	Marc E. McDill		1997
Forest Resources	Larry H. McCormick		1976
Forest Resources Extension	James C. Finley		1975
Forest Science	Robert S. Bond		1977
Forestry	Hugh P. Baker	1907	
Forestry (Extension)	C. R. Anderson	1916	
Forestry (Visiting Lecturer)	Bernhard E. Fernow	1906	
Forestry and Environmental Resources Conservation	Arthur A. Davis		1984
Forestry and Statistics	Peter E. Dress		1958
Molecular Genetics	John Carlson		1997
Natural Resource Policy	Grace Wang		1998
Natural Resources	Larry A. Nielsen		1994
Silviculture	Joshua L. Deen	1933	
Urban and Community Forestry	William F. Elmendorf		2002
Watershed Management	William E. Sopper		1960
Wildlife and Fisheries			
Aquatic Biology	Hunter Carrick		2001
Aquatic Ecology	Dean E. Arnold		1982
Fisheries Management	C. Paola Ferreri		1995
Fishery Science	Jay R. Stauffer Jr.		1984
Ichthyology	Jay R. Stauffer Jr.		1994
Wildlife and Wetlands	Robert P. Brooks		1998
Wildlife Conservation	Richard H. Yahner		1990
Wildlife Ecology	Robert P. Brooks		1983
Wildlife Management	James S. Lindzey		1965
Wildlife Resources	Margaret Brittingham		1988
Wildlife Science	Gerald L. Storm		1972

Table 5   Continued

Title	Faculty	Before 1957	After 1956
Wildlife Technology	Robert P. Brooks		1980
Wood Products			
Forest Products	Newell A. Norton	1941	
Forest Products Marketing	Paul M. Smith		1991
Lumbering	W. G. Edwards	1923	
Wood Products Business Management	Judd H. Michael		2000
Wood Products Engineering	John J. Janowiak		1995
Wood Products Operations	Charles Ray		2002
Wood Science and Technology	Robert C. Baldwin		1968
Wood Technology	Richard N. Jorgensen	1949	
Wood Utilization	George R. Green	1921	

titles were designated among the 113 faculty hired since then. All twelve of the titles in wildlife and fisheries subjects were new, the first of these positions having been established in 1970.

Two endowed professorial chairs were created through the largesse of benefactors. The Maurice K. Goddard Chair in Forestry and Environmental Resource Conservation was first filled in 1985, and the Joseph E. Ibberson Chair in Forest Resources Management in 2002 (Tables 6 and 7). These professors have important responsibilities in outreach as well as in teaching and research. The Goddard chair provides leadership on public policy related to environmental issues. The Ibberson chair enhances the sustainable management of private forest landowners through contacts with students, consultants, government agencies, and the public. A third

Table 6   Maurice K. Goddard Professors of Forestry and Environmental Resource Conservation

Years	Professor	Specialty
1985–1987	Arthur A. Davis	resource management and development
1988–1991	Benjamin A. Jayne	forest products, natural resource management
1991–1994	Steven Thorne	forest policy, environmental law
1995–2000	Caren E. Glotfelty	water resource management
2001–present	Robert McKinstry	environmental law and litigation

Table 7   Joseph E. Ibberson Professor of Forest Resources Management

Years	Professor	Specialty
2002–present	Harry V. Wiant Jr.	private forestland management, biometrics

endowment, given by alumnus John T. Steimer, supports the Nancy and John Steimer Professorship, administered by the College of Agricultural Sciences, held by Marc D. Abrams beginning in 2001. Joseph E. Ibberson committed to a second endowed chair in 2003 through his will, this one to be in Urban and Community Forestry when the chair is funded.

Special efforts to diversify the faculty have been quite successful in recent years, despite the limited pool of qualified women and ethnic minorities. Faculty search committees have been diligent and proactive in searching for the best applicants on those occasions when a faculty position could be filled. All recently hired faculty came with top-notch qualifications and collectively held degrees from many different universities. The first woman to join the faculty was Margaret Brittingham, in 1988. Until then all faculty were white males, reflecting the dominance of white men in natural resources professions before 1970. In 2005 four of the twenty-five tenure-track faculty were women, an increase that occurred despite limited opportunities to fill positions and with no decrease in quality.

The turnover in faculty in the early days, surprisingly, was much more rapid than in the second fifty years. Of the seventy-six faculty employed before 1957, forty-three (57 percent) served fewer than five years, including twenty-three who were on the faculty for only one year. Among those having long tenures that ended before 1957, the longest were William Edwards, who served for thirty-four years, and John Ferguson, for twenty-eight years.

Nine who were on the faculty both before and after 1957 exceeded twenty-nine years of service, namely, Ronald Bartoo (31 years), Henry Chisman (41 years), H. Norton Cope (30 years), Henry Gerhold (50 years to date), Rex Melton (41 years), William Sopper (39 years), Wilber Ward (32 years), Wallace White (35 years), and Robert Wingard (31 years). Professors Cope and White were the earliest of these to be employed, both in 1929.

Longer tenures on the faculty have been typical more recently. Excluding current faculty hired after 2001, only twenty-two (21 percent) of the 107 whose employment started after 1956 had served on the faculty for fewer than five years by 2006. Ten faculty who were employed in 1957 or afterward had served for twenty-nine or more years by 2006. They were Paul Blankenhorn (32 years to date), Todd Bowersox (37 years), David DeWalle (38 years to date), James Finley (32 years to date), Russell Hutnik (30 years), James Lynch (31 years), Larry McCormick (36 years), William

57

Sharpe (35 years to date), Kim Steiner (33 years to date), and Charles Strauss (46 years to date).

The memories that students cherish about their favorite professors, and the most problematic ones, no doubt are as different as the individuals who made up the faculty and the personalities of the students who studied with them. Whenever alumni gather, they never tire of telling stories about their most memorable experiences.

7

FACILITIES

Programmatic facilities of the School of Forest Resources have headquarters on three Penn State campuses—Mont Alto, University Park, and DuBois. The educational and research activities of students and faculties also extend into various forested lands and bodies of water, some nearby, others as distant as Australia, China, Germany, Malawi, India, and many other countries.

The oldest building in the Penn State system, Wiestling Hall, was built about 1803, even before the university was founded. In use at Penn State Mont Alto since 1903, Wiestling was used first as a classroom of the Pennsylvania State Forest Academy and also for lodging and meals. Fifty years ago it was the dining hall, and more recently it was reconditioned for use as administrative offices and a student activities center. For many year classes were taught in Science Hall (Fig. 12).

In 1929, when the Forest Academy became part of Pennsylvania State College, forestry classes were offered at Mont Alto for all entering freshmen Penn State forestry students. In 1963 Penn State Mont Alto became a Commonwealth Campus, offering the first one or two years of many Penn State degrees, as well as some associate degrees, including forest technology. In 1997 Mont Alto joined Penn State's Commonwealth Colleges and began offering various bachelor's degrees. Now the Mont Alto campus has three classroom buildings and four residence halls, including Conklin Hall, which forestry students helped to build from 1907 to 1909. A commemorative marker outside Conklin Hall states, "No matter what the future, the days here will be the ones remembered when age brings quiet contemplation." Also on the campus are a library, an arboretum, a dining hall, a bookstore, and a chapel built in 1854. The eighty-thousand-acre Michaux and Mont Alto State Forests and the thousand-acre Waynesboro Watershed are readily accessible for fieldtrips. As part of Mont Alto's centennial celebration Joan M. Hocking edited recollections of

FIG. 12   Science Hall at the Mont Alto Campus. College of Agricultural Sciences
photo.

alumni and faculty in *Centennial Voices, the Spirit of Mont Alto, a Continuing
Story* (2003).

When the School of Forest Resources started in 1907 as the Department of Forestry in the Pennsylvania State College, classes were taught in
the original Forestry Building (Fig. 13), also known as Hemlock Hall
(which actually was the second Hemlock Hall), the Old Green Shack, the
Pea-Green Shack, and Fergie's Woodshed. The drafty building was con-
structed in 1906 entirely of wood, mostly hemlock lumber, which was the
cheapest on the market. So it is no wonder that some of the students saw
it as a firetrap, as did administrators of the School of Agriculture. They
turned down a request for wallboard to cover cracks in the walls, believing
the building would burn down sooner or later. Fires then were not uncommon, and fires did destroy Main Engineering and the Horticulture
Building. John Ferguson later persevered in obtaining wallboard from
Agriculture administrators, but he had to install it himself. This took him
the better part of a summer, and he had to buy the nails at his own expense.
Toilet facilities consisted of a single seat, later "modernized" to seat three.
Students were employed as janitors and tended the furnace. The Forestry
Building was infested with rats, so when Bill Edwards was a student janitor

he kept a club always within reach. Edwards later became a professor and presumably left the "education" of rats to others.

A forest tree nursery installed in 1908 lay behind the Forestry Building. Students raised thousands of seedlings there and shipped them out for forest plantings. Larger trees were planted on campus and in town—for example, tulip poplars along Fairmount Avenue. Later faculty and students operated nurseries for research purposes in Stone Valley and along Fox Hollow Road, north of campus. At various times the Bureau of Forestry also made available its Penn Nursery at Potters Mills.

For three decades the old Forestry Building was the busiest, most crowded building on campus. Students and professors came into intimate contact, and the friendliest relations existed. Ferguson recorded that "The

FIG. 13   Fergie's Woodshed. College of Agricultural Sciences photo.

61

Profs knew their studes [*sic*] and the studes knew their Profs, and it was difficult for either to get away with much or to appear to be more than they really were." Fergie's Woodshed was dismantled in 1940, a few weeks before the alumni homecoming and housewarming of the new Forestry Building (Fig. 14) on October 11 and 12, 1940. After special messages from Gifford Pinchot, Hugh P. Baker, and John A. Ferguson, the audience paid a standing tribute to Fergie.

From 1940 until 2005 the students and faculty occupied the new Forestry Building, renamed Ferguson Building in 1967 in honor of John A. Ferguson; his widow and daughter attended the ceremony. The forestry alumni had requested the name Ferguson Hall in 1947, but the board of trustees rejected the proposal because of their policy against naming buildings for living people. The three-story brick building contained classrooms, faculty and staff offices, some small laboratories, and a library. Two huge, upright Kodiak bears and a moose head adorned a meeting room used for faculty meetings and other gatherings. Outside the rear wall Xi Sigma Pi members mounted two peaveys and a steering oar, a relic from the last log raft to float down the west branch of the Susquehanna River in March 1938. That trip was to commemorate a past generation of river men who ferried log rafts to market. But the ill-fated raft crashed into a bridge pier near Muncy and seven of the forty-eight passengers drowned. Sometime after 1968 the steering oar was moved to the Lumber Museum west of Galeton.

The next expansion of space for faculty, students, and staff originated with M. K. Goddard's ideas for a forestry center, though it did not turn out quite as he had envisioned it. The Forest Resources Laboratory, completed in 1966, provided additional classrooms, offices, and research facilities. It was built at the east end of campus instead of the more distant location that Goddard had proposed. More space was found later, in four other buildings, to accommodate further growth. The Forest Resources Laboratory was retained by the School after 2006, when the faculty and activities were consolidated in the new ninety-eight-thousand-square-foot Forest Resources Building. Ferguson Building was destined for other departmental uses by the College of Agricultural Sciences.

Summer camps with tents for housing have been held at various locations in Pennsylvania, including Foxburg, Lamar, Stone Valley, Ralston, Ludlow, and Endeavor. Some of the camps were within ten to fifteen miles of State College, considered a walking distance; so on weekends students walked to State College for dances and other forms of pleasure. Blue Jay

FIG. 14 Ferguson Building in 1952. College of Agricultural Sciences photo.

Camp near Marienville was the site of summer camps from 1939 to 1960, except for the World War II years. Blue Jay was a former government camp for transients built in 1935 like a CCC camp. The U.S. Forest Service made the camp available through an agreement with the university. In 1947 the eight-week camp for sophomores resumed at Blue Jay, and a four-week camp was started in Stone Valley for students transferring into forestry from other majors. At Blue Jay the second-year forestry students spent four weeks in a practical forestry course that also included fieldtrips, and four weeks in a surveying course that was also taken by civil engineering students. The summer instruction in forest inventory, management plans, and surveying was moved to Mont Alto in 1961, then to University Park, and finally to Stone Valley, as financing could not be found to renovate the deteriorating Blue Jay buildings. Curricular changes that resulted from dropping summer camp after 1966 were hotly debated for some years by faculty, alumni, and employers, who harbored feelings of nostalgia and lingering regrets about the loss of a memorable, valuable experience.

The School of Forest Resources manages about 8,500 acres of forestland, which are intensively used for teaching, research, and demonstration. The forests are also open to the public for a wide variety of activities such as hunting, hiking, bird watching, and mountain biking. The largest forest, the 6,775-acre Stone Valley Forest located in northern Huntingdon County, is about a twenty-minute drive from State College. The U.S. Resettlement Administration acquired much of that land in the 1930s and later turned it over to the U.S. Forest Service, which made it available in 1940. Donald D. Stevenson, H. Arthur Meyer, and Ronald A. Bartoo completed a management plan in 1943. The Forest Service officially deeded it to Pennsylvania State College in 1954 and 1955 for use as an outdoor laboratory. Professors Meyer and Bartoo revised the first management plan in 1949, and Rex E. Melton supervised several subsequent revisions. Inventories of the entire forest were completed in 1988 and 2001 and a fifty-year management plan was completed for the entire forest in 1989 by Joseph A. Harding, director of Forest Lands, with subsequent revisions in 2002. The College Farm Woodlands were organized in 1938 and a management plan was prepared. Recently renamed the Spring Creek Forest, the twelve-hundred-acre forest consists of various woodlots within a few miles of Penn State's main campus. The four-hundred-acre Weaver Forest located in western Centre County near the town of Marengo was obtained by the School of Forest Resources in 1989. Other forest properties given to the School include the fifty-acre Laurel Haven Education Center in Julian, a seventy-acre Trimble property near Wyalusing, and a fourteen-acre property a few miles west of State College donated by Mrs. Jean Womer. Sawmills operated by the School at various times were located near Fergie's Woodshed, in the College Woodlands, in Stone Valley Forest, and at the Forest Resources Laboratory. Currently the School's forestlands are actively managed for multiple uses, including timber pro-

FIG. 15 Summer camp instructors, including John A. Ferguson wearing suspenders. School of Forest Resources negative #811, Penn State University Archives, Pennsylvania State University Libraries.

FIG. 16 Forestry class at summer camp. School of Forest Resources negative #945, Penn State University Archives, Pennsylvania State University Libraries.

FIG. 17 Students relaxing at summer camp with banjo, fishing pole, and mounted snakeskin. School of Forest Resources negative #195, Penn State University Archives, Pennsylvania State University Libraries.

FIG. 18 Blue Jay Summer Camp faculty *(left to right)* Rex Melton, Wib Ward, Ron Bartoo, Merwin Humphrey. School of Forest Resources photo.

duction, watershed protection, wildlife habitat, and recreational opportunities.

The Penn State DuBois campus, founded in 1935, has provided facilities for the wildlife technology program since 1970. Instruction takes place in classrooms as well as at nearby Moshannon State Forest, the Allegheny National Forest, several state parks, an environmental center, a hunting preserve, and a bison ranch.

In 1998 alumnus Louis Schatz pledged $5.6 million from his estate to endow the Schatz Center for Tree Molecular Genetics in the School of Forest Resources. Through endowments for a professorship in tree genetics, a postdoctoral fellowship, visiting scholar support, undergraduate awards, colloquia, and library collections, the Schatz Center provides funding for research and education in forest genetics and related technologies at University Park and the Mont Alto campus. The Schatz Center endowments also supported construction of the new Forest Resources Building. The Schatz genetics laboratory's high throughput facility has the capacity to sequence more than a hundred thousand DNA clones per year, that is, more than 70 million bases of new DNA sequence. Until 2005 the Schatz Center was strategically located in the Wartik Laboratory, where the Biotechnology Institute's shared technology facilities for DNA micro-arrays, nucleic acids, and hybridoma services were located, and then for a year in the Life Sciences Building, before moving to the new Forest Resources Building.

Construction of the new Forest Resources Building began in August 2004; it was completed in December 2005 and occupied during March to June 2006 (Fig. 20). For the first time it houses all three professional programs under one roof, including thirty-seven faculty and twenty-one staff, serving about three hundred undergraduates and one hundred graduate students. Before then the School's people were housed in seven buildings: the Ferguson Building, Forest Resources Laboratory, Merkle Laboratory, Land and Water Building, Life Sciences Building, Henning Building, and an office building in State College; in addition, fish laboratories were located at Rock Springs. The School retained the Forest Resources Laboratory for wood products engineering and materials preparation, the greenhouses, the forestlands operations office, and the Center for Watershed Stewardship graduate program.

A crowd of about 150 gathered for the ceremonial groundbreaking for the new Forest Resources Building on Friday, October 29, 2004. They included invited guests, officials of the Gilbane Building Company, mem-

bers of Bower, Lewis, Thrower Architects, the Bureau of Forestry, and
Penn State, along with faculty, students, and staff of the School of Forest
Resources. President Graham Spanier, Agricultural Sciences dean Robert
Steele, School director Charles Strauss, and Michael Lester of the Depart-
ment of Conservation and Natural Resources offered brief remarks and
posed with ceremonial shovels. Students were on hand to greet and direct
guests, and at the conclusion of the remarks gave the rousing cheer, "We
Are . . . Penn State!"

A topping-off tree was erected atop the frame of the new building (Fig.
19) on December 17, in keeping with a long-standing tradition of iron-
workers. Instead of the usual small evergreen tree, a thirty-foot Douglas-
fir exemplified research of the School of Forest Resources, besides serving
as a symbol of the topping-off ceremony. The Douglas-fir was grown as
part of the genetics research and given by the School to the building contractor. The Pennsylvania Tree Improvement Program has been collaborating in developing genetically improved varieties of Christmas trees, and
also in harvesting seed-bearing cones from seed orchards.

Laminated wooden beams also form part of the building structure. The
wooden beams were fabricated by RidgidPly Rafters, Inc., using red maple
lumber from Pennsylvania sawmills. The Pennsylvania Forest Products
Association coordinated the project, Lewis Lumber Company planed the
lumber, and the material was kiln-dried by the School of Forest Resources
and Pennsylvania House. Faculty of the School also provided technical
specifications for the beams, based on their research on glulam beams for
timber bridges.

The new building consists of four stories and a lower floor, encompass-
ing about ninety-eight thousand square feet. That is 50 percent more than
the space that existed in Ferguson Building and the Forest Resources Laboratory combined. Teaching and outreach facilities encompass nearly 30
percent of the new building; research facilities, 40 percent; and offices for
faculty, staff, and graduate students, 30 percent. Teaching areas include
four teaching laboratories; two technology classrooms; the Steimer Auditorium, with a 150-seat capacity; two undergraduate computer labs; and a
GIS lab for graduate students. Research spaces consist of laboratories for
forestry, fisheries, water resources, wildlife, and wood products. Outreach
facilities include a thirty-five-seat conference room with video teleconfere-
ncing capability, five meeting rooms with state-of-the-art communication
systems, a publication production room, and the York Group Wood Products Evaluation Laboratory. For faculty, staff, students, and visitors there

FIG. 19 Topping-off tree being erected on the new Forest Resources Building in 2005. Photo by H. D. Gerhold.

are offices; the Edwards Student Activities Center; the Pennsylvania Forest Products Association Atrium, a four-story, glass-enclosed common area serving students, staff, and faculty; and the Alumni Plaza, which features a landscaped setting for outdoor events and study.

Many organizations, companies, alumni, and friends of the School have made financial contributions toward the $6 million budgeted for philanthropic support of the total cost. Nancy and John Steimer contributed more than $1 million for planning and construction, in particular for the

Steimer Auditorium. An earlier gift from Louis Schatz toward tree genetics included $1 million for the tree genetics laboratory.

One of the more visually engaging gifts is the $700,000 value of hardwood panels, seating areas, stair casings, architectural millwork, and laminated beams installed throughout the building. The Pennsylvania Forest Products Association provided the warmth and charm of cherry, oak, ash, and other hardwoods to create an architectural symbol that is unique within the campus. Thus our building will serve as a showcase for Pennsylvania hardwoods.

Classrooms, laboratories, and offices have been named through financial contributions, in keeping with university policy. The Weaber Corporation, Pennsylvania's largest sawmill and integrated wood products plant, provided a gift for the wood physics laboratory to recognize the work of Paul Blankenhorn, professor of wood science and associate director of academic programs, for his teaching, research, and outreach contributions to Pennsylvania's wood industries. The Richard King Mellon Foundation gave a gift for a forest hydrology suite recognizing the work of William E. Sharpe, professor of forest hydrology, whose efforts have led to substantial improvements in residential water conservation and heightened awareness of the environmental impacts of acid rain. The F. A. Bartlett Tree Expert Company has pledged support for the construction of a high-tech classroom named in honor of alumnus John C. "Jack" Good, executive director of the Bartlett Foundation, with state-of-the-art computer projection equipment and computer access for students at every desk. The Collins Companies, founded in 1855 when T. D. Collins began timber operations in Pennsylvania and nationally known for its commitment to sustainable forestry, have pledged support toward the construction and naming of the wood products teaching lab. Edward and Pat Kocjancic, in appreciation of Ed's forestry education and their personal and professional ties with Penn State, have provided financing for naming the forest soil and water teaching laboratory. In a similar fashion, Bruce and Jean Edwards have named the student center as a tribute to Bruce's education and their appreciation of the School of Forest Resources and the university. A gift of the Danzer Corporation, an international leader in the manufacture and marketing of hardwood lumber, dimension, and veneer products, supports the construction and naming of the Wood Products Marketing Laboratory.

A unique aspect of the development initiatives was the banding together of support by members of professional organizations. The Pennsylvania Forestry Association gathered sufficient funds to name the director's office. Similarly, certain members of the Association of Consulting Foresters have named the Ibberson Chair in Forest Management Office, as have members of the Pennsylvania Chapter of the Society of American Foresters in naming the Goddard Chair Office, members of the Penn-York Lumbermen's Club in naming a wood products faculty office, and alumni of Tau Phi Delta in naming the Strauss Faculty Office.

The $30.5 million structure is a vital facility for ensuring that Penn State's School of Forest Resources will continue to recruit and retain the highest-caliber faculty and students, offer a top-quality contemporary education, and provide dynamic research and specialized technology transfer for forest-related resource interests throughout Pennsylvania and adjoining regions. More than five hundred guests, alumni, faculty, and students attended the dedication ceremony on September 8, 2006.

Directly across Park Avenue from the Forest Resources Building, the 395-acre Arboretum at Penn State is under development. Kim Steiner, director of the arboretum, is making plans for a unique facility for the study and enjoyment of plants and plant communities in an urbanizing environment. There are plans for an education center, a conservatory, demonstration and specialty gardens, a pond and fountain, and a pavilion overlooking natural plant communities of the region. In September 2005 a thirty-three-foot white oak was dedicated as a "witness tree" to the forthcoming development of the arboretum. Horticulture alumnus George K. Biemesderfer, owner of Green Acres Nursery, donated the oak

FIG. 20   The new Forest Resources Building in 2006. Photo by H. D. Gerhold.

in honor of Charles Hosler, former vice president for research and dean of the graduate school, and his late wife. Within the arboretum the Bellefonte Central Rail-Trail bicycle and pedestrian path was completed in 2005, built on the bed of the Bellefonte Central Railroad, which ceased operation in 1974. The first flowerbeds will be built in the arboretum a year after the new Forest Resources Building was occupied in 2006.

8

ACADEMIC CURRICULA

The forestry curricula at Penn State, ever changing, have always had elements aimed at both the theory and practice of forestry in ways that are biologically sound, economically feasible, and socially acceptable. Regardless of which curriculum alumni experienced, they will look back on it as challenging, comprehensive, and probably containing some courses they would just as soon have skipped.

Accreditation of curricula has been helpful in maintaining quality, revising contents, and garnering support from the college and university. The Society of American Foresters first accredited professional forestry curricula in 1935, and Penn State's was one of fourteen approved from twenty evaluated. The evaluators were critical, however, of the inadequate physical plant, the department's heavy teaching load, and its modest research output, problems that persisted for many years despite efforts to remedy them. The curriculum was reaccredited in 1943, 1950, 1956, and at frequent intervals since then. The SAF conducted the most recent accreditation review in 2003, jointly with the Society of Wood Science and Technology, which evaluated the wood products baccalaureate program. Under the forest science major, the forest biology and forest management options were reaccredited, and the urban forestry option was accredited for the first time. In the wood products major the processing and manufacturing option was reaccredited, and the business and marketing option was accredited for the first time.

Faculty members have revised the curricula periodically over the years and have added new majors and new degree programs, both undergraduate and graduate (Table 8). The wood utilization major was added in 1942; the wildlife science major became a reality in 1981 and expanded to wildlife and fisheries science in 1988. New technologies have been incorporated in courses, entirely new courses have replaced others, and curricula

Table 8 Principal Events in Curricula and Majors

Year	Event Related to Curriculum or Major
1907	Professional forestry instruction began at Penn State, one of seven majors in the School of Agriculture.
1908	Summer camps began, located in the vicinity of State College or Mont Alto or sometimes elsewhere. Students attended for two weeks, later eight weeks, after their freshman, sophomore, or junior year, depending on revisions in the curriculum. From 1930 to 1933 summer camp was held at the Allegheny National Forest; in 1934–38 at Mont Alto; in 1939–1941 and 1947–1960 at Blue Jay Camp near Marienville; in 1961 summer camp moved to Mont Alto and later operated from University Park and Stone Valley, for the last time in 1966.
1913	First M.S degree in forestry conferred.
1929	Four-year forestry curriculum at Mont Alto discontinued (formerly two-year, 1903–5, then three-year, 1904–23). Penn State freshmen started at Mont Alto, also two-year ranger students. Baccalaureate students continued at State College, returning to Mont Alto following their sophomore year for an eight-week forest management camp.
1929	Two-year ranger course first offered.
1935	Penn State one of eight professional forestry curricula accredited by the Society of American Foresters, for the first time, in the highest category. Reaccredited in 1943, 1950, 1956, and at frequent intervals since then.
1939	First M.S. degree in wildlife management conferred.
1942	Two-year ranger course discontinued.
1942	Wood utilization curriculum established, first implemented after World War II.
1945	Master of Forestry degree awarded for the first time.
1947	Summer camp at Stone Valley started for transfer students.
1961	Forestry major changed to majors in forest science and forest technology, wood utilization changed to wood science.
1961	Wildlife management graduate program transferred from Biology Department to School of Forestry.
1962	Last entire class of forestry freshmen matriculated at Mont Alto.
1963	Associate degree program in forest technology started at Mont Alto campus.
1963	Forestry curriculum revised substantially, limited to 126 credits; forestry and wildlife courses omitted from first two years to accommodate students at various Commonwealth Campuses.
1963	Mont Alto became Commonwealth Campus, admitting other majors and associate degree students.
1966	Forest science and forest technology majors combined into forest science.
1967	Ph.D. in forest resources approved.
1970	Associate degree program in wildlife technology started at DuBois Campus.
1971	Environmental resources management interdepartmental major installed by College of Agriculture, with involvement of forestry faculty.
1972	First Ph.D. degree in forest resources conferred.
1974	Master of Forestry changed to Master of Forest Resources.

1974   Course (FOR 200) instituted to provide advice and orientation about career options and course choices, with fieldtrips to various kinds of employers.
1974   M.S. in wildlife management, formerly interdepartmental, authorized within School of Forest Resources.
1975   Master of Forest Resources degree program approved; first M.F.R degree conferred in 1976.
1975   Wood science major changed to forest products and greatly revised.
1978   Master of Agriculture degree authorized in forest resources.
1981   Wildlife science major established.
1981   School of Forest Resources given principal administrative responsibility for environmental resources management major.
1986   Educational objectives of forest science curriculum defined explicitly.
1988   B.S. in wildlife science changed to wildlife and fisheries science.
1990   Ph.D. and M.F.R. degrees approved in wildlife and fisheries science.
1992   Forest products major revised and changed to wood products with two options, namely, wood products business and marketing, and wood products processing and manufacturing.
1996   Forest science major revised with four options, namely, forest biology, forest management, urban forestry, and watershed management.
1997   Student exchange program established with the faculty of forestry, University of Freiburg, Germany.
1998   Graduate option in watershed stewardship started by School of Forest Resources and Department of Landscape Architecture.
2001   Wildlife and fisheries science major revised with two options, namely, fisheries and wildlife.

have been broadened through university-wide requirements in humanities and arts, cultural diversity, and communication skills.

Significant technological improvements in teaching were made in the 1990s. A computer studio installed in Ferguson Building had computer workstations linked with the university network. Instructors used these in teaching, and students accessed the library and the internet. Professors created internet websites for several courses. Global positioning systems (GPS) have largely replaced plane surveying. Geographic information systems (GIS) came into regular use in several courses. Other advanced technologies include a universal testing machine with applications in wood products courses, and a state-of-the-art electrofishing boat used in fisheries courses. Electronic mail enables rapid communication with advisees and students enrolled in particular courses, as well as generally among students, faculty, and staff. Students now enroll in courses by phone or computer, a major departure from the slow, cumbersome methods of the past.

In 1971 the College of Agriculture initiated an interdepartmental B.S. degree in environmental resources management (ERM), in response to urgent social concerns in the 1960s about effects of pollution on the environment. Forestry enrollments soared, too, causing overcrowded classrooms and an overburdened faculty. The School was a major participant in the ERM program. In 1981 the School was given shared administrative responsibility for the program, under the aegis of the college's associate dean of resident education. Later, other units of the college also have shared in its administration. The erm major had the largest enrollments in the college for many years, peaking near seven hundred during the 1990s but then declining precipitously to fewer then one hundred students by 2004.

In 1997 a study-abroad program was established with the faculty of forestry at the University of Freiburg. Penn State and Freiburg students have had reciprocal two-week visits in alternating years, accompanied by faculty. More recently the course that our students take has expanded to a two-credit program of study over a fifteen-week semester, followed by a ten-day study tour in southern Germany highlighted by visits to forests, wood industries, and cultural features. A formal credit-earning exchange program also is available to students who wish to take courses at either university.

SUBPROFESSIONAL AND ASSOCIATE DEGREE PROGRAMS

From 1929 to 1942 a two-year ranger course was taught, mostly at Mont Alto but in some years partly at State College. Even before then, starting in 1920, veterans of World War I were able to take a two-year vocational forestry course. The curriculum consisted mainly of practical forestry courses and training in technical skills. During this period 122 men, ranging from four to fourteen per year, received two-year certificates.

The Forestry School launched an associate degree program in forest technology in 1963, with a separate faculty at the Mont Alto campus. This is when Mont Alto became one of the university's Commonwealth Campuses, and when the B.S. curriculum was revised substantially. The forest technology program trained forest technicians in forest operations and basic forest management procedures. The curriculum was designed to be distinctive when compared with the baccalaureate course of study. Incoming classes exceeded one hundred by the mid-1970s, then decreased dramatically during the 1980s to as low as twenty, and climbed again during the 1990s. The program received recognition by the Society of American Foresters in conjunction with the Council of Eastern Forest Technician Schools, and also by the state civil service system.

In 1970 a complementary associate degree program in wildlife technology was started at the DuBois campus with a similar purpose, to train wildlife technicians. The students spend considerable time in the field in plant and animal identification, natural resource inventories, and mapping and census techniques. Enrollments at DuBois have fluctuated, too. In 1999 the wildlife technology program was nationally accredited by the North American Wildlife Technology Association.

Under the Commonwealth College organization, the School of Forest Resources has continued to provide professional guidance to these two programs. The Mont Alto and Dubois campuses have the principal responsibility for them, however.

CURRICULUM IN FOREST SCIENCE

George Wirt drafted the original curriculum of the Forest Academy at Mont Alto, using as references his knowledge of the Biltmore School curriculum, the bulletins of Cornell and Yale universities, and a U.S. government bulletin that contained European forestry curricula. Wirt wrote, "I went far up into Mont Alto park and with much prayer and meditation, after many hours a tentative draft of a curriculum was formulated" (1953, 54). A year later, the initial two-year curriculum was lengthened to three years. J. T. Rothrock and Forestry Commissioner Robert S. Conklin reviewed the draft with Wirt and they agreed upon a three-year, year-round program with only a week out in August and one week at the Christmas season.

At Penn State a four-year course of study in forestry was authorized in 1905 but not implemented until 1907. In the preceding twenty years J. T. Rothrock and William Buckhout had presented forestry lectures, but not a complete course of study. Bernhard Fernow gave the initial lectures of the professional program in 1907, having previously developed a short-lived forestry curriculum at Cornell University. Hugh Baker, who had organized the forestry curriculum at Iowa State College, replaced Fernow after one semester and infused professional forestry instruction at Penn State with his own ideas. John Ferguson joined Baker in 1908. As head of the department from 1913 to 1937, Ferguson undoubtedly had a most profound effect on the curriculum in the early years. The courses were compatible with the common curriculum followed by all first- and second-year students in the School of Agriculture. Ferguson attended several meetings where leaders of forestry schools discussed the scope and character of professional training in forestry. In 1909 representatives from California, Harvard, Iowa, Michigan, Minnesota, Toronto, and Yale met at Pinchot's home in Washington, D.C. They met again at a conference in 1911 to standardize training, and yet again in 1920 at Yale.

In 1931, after the Mont Alto and Penn State forestry programs had been combined, John Ferguson described a unique feature that persisted until 1963, though with periodic modifications. The plan for training professional foresters at Penn State, he wrote, "differs radically from that in effect in the other twenty-odd professional forest schools in the country." Those schools gave freshmen and sophomores a thorough knowledge of

FIG. 21   A class of forestry students studying wood identification in "Fergie's Woodshed." School of Forest Resources photo.

the fundamental sciences underlying the science of forestry and then built forestry knowledge on that foundation in the junior and senior years. At Penn State the study of fundamental sciences at first was delayed until the students gained an intimate knowledge of the forest. In the freshman year at Mont Alto students spent three days per week outdoors learning about tree identification, nurseries, reforestation, timber estimating, surveying, saw-milling, wildlife, forest ecology, and firefighting. The expectation was that they would better appreciate the necessity of studying basic sciences after gaining an appreciation of the "forest laboratory." Required and elective forestry courses in the last two years enabled students to specialize in professional forestry, private forestry, lumber industry, or wood utilization. By 1937 ten specialties were available.

The forestry curriculum has undergone occasional name changes and frequent revisions in the number of credits needed, particular course requirements, and course contents both at Mont Alto and at State College/University Park. Only some of the more important changes can be chronicled here without getting immersed in endless minutiae.

A simplified overview of credit requirements by subject matter in six meaningful years gives some insight (Table 9). In 1911 the original Penn State curriculum was modified, and its courses represent the forestry curriculum in the early years. A comparison of the 1928 and 1930 curricula indicates revisions that accommodated students affected by the merger of the Mont Alto and Penn State programs. The midpoint of one hundred years was 1957, and that year's curriculum contrasts with the dramatic changes in 1963. Finally, the current curriculum is not greatly different from the four forest science options that were adopted in 1996. Total credits ranged from 165 to 169 in the early years, declined to 148 by 1957, and then decreased again to 126 to meet a university-wide mandate in 1963.

Within the declining credit totals were some other significant changes in subject matter. Rhetoric or English credits changed a bit, being high initially and then dropping to twelve or thirteen for many years, and increasing recently with a return of emphasis on communication abilities. Foreign languages were required initially so that students would have access to German and French forestry texts, the only ones available at first; forestry textbooks by American authors were uncommon before 1910. The basic sciences decreased gradually, and course contents have changed somewhat. Mathematics credits have been relatively stable, but calculus is now required as a basis for statistics. Surveying is no longer considered essential, reflecting changes in professional responsibilities of foresters.

79

FIG. 22   Forestry students working on a woods road with Professor John A. Ferguson *(left of center)*, smoking a pipe. School of Forest Resources negative #191, Penn State University Archives, Pennsylvania State University Libraries.

FIG. 23   Class of 1912 in State College Transportation vehicles on fieldtrip to Greenwood Furnace Nursery, May 1911. School of Forest Resources negative #826, Penn State University Archives, Pennsylvania State University Libraries.

FIG. 24   Students learning about packhorses at "Fergie's Woodshed." School of Forest Resources negative #242, Penn State University Archives, Pennsylvania State University Libraries.

FIG. 25   Professor C. H. Strauss and his students during a timber inventory practicum in the forest, circa 1996.

Table 9   Changes in the Forestry Curricula at State College/University Park (summaries of credits by course categories in selected years)[1]

Course Categories	1911	1928*	1930*	1957	1963	2005
			credits			
1. English, writing, speaking	17	12	13	12	12	15
German, French, Spanish	12					
Writing-intensive courses					3	
2. Biological sciences	15	12	8	11	9	4–8
Chemistry, physics	17	18	12	12	14	4–7
Geology, soils, meteorology	9	7	7	8		3–15
3. Mathematics	5	4	4	6	6	4–6
Statistics, computer science					4	5–7
Surveying, photogrammetry	6	6	8	10		0–3
4. Social sciences, arts, humanities	12	9	9	9	12	18
5. Professional, vocational	71	82	66	64	34	47–69
6. Camp: freshman or sophomore	F	FS	FS	S	S	
7. Electives		6	32	6	31	3
8. Physical education	4	5	5	4	4	3
9. ROTC	1	4	4	6		
10. Total credits, including camp	169	165	168	148	126	129

1. Courses in 1911 represent the forestry curriculum in the early years, after some modifications. The 1928 and 1930 curricula indicate requirements before and after the merger of the Mont Alto and Penn State programs. The 1957 curriculum represents a midpoint of the first hundred years. Dramatic changes were made in 1963. The current curriculum of 2005 is not greatly different from the four forest science options implemented in 1996.

* The 1928 curriculum had options in forestry, wood utilization, lumber industry, and city forestry; city forestry was changed to private forestry in 1930.

The social sciences have become more important, as public involvement in forest planning has increased.

Forestry courses have always been a major, though declining, part of the curriculum. That was true even in the years after 1963, when most of the elective credits consisted of forestry or closely related courses that had to be approved by advisors. But then freshmen no longer were required to enroll at Mont Alto, or to take any forestry courses until later. The downward trend in vocational and professional courses was reversed recently, after options within the forest science major were introduced in 1996. Summer camp courses ended in 1966, and some of that practical experience has been incorporated in other professional courses. Skills such as packing horses, sharpening axes, filing cross-cut saws, and throwing two-chain trailer tapes were dropped long ago. But today's students must learn how to use GPS equipment, field data recorders, and other technological devices. Many courses have fieldtrips, most of them within an hour's drive and others to more distant locations, lasting a full day. Students also have opportunities to learn about natural resources elsewhere through tours to other states, or even through travel to Germany.

Elective credits increased in 1929 to accommodate the Mont Alto–Penn State merger, and again when the curriculum was liberalized in 1963. Then in 1996 some elective credits were replaced by choices among professionally related courses that were appropriate for the various options. There has been little change in physical education credits, but students now can choose among many courses. Military course requirements had ended by 1963.

Fifty years ago the faculty was well aware that a new era of forestry education was dawning, and changes under way were described by Ronald Bartoo (1967), head of the Department of Forestry and Wildlife. By then the paramount mission of foresters to reestablish, protect, and conserve natural resources in Pennsylvania and elsewhere had been largely fulfilled. The perceived threat of timber famine and the custodial concept of forestry were fading. The public demand for benefits from forests other than timber, such as recreation opportunities, pure water, and wildlife, was increasing. Greater attention to managerial and social aspects of forestry was affecting the ways in which foresters carried out their changing responsibilities.

Accordingly, the faculty made dramatic changes in the forestry curriculum, especially in 1963, and further adjustments continued for years afterward. Gaining an intimate knowledge of forestry as freshmen or even sophomores no longer was feasible, as many students started at Commonwealth Campuses where no forestry courses were taught. To accommodate them, the first forestry courses were scheduled in the junior year at first; later they were advanced to the sophomore year, requiring all forest science majors to enroll at University Park. There was considerable flexibility in the curriculum, which enabled students to select electives by which they could specialize in subfields of forestry that suited their career interests.

The idea of having faculty advisors who would counsel students in selecting the most appropriate electives for their professional interests, an innovation of the 1963 curriculum, was effective for only a minority of students, but it took a while to realize this. Many students were not sufficiently focused or did not bother to consult their advisors, especially when it became possible to register independently by phone or computer. When a review of transcripts showed a large number of questionable courses

FIG. 26   Forestry students on a southern fieldtrip, sitting on a cypress log in Georgia, 1914. School of Forest Resources negative #584, Penn State University Archives, Pennsylvania State University Libraries.

FIG. 27   School of Forest Resources students on a southern fieldtrip in 1986. Photo by K. C. Steiner.

FIG. 28   School of Forest Resources students on a trip to Germany in 1999. Photo by Susie Steiner.

FIG. 29   Forest Resources students on a visit to Society of American Foresters headquarters in Washington, D.C., in 1988. Photo by K. C. Steiner.

being permitted for technical electives, the faculty greatly reduced the credits in this category and specified more requirements.

The faculty also investigated other ways by which the curriculum could be revised to improve the effectiveness of advising and adapt to emerging changes in the forestry profession. In 1985–86 the forest science faculty developed sixteen pages of educational objectives that listed specific essential knowledge that students should acquire from their professional or technical courses, and the courses in which students were exposed to each of the objectives. The document was viewed as a starting point for curriculum review. The list was sent to fifty-eight senior forestry professionals for commentary, and the comments received from twenty-four of them were helpful in making revisions. The process and the final product were described in a 1987 article in the *Journal of Forestry*, reprints of which were in great demand.

By the early 1990s it was evident that the forestry profession was changing in extraordinary ways. "Ecosystems" became a buzzword. Discussions in the *Journal of Forestry* and at national meetings showed strong divisions within the profession between those interested mainly in timber and those interested in other forest values. The U.S. Forest Service was hiring fewer foresters and more historians, archaeologists, social scientists, and geographers. Timber output from federal lands had begun a long and precipitous decline, and the logging industry in the West was beginning to suffer.

Against the backdrop of these emerging trends, a "summit" on forestry education was held in 1991 in Denver with delegates from industry, federal and state agencies, and nearly all the U.S. forestry schools. The title of the conference was "Forest Resource Management in the 21st Century: Will Forestry Education Meet the Challenge?" Al Sullivan, Rob Brooks, and Kim Steiner attended on behalf of Penn State. Among the conclusions were suggestions that forestry curricula should (1) have a broader resource focus than timber, (2) emphasize critical thinking and problem-solving skills, (3) provide more coverage of the social sciences and integration of social and biophysical sciences, and (4) move toward specialization in graduate school rather than at the undergraduate level.

The Denver education summit was the first of many national meetings on forestry education in the past fifteen years, a period of unprecedented dialogue about what forestry education is and ought to be. Many members of the School faculty have participated in these meetings. Kim Steiner founded the Biennial Conference on University Education in Natural Resources with an inaugural meeting at Penn State in 1996. As originally hoped, other universities have taken up the baton, and subsequent meetings have been hosted by Utah State University (1998), the University of Missouri (2000), North Carolina State University (2002), Northern Arizona University (2004), and Michigan State University (2006). For the first time, educators from across the nation have come together regularly to discuss teaching and curricular issues in forestry and allied disciplines. Attendance is typically eighty to a hundred. Other significant meetings on forestry education during this period included one in Syracuse, New York, in 1994 (sponsored by the Society of American Foresters and the National Association of Professional Forestry Schools and Colleges [NAPFSC]), one in Washington, D.C., in March 1999 (sponsored by the Pinchot Institute for Conservation), and several associated with NAPFSC in which revisions to the SAF accreditation criteria were discussed.

Several members of our faculty who had been active on the national scene began to worry in the 1990s about whether the existing forestry curriculum was enough to sustain School enrollments in the years ahead. The resulting twelve-member Task Force on Undergraduate Education, led by Kim Steiner, met biweekly to develop a new major, named renewable natural resources management (NRM). The intent was to address the educational needs of contemporary managers of renewable natural resources, primarily those employed by organizations with diverse management goals. Four new courses were to (1) introduce the integrated management of forests, wildlife, and water; (2) explain how organisms and their environments function as ecological systems; (3) use analytical and inferential techniques for manipulating data through geographic information systems; and (4) synthesize problem-solving methods applied to natural resources management in biological, economic, social, and political contexts. The proposed curriculum was discussed thoroughly and ultimately was endorsed by the School's advisory board in 1992 and approved by the School faculty in 1993.

The task force also proposed that additional faculty members were needed for the curriculum, but the college was not willing to create these positions because of financial constraints. A stalemate ensued, and the NRM major was not implemented. Not all faculty of the School were disappointed, as some were concerned that NRM would weaken the professional integrity of the forest science major. Furthermore, no one could predict the employment market for NRM graduates.

At subsequent national meetings on forestry education there were discussions of the NRM curriculum and the process by which it was developed.

Whether influenced by Penn State's experience or not, many forestry schools and colleges implemented NRM-like curricula in the 1990s. The discussions also may have given impetus to a revision of the forest science major.

An eight-member curriculum review committee chaired by Charles Strauss developed alternative recommendations for strengthening the forest science major. The proposed revision aimed to maintain its versatility and integrity and provide more structure to the curriculum around four defined career tracks. In 1996, after some debate, the faculty approved and implemented four options within the forest science major that would better prepare students for well-defined career opportunities. The options were identified as forest management, forest biology (research oriented for those considering graduate studies), urban forestry, and watershed management. The multidisciplinary forest management option maintained the broad, integrated learning experience of traditional forestry, giving students the sound foundation they need for professional development. The other three options provided opportunities to specialize in closely related fields supported by the expertise of the existing faculty. The watershed management option was designed to qualify students for federal employment as hydrologists; because those stringent requirements placed constraints on forestry courses that could be included, it was the only option that could not qualify for accreditation by the Society of American Foresters. This was not the first time there had been options in the curriculum. In 1928 electives enabled students to specialize in forestry, wood utilization, lumber industry, or city forestry (Table 9). But in 1996 the faculty was not aware of the city forestry precedent, and urban forestry was thought to be a novel and emerging professional area.

Perhaps the new curricular revisions had a positive effect, because Penn State's forestry enrollments continued to be strong until 2000. Nationally, forestry enrollments began to trend downward in 1995, and this trend continued unabated until recently. Some traditionally strong forestry programs now have very low enrollments but continue to maintain their administrative independence. Others that had formerly stood as distinct departments or colleges have merged with other agriculture departments or colleges in order to maintain program viability. At some prominent universities the accredited forestry curriculum has been reduced to an option or a track within a major such as environmental sciences or natural resources. Also, there has been a pattern of forestry enrollments declining more at large, prestigious state and private universities than at smaller, more professionally oriented schools.

The challenge to forestry education now is to maintain its professional base while adapting to the contemporary, more comprehensive aspects of managing natural resources. On a national level, forestry education has probably never seen such a transformation since the rapid proliferation of programs in the early decades of the last century. Many programs remain very robust, despite problems with lower enrollments and the changing interests of students. Although Penn State's baccalaureate forestry enrollments have declined in all three majors, the total enrollment is still among the largest nationally.

CURRICULUM IN WOOD PRODUCTS

The wood utilization curriculum, initiated to provide an engineering option in forestry, was approved in 1942 but not started until after World War II; the first degrees were awarded in 1948. Four exceptional faculty members developed and taught this program: Newell A. Norton, Wallace E. White, William T. Nearn, and Richard N. Jorgensen. Norton served as an administrative coordinator of the "wood ute" faculty. He and Bill Nearn taught basic courses in wood products and manufacturing systems. "Doc" White taught both forestry and wood ute students about microscopic properties of wood and wood identification. Bill Nearn and Dick Jorgensen taught the advanced courses in drying, preservative treatments, wood engineering, adhesives, and composite products. Jorgensen subsequently pursued a research career with the U.S. Forest Service. Nearn, intrigued by the allure of private industry, joined the Weyerhaeuser Corporation and conducted research for developing engineered wood products.

Changes in the name of this curriculum reflected shifts in emphasis involving instruction, recruitment of students, and employment opportunities for graduates (Table 10). The curriculum was revised in 1961 and its name changed to wood science, broadened to forest products in 1975, and in 1992 focused on wood products with two options: business and marketing, and processing and manufacturing. It is noteworthy that the success of options in wood products was later copied by the forest science and wildlife and fisheries faculties.

Difficulty in recruiting students for this major has been a recurring

Table 10 Changes in the Wood Products Curricula at State College/University Park (summaries of credits by course categories in selected years)

Course Categories	1943 Wood Utilization	1965 Wood Technology	1969 Wood Science	1975 Forest Products	1992 Wood Products Process. & Manufact.	Business & Marketing
1. English, Writing, Speech	15	15	12	12	12	12
2. Biological and Physical Sciences	24	27	25	25	18	9
3. Mathematics and Statistics	20	15	13	12	12	12
4. Social Sciences, Arts, Humanities	3	9	12	12	18	18
5. Professional wood products & related	72	56	34	32	31	22
6. Electives and supporting courses	3	21	30	30	30	48
7. Physical Education	4	4	4	4	4	4
8. ROTC	6					
9. Total Credits	147	147	130	127	125	125

problem, in contrast to employment opportunities and salaries for its graduates, which have been superior to those of other majors in the School. Wood products could be characterized as a niche curriculum, in which fundamental engineering and business principles are applied to the particulars of the product and marketing systems found within the complex wood industries. Few freshmen entering Penn State are aware of this major. Typically a large majority of the students enter as transfers from the Colleges of Engineering or Business. Thus wood products is considered a "discovery major." Nonetheless, its graduates are recognized as well trained and in demand by the myriad companies within this broad industry.

Forty years ago Penn State president Eric Walker, an engineer, prophesied, "In spite of developments in recent years in the production and use of new materials, lumber remains man's chief building material, and there is every prospect that it will continue to hold the supremacy it has held for centuries against the competition of brick, stone, steel, aluminum, and other materials." Since then wood scientists, engineers, and businessmen have ingeniously adapted and marketed solid and composite wood products in meeting the expanded needs of society worldwide, needs that have largely been met within the sustained capability of the world's forests.

CURRICULUM IN WILDLIFE AND FISHERIES SCIENCE

Wildlife interests prevailed among faculty and students from the time of George R. Green, who was on the faculty from 1912 to 1924, and probably earlier. Collecting snakes, birds, and other wildlife, he turned his lab into a "virtual zoo." Hundreds came on Sundays and holidays to see his creatures. Green obtained two bears from the Game Commission, to see if they would breed in captivity—they did not. The gentle female, named Tiny, would enter the Forestry Building when a window was opened and wander into classrooms and offices. Everyone loved her except the stenographer, who would yell and take to the top of her desk when she heard claws clattering down the hall. Once, during a lecture by the distinguished Professor Chapman of Yale, Tiny made a fuss and was let in. The bear sniffed around Chapman's feet as he gave his lecture, unperturbed. On one occasion Professor Green gave a talk before the Teachers' Institute in Johnstown. As he moved around the room with snakes coiled around his arms, several women left the room and one fainted. "It was a great success," he declared. Green was made head of the Department of Nature

Education when the School of Education was established. His zoo and all of the books about nature went with him.

The B.S. degree program in wildlife science started in 1981, but forestry students took courses in wildlife long before then, and of course both students and faculty frequently engaged in hunting and fishing. Zoology was part of the forestry curriculum already in 1911, but there was no course titled wildlife. In 1937 the Cooperative Wildlife Research Unit was established at the university, though not within the Department of Forestry at that time. The first M.S. degree in wildlife management was conferred by the Zoology Department in 1939, indicating that wildlife courses were being taught; range management was taught in the Forestry Department.

In 1959 the faculty began looking seriously into the feasibility of undergraduate specialties in wildlife management, and also watershed management and recreation management. In 1961 the wildlife management graduate program was transferred from the Biology Department to the School of Forest Resources, and the College of Agriculture somewhat reluctantly approved a position in wildlife management. John L. George was appointed in 1963 as the School's first faculty member in wildlife management, and he began a vigorous campaign to expand wildlife interests in the School.

A series of developments gave visibility to wildlife education and culminated in a comprehensive program. The first substantial evidence came in 1965, when the Department of Forest Management was renamed the Department of Forestry and Wildlife. Expansion of the wildlife teaching faculty got under way in 1967. In 1970 the associate degree program in wildlife technology was started at the DuBois campus. The School of Forest Resources received approval to use the wildlife label on courses in 1971, and the School was authorized in 1974 as the sole unit to offer an M.S. degree in wildlife management. The wildlife science B.S. major was first offered in 1981. Until then forestry students could take electives in biology and wildlife to qualify as wildlife biologists in federal Civil Service rosters. In 1982 the Cooperative Fisheries Research Unit was transferred to the School and combined with the wildlife unit. The wildlife science B.S. major was restructured and became the wildlife and fisheries science major in 1988; in 2001 separate options in wildlife and fisheries were created (Table 11). The finale occurred in 1990, when the Ph.D. program in wildlife and fisheries science was approved.

Table 11 Changes in the Wildlife Curricula at University Park (summaries of credits by course categories in selected years)

Course Categories	1981	1988	2001 Wildlife	Fisheries
1. English	12	9	9	9
2. Biology	22	29	18–19	18–20
3. Chemistry and	10	7	7	7
Physics	0	4	4	4
4. Mathematics, Statistics, Computer Science	15	15	12	12
5. Social Sciences, Arts, Humanities	18	21	21	21
6. Wildlife and Fisheries	15	16	24–25	25
7. Electives	28–29	24–27	19	19
8. Physical Education	4	4	3	3
9. ROTC (optional)	6	3	3	3
10. Total	130	132	120	122

GRADUATE DEGREE PROGRAMS

The graduate program was quite modest at first, with one to three master's degrees conferred annually from 1913 to 1946. The numbers increased somewhat after 1947, and have grown more dramatically since 1972. In recent years approximately one hundred active graduate students have enrolled annually. About one-quarter of them work toward the Ph.D. degree, and some 35 percent of the graduate students have been women. The strong interdisciplinary orientation of the faculty is indicated by the considerable numbers of graduate students they advise in multidisciplinary majors such as ecology or environmental pollution control, which are outside the School's two graduate majors, forest resources and wildlife and fisheries science.

The history of graduate degrees begins in 1913, when the first two M.S. degrees in forestry were conferred at Penn State. One thesis was on range management, not at all a topic considered important in the Northeast, and the other was about the relationship of the resources of a national forest to the community, a subject of renewed attention today. In 1939 the first of many theses on wildlife appeared, this one on the winter foods of deer, about the time when excessive browsing was first recognized as a serious problem. Research conducted by graduate students and faculty is expected to be at the cutting edge of science and technology, and this long-standing tradition continues. The graduate committee for each student helps in designing a program of study and research suited to the student's interests, and supervises progress toward clearly defined objectives that meet requirements of the graduate school and the School of Forest Resources.

The Master of Forestry degree was first granted in 1945, providing advanced professional education at first in forestry or wood utilization and later also in wildlife science. In 1975 its requirements were revised and its name was changed to Master of Forest Resources, consistent with the name of the School, which had been changed ten years earlier.

M.S. degrees in wildlife management at first were administered in the Biology Department, and then this interdepartmental program was transferred to the School of Forestry in 1961. The School of Forest Resources became solely responsible in 1974, and the name of the degree was changed in 1988 to wildlife and fisheries science.

The graduate school authorized the Ph.D. degree in forest resources in 1967, and the first Ph.D. was awarded in 1972. In 1990 the Ph.D. and M.F.R. degrees were approved in wildlife and fisheries science.

Faculty of the School also supervise graduate students in multidisciplinary graduate programs, including biotechnology, ecology, environmental pollution control, genetics, integrative biosciences, operations research, and plant physiology. Ecology has been the most popular of these, especially for students with wildlife interests. The breadth of interests and involvement with other departments and colleges of the university has been growing steadily.

The Center for Watershed Stewardship was started in 1998 by the School of Forest Resources and the Department of Landscape Architecture. It was funded through a grant from the Howard Heinz Endowment. The center's purpose is to create the next generation of watershed professionals by combining interdisciplinary capabilities with strong disciplinary bases in a community-oriented context. The center's programs include graduate studies in watershed stewardship and a continuing education program of short courses for natural resources professionals and community leaders. In the second year of the graduate curriculum students participate as teams in a "Keystone Project," which gives them real-world experience in watershed planning.

A joint degree program with the Dickinson School of Law was approved in 2003. Students in the program can receive a degree of Juris Doctor (J.D.) from Dickinson and a master's degree or a Ph.D. from Penn

State in forest resources or wildlife and fisheries science. The joint degree program typically entails five semesters in residence at Dickinson plus as many semesters at Penn State as required for the particular degree. The Goddard chair professor has been designated as the advisor in the School of Forest Resources.

9

STUDENT RECRUITMENT, ENROLLMENTS, GRADUATION RATES, AND PLACEMENT

Until recently, efforts to recruit students typically have been low key, relying mainly on printed materials of the School of Forest Resources, college, and university. But a more aggressive approach has become a priority in recent years, in an attempt to counteract declining enrollments that occurred especially during the 1980s and again in recent years. The School's Undergraduate Programs Office coordinates regular contacts on campus with the Division of Undergraduate Studies, which advises students who are undecided about their major, and with the Colleges of Business and Engineering. Off-campus visits regularly include university campuses at Mont Alto, DuBois, Williamsport, and Altoona, and we tie in with College of Agricultural Sciences recruitment on other campuses and in high schools. We also encourage various professional groups and alumni to help recruit for us.

The School's current proactive marketing strategy aims to increase the number, quality, and diversity of our enrollments. One way is to provide personal interaction with potential students and their parents, along with high-quality advising and placement services for enrolled students. Another part of the strategy is to more effectively use various marketing approaches and media, including the internet, printed material, closer coordination with the Division of Undergraduate Studies advisors, continued cooperation with related two-year programs at Mont Alto, DuBois, and Penn College, and other targeted face-to-face recruiting activities.

Scholarships are one means of encouraging well-qualified students to enroll. Scholarships also provide an incentive for better scholarship and can aid in the retention of good students. The number of awards made to undergraduate forest resources students by the School's scholarship committee grew from thirty-six in 1990–91 to eighty in 2004–5, and their total value increased from $30,000 to $133,922. Accordingly, the average award in 2004–5 was $1,661. Individual awards ranged from $500 to $5,000. In addition, our students compete for scholarships at the college and university levels.

Graduate assistantships and fellowships are vital for recruiting well-qualified graduate students. Nearly every graduate student has such financial support, which includes a competitive stipend and tuition waiver. In return, graduate assistants help faculty in teaching undergraduate courses and also are assigned duties in research projects or extension activities.

From rather modest beginnings, the number of students enrolled and graduating in forestry accelerated in the School's early decades. In 1909, when there were ten forestry schools nationwide, forty-seven forestry students received bachelors degrees in the United States; seventeen (36.2 percent) of these were awarded in Pennsylvania, thirteen at the Mont Alto Academy and four at Penn State. In 1939, when there were eighteen accredited forestry programs and nine others in the country, 1,102 received undergraduate degrees in forestry, 102 (9.3 percent) of which were B.S. degrees at Penn State. These figures and graduation rates by decade (Table 12) indicate the early prominence of forestry education in Pennsylvania and its continuing importance nationally, even as many more institutions started forestry programs.

Consistent with the growth of forestry and related professions, there has been a great increase in forestry enrollments and degree programs, and also occasional retrenchments over the years, notably those during World Wars I and II. Many students enlisted for the various armed forces or were drafted. After the conflicts, veterans made up the preponderance of the large classes for several years, induced particularly, after World War II, by benefits of the GI Bill of Rights. Their common bond of military service and the necessity of adapting to academic challenges at Mont Alto served to develop a special camaraderie in these postwar classes.

Fifty years ago, in 1956, the total enrollment of 329 men in forestry at Penn State consisted of 114 freshmen at Mont Alto, 197 sophomores and upperclassmen at University Park, 17 graduate students, and 1 special student. In fall 2006 92 students were enrolled in forest science, 120 in wildlife and fisheries, 20 in wood products, and there were 88 graduate students. The total of 320 students included 83 women, representing 34 percent of the graduate students and 23 percent of the undergraduates. There had been a steady decline in undergraduates since 1999, a recent peak year, when the total enrollment was 633, including 73 graduate students.

A summary by decades of degrees in forest resources awarded at Penn

97

FIG. 30   All of the forestry students enrolled in 1912 assembled at "Fergie's Woodshed." School of Forest Resources negative #860, Penn State University Archives, Pennsylvania State University Libraries.

State and the Mont Alto Academy (Table 12) gives an overview of the trends. The number of graduates during the first three decades was modest and relatively stable, with somewhat larger numbers at Penn State than at Mont Alto. A large increase in graduates after 1935 was stimulated by the Civilian Conservation Corps. The numbers declined below fifty from 1943 to 1949 and 1956 to 1957 owing to the wars, and reached very high levels between 1966 and 1980 (Appendix B-1). The peak years were 1977–79, when an average of 242 degrees per year were conferred, 50 percent in forest science, 10 percent in wood science, 16 percent each in forest technology and wildlife technology; 8 percent were graduate degrees. A strong decline was under way in 1981 and continued until 1992, when the number of degrees increased again. From 1987 until 2001 more degrees were awarded every year in the wildlife major, ranging from twenty-six to seventy-one, than in forest science. Recent baccalaureate graduation rates have decreased again since 2000, from 125 in the three majors to eighty-one in 2005. Graduate degrees, both master's and doctoral, have increased greatly since the 1960s. In the past decade two-year degrees represented 28 percent of the total number awarded, baccalaureate degrees 62 percent, and graduate degrees 10 percent.

Table 12 Undergraduate and Graduate Degrees Awarded, Summarized by Decade (baccalaureate degrees conferred by Penn State include those in majors currently named Forest Science [FOR], Wood Products [WP], and Wildlife and Fisheries Science [WFS])

Years	Two-year Degrees		Baccalaurate Degrees				Graduate Degrees		Total
	Forestry	Wildlife	Academy	FOR	WP	WFS	Master's	Ph.D.	
1906–1915			79	110			2		191
1916–1925			86	93			1		180
1926–1935	49*		78	191			6		324
1936–1945	73*			544			7		624
1946–1955				562	61		63		686
1956–1965	15			592	66		84		757
1966–1975	375	100		671	66		142	4	1,358
1976–1985	324	349		778	203	24	158	26	1,862
1986–1995	118	139		214	55	330	109	32	997
1996–2005	200	248		368	113	507	127	39	1,602
1906–2005	1,154	836	243	4,123	564	861	699	101	8,581

*Ranger course graduates

Forestry was an almost exclusively male domain until the 1960s, throughout the nation as well as at Penn State. In 1969 the first female, Sophia Lecznar, received an M.S. degree in forest resources at Penn State; and in 1973, for the first time here, the B.S. degree in forest science was conferred on a woman, Patricia A. Remy. The first female forester hired by Pennsylvania's Bureau of Forestry, in 1984, was our alumna Amy Griffith, whose father also worked for the bureau. Not until 1995 did our first female students receive doctoral degrees; appropriately, though not by design, one specialized in forestry (Callie Pickens), one in wildlife (Luise K. Davis), and one in wood products (Lucie K. Ozanne).

Students graduating from the school's three majors have experienced strong placement opportunities, according to annual employment surveys conducted one or two years after graduation. During the latest five years of available data, 1998 to 2003, 88 percent of graduates were engaged in professional positions, including 17 percent in graduate studies; most of the remainder had blue-collar jobs, and a few were unemployed. Comparable figures for the previous twenty-five years were 84 percent in professional positions, including 15 percent in graduate studies. Annual data have been somewhat cyclical, with low points of professional employment in 1973 (67 percent) and 1993 (57 percent) associated with major recessions in the U.S. economy. Starting salaries for 2003–4 were approximately $30,000 for those employed in forest management; 40,000 in other types of management, engineering, or sales, mostly in the wood products industries; and $25,800 in wildlife or fisheries management. For the twenty-five-year period 1973–98, comparable starting salaries were $22,000, $27,500, and $13,500, respectively.

Our alumni are located in many states and countries, although many remain in Pennsylvania. In 2005 the Penn State Alumni Association had addresses for 4,662 alumni of the School of Forest Resources, not including additional alumni who had received degrees in intercollege graduate programs. Of these, 4,616 (99 percent) were located in the United States, including 2,456 (53 percent) in Pennsylvania, and 46 (1 percent) in other countries. Our alumni resided in every county in Pennsylvania and in every state in the nation. Pennsylvania counties with the largest numbers were Centre (264), Allegheny (125), and Montgomery (101); others with sizable contingents were York (95), Lancaster (82), Westmoreland (82), Cumberland (79), Chester (76), Berks (67), Dauphin (67), Luzerne (51), and McKean (51). The leading states were Pennsylvania (2,456), Virginia (204), Maryland (145), New York (133), Florida (125), Oregon (111), and

North Carolina (104); next came Colorado (91), California (83), New Jersey (77), Washington (70), Georgia (64), South Carolina (63), Ohio (60), and Texas (55). The forty-six alumni in other countries were distributed among twenty-five nations; eleven (24 percent) of these were in Canada; India, Taiwan, and Thailand had three (7 percent) each; and one or two alumni were in each of the other countries.

10

STUDENT ORGANIZATIONS

Much of the information about student organizations came from the *Sylvan*, the yearbook initially published by the student Forestry Society and later by the staff, which included students in all majors. Faculty members who have served recently as advisors to the various organizations added to the descriptions. Activities of the student organizations have varied over the years, so recollections of former members may differ from these accounts.

The student Forestry Society was organized by Professor Baker in 1909, soon after the Department of Forestry came into existence. Its original purpose was to enable students to air their views on forestry topics; accordingly, students presented one or more papers at each meeting, the best of them receiving prizes. Later, interest in papers dwindled and they were replaced by outside speakers. In the early years the Forestry Society sponsored the U.S. Pack Master, who spent a month teaching students the art of packing horses. There was a welcoming campfire for freshmen in the fall and a farewell banquet for graduating seniors. The forty-fourth annual banquet was held in 1956, which suggests that the first banquet was held in 1912, or earlier if any years were skipped. Usually a prominent academic or governmental speaker was featured, and sometimes a skit poked fun at students and faculty members; Professor Merwin Humphrey was a memorable provocateur and participant. For many years, starting in 1934 with some lapses, the Forestry Society published the *Sylvan*, although the first issue was named the *Penn State Forester*. The *Sylvan* presented photographs of the students and faculty, articles about professional forestry, descriptions of student activities, and assorted comments about classmates and teachers, lame jokes, and even "pomes." A woodsmen team entered competitions involving woodsy skills with teams from Mont Alto and from other universities, typically West Virginia and Syracuse. The tristate field days in the spring at one of the universities featured tree felling, log sawing, chopping, the chain throw, and a variety of other activities. They usually culminated in a picnic and late-night party; so the bus trip home on Sunday was a quieter affair. One event in the distant past was a run to McAlevys Fort and back, a roundtrip distance of about thirty miles that included a climb of eight hundred feet over Tussey Mountain in both directions; students must have been more rugged in those days. The forestry ball was held for many years, at first outdoors near Fergie's Woodshed, then in the Armory, and later in Rec Hall and the student union building. Other activities included Christmas tree and firewood sales, participating in Red Cross blood drives, work projects in local parks, intramural sports, and trips to various places of interest. The Forestry Society became a student chapter of the Society of American Foresters in 1993, and students have attended regional and national conventions. Penn State's student chapter has won national recognition, including the 2002–3 Outstanding Student Chapter Award and second place for the 2003–4 award. The chapter also won second-place awards for its website in both years. In 2005 the chapter's team won first place in the Quiz Bowl at the SAF national convention among thirty schools that participated, and again second place in the website competition.

The Eta chapter of Xi Sigma Pi, the national forestry honor society, began at Penn State in 1924 through the efforts of Professor Hugh Baker. Professor Harold Newins of the Oregon Forest School established the chapter and soon afterward joined the Penn State faculty. The purpose of this international organization, founded at the University of Washington in 1908, is to maintain high scholarship, build up the forestry profession, and promote fraternal relations among those engaged in forest activities. Students nominated for membership assemble pledge books and collect signatures of faculty and student members as a means of getting better acquainted. They also work on a pledge project, such as measuring experimental plantations or other projects that are helpful to the School. Other activities have included working on research projects, sponsoring speakers, and maintaining plaques that list awardees and faculty of the School. Each year society members select a student for the Outstanding Forestry Senior Award.

The student chapter of the Forest Products Research Society provides a way for students to share their interests in professional matters related to wood and other forest products. In recent years the Penn State chapter has joined students from Virginia Tech in a weekend excursion to the High Point, North Carolina, center of the furniture industry. Club activi-

FIG. 31   Tree-felling event at tri-state field day. Photo by C. H. Strauss.

FIG. 32   Axe throw at tri-state field day. Photo by C. H. Strauss.

ties have included fieldtrips to forest products industries, discussions with professionals, and a canoe-building contest. Dr. Nicole Brown initiated a new form of competition among students and faculty, the cardboard canoe race staged at Lake Perez in Stone Valley. Pairs of contestants have two hours to construct their craft from two 4 x 6 foot sheets of cardboard and a roll of duct tape, and paddle it over a hundred-yard course. Some even make it back to the dock.

Tau Phi Delta is a national social professional fraternity for students interested in forestry and the outdoors. First chartered as a forestry club in 1922, its purpose is to promote a lively interest in forestry activities and in high scholarship. The local "Treehouse" is the only remaining chapter in the nation. It has evolved from strictly forestry members to include others in environmentally related fields. Faculty advisors have included Maurice Goddard, Wallace White, Ronald Bartoo, Wayne Murphey, Peter Dress, and Charles Strauss. Social activities have included sponsoring a School picnic in the spring, theme parties, hayrides, skiing, deer and bear hunts, and fishing trips. In 1967 Tau Phi Delta acquired a new fraternity house at 427 East Fairmount Avenue; subsequent improvements included red oak paneling installed by the members from trees they had felled and milled. The fraternity has taken pride in serving the community, winning more than thirty Red Cross blood drives among fraternities, establishing the W. James Evans Memorial Arboretum, and assisting State College Borough and the Game and Fish Commissions with cleanups, among other activities. State College Borough declared April 21, 2003, Tau Phi Delta Day, recognizing that the fraternity had proven its worth as "good neighbors" to the community.

The Lumber Jills, an association of forestry students' wives, was organized in 1959 through the initiative of Hazyl Fletcher, wife of director Peter Fletcher. The club promoted fellowship, helped strengthen student-faculty relationships, and acquainted members with the forestry profession. In 1962 the group joined with similar organizations at other universities, twenty-two eventually, to form the National Association of Forestry Students' Wives; the Penn State Lumber Jills served as historians. NAFSW met annually until 1968, after which it was dissolved because the broader society was changing. "Dutiful wives" were progressing toward equal partnership with their husbands or careers of their own.

The Penn State student chapter of the Wildlife Society, chartered in 1964, is an organization of students and faculty with the goal of increasing public awareness of wildlife management values and issues. The Wildlife

Society has hosted speakers in the wildlife and fisheries fields, arranged trips to interesting places such as Hawk Mountain Bird Sanctuary and Elk County, assisted the Pennsylvania Game Commission at bear and deer check stations, participated in habitat restoration and watershed assessment projects, and participated in the wildlife conclave of the Wildlife Society's northeast section. The organization also has been engaged in wildlife and natural resource education for the public though outreach programs such as Pennsylvania Wildlife 4-H and workshops held at Shavers Creek Environmental Center.

The Penn State student chapter of the American Fisheries Society was founded in 1997. It provides a forum for students to learn about fisheries-related topics by hosting speakers and sponsoring fieldtrips. The chapter has coordinated Red Cross first aid and CPR training and certification for students and faculty.

The Penn State student chapter of the American Water Resources Association was formed in 1989 by students with interests in water resources issues. Members include graduate and undergraduate students from the School of Forest Resources and water-related majors across campus. The AWRA student chapter has routinely sponsored water resources seminars, fieldtrips, and community service programs such as educational field days for local junior high school students. The Penn State student chapter won the National Outstanding Student Chapter Award in 1991, 1992, and 1998.

Graduate students of the School formed the Natural Resources Graduate Student Organization in 1993 as a professional and social organization through which they could become better acquainted with each other and pursue their common interests. In 2004 they reestablished themselves as the School of Forest Resources Graduate Student Organization. They have joined similar groups across the campus in addressing issues related to teaching responsibilities, representation by unions, and other workforce concerns. Their meetings with the director have brought improvements to the School, such as better access to computers and professional development seminars on job searching, women's issues, and funding sources.

This rich assortment of student organizations is a vital part of the School's tradition. Through their participation students can develop their skills, teamwork, and leadership talents and thus enhance their prospects in professional careers.

11

RESEARCH

The scientific knowledge of forestry that students acquire and practitioners apply is created by research and scholarship, both formal and informal. New knowledge has been generated not only at universities, of course, but also through the research of government agencies and industrial organizations. The experiences of practicing foresters also are a source of useful knowledge.

Research at universities becomes manifest through publications of faculty and graduate students, as they pursue their professional interests and build scholarly reputations. For faculty to gain promotions they must also become proficient at obtaining research grants, as grants have become the principal means of financing research. Graduate students learn how to do research through their own projects, guided by their professors. So research at universities tends to be more individualistic and opportunistic, and less oriented toward the practical objectives of government agencies or industries, though it is sometimes influenced and often supported by them. The objectives of research projects also cater to the interests of private forest landowners (in that they own the majority of forest properties), municipalities, and various groups that use forests for recreation and other purposes. Professors and students have a symbiotic relationship in their research. Professors provide insights, facilities, and continuity for a series of related studies, while students often inject novelty, creativity, youthful enthusiasm, and occasionally even a new direction.

In the early days, the only textbooks on forestry were in German or French, and new knowledge applicable to North American forests was sorely needed. Books and other publications written by Fernow and Illick in the early 1900s are good examples of initial American forestry publications. Although the main academic emphasis at that time was on undergraduate education, research got under way almost from the beginnings at Mont Alto and Penn State. Experimental pine and hardwood plantations were planted in the vicinity of Mont Alto by 1906. By 1930, when the Pennsylvania Forest Research Institute opened at Mont Alto with Willis M. Baker as director, eighty-four study plots and demonstrations had been established. The first faculty member at Penn State whose title included the words "forestry research" was Arthur C. McIntyre, employed from 1927 to 1936. The implication was that his main responsibility was to conduct research, on a wide variety of topics, whereas most faculty would concentrate on teaching. Forestry research has appeared in the titles of just three others: Donald D. Stevenson, employed 1935 to 1945; Raymond R. Moore, 1936 to 1937; and Ronald A. Bartoo, 1937 to 1968. There also have been other faculty members whose principal responsibility has been research.

During the first five decades, research in the School was rather limited. The faculty was small, their efforts were directed mainly at educating students, and research funds were scarce. Laboratory experiments and statistical analyses were uncommon. Specialized fields such as watershed management, genetics, soils, products marketing, and fisheries came along later, as part of the proliferation of research.

An important event in 1956 alienated research relationships between the School of Forestry and the Bureau of Forestry. Joseph Ibberson attended a meeting in the office of Maurice Goddard, and he provided the following account of what happened. Goddard had become secretary of the Department of Forests and Waters a year earlier. William Bramble presumably had persuaded Goddard that forestry research should be conducted at Penn State and not by the Bureau of Forestry. In any case, that decision was made at the meeting, and vocally supported by the Penn State participants, including President Milton Eisenhower, Dean of Agriculture Lyman Jackson, Agricultural Experiment Station Head Mike Farrell, and Professor Bramble. Soon afterward Goddard renamed Ibberson's Division of Research the Division of Forest Advisory Services. He also transferred to Penn State many boxes of research records and $100,000 so that Wilber Ward and others could summarize the silvicultural research results of the bureau, with the proviso that they would bring them to a conclusion. A closer research relationship between the School of Forest Resources and the Bureau of Forestry has been fostered since then by both parties, with collaboration and financial support in many projects.

The pace of research accelerated greatly after 1960, when Director Peter Fletcher started pressuring the faculty to strengthen research efforts and to seek grants that would provide greater support. This new expectation jolted some faculty, who had become accustomed to reliance on very modest funding from the College of Agriculture for their small research projects. Fletcher and Assistant Director Robert McDermott, Fletcher's close friend and confidant, were determined to improve the School's reputation through research. They recognized that the growing availability of grant funds presented the best prospects for increasing research budgets. Furthermore, research productivity was·becoming increasingly important to the faculty and administrators as a means of achieving tenure and promotions. In 1975 the university instituted new regulations for promotion and tenure that exerted greater pressure on faculty to publish research results in prestigious journals.

Subsequent directors since Fletcher also have facilitated the ability of faculty to secure grants. So has the Agricultural Experiment Station, by dramatically improving its service to faculty in preparing and submitting grant proposals. The younger faculty and those hired more recently also responded to the challenge, and have been very successful. Grants awarded to faculty have increased dramatically in recent years (Table 13), coming from a wide variety of sources but primarily from state and federal agencies. Since 1984 grants to our faculty have been greater than the sum of state and federal research appropriations every year. State appropriations allocated to the School for research increased 175 percent from 1983–84 to 1992–93, in contrast to 14 percent between 1993 and 2005–6. Federal research appropriations increased 20 percent and 46 percent for the same periods. Thus, since 1993 federal and state support for research has increased only modestly. In fact, since 1990 the purchasing power of state and federal research support actually has decreased because of inflation. During fiscal year 2003–4, faculty generated ninety-nine proposals totaling $22 million, and attracted more than $5.7 million in new awards to the School. Grants have made it possible not only to increase the quantity and diversity of research but also to improve its quality and to provide support for more graduate students.

Table 13 Annual Research Budgets Showing State Appropriations, Federal Formula Funds, and Grants Awarded to Faculty in Representative Selected Years (in thousands of dollars)

Year	State	Federal	Faculty Grants	Total
1983–1984	317	260	520	1,507
1992–1993	875	313	2,443	3,641
2003–2004	1,114	416	5,711	7,241
2005–2006	996	460	data incomplete	

Faculty members in the School of Forest Resources conduct research and scholarly work in a wide range of disciplines and interdisciplinary areas, either as principal investigators or as part of a collaborative team. The sources of financial support have had definite impacts on the kinds of research they have pursued. Securing financial support has been easier for basic research, which some practitioners regard as impractical, than for applied research.

The current research program is a complex mix of individual and inter-disciplinary programs. Faculty members take the initiative in devising individual and collaborative projects and securing financial support through grants or the Agricultural Experiment Station. In some cases collaboration has been formalized. Four faculty members hold joint appointments with the Penn State Institutes for the Environment, and one faculty member has a joint appointment with the Life Sciences Consortium. The School of Forest Resources also houses the Pennsylvania Cooperative Fish and Wildlife Research Unit, a group of two federal scientists who hold graduate faculty status and advise graduate students; a regional office of the National Park Service with five scientists; a research unit of The American Chestnut Foundation with one scientist; and a regional office of the Nature Conservancy with one scientist.

Graduate students have been a vital part of the School's research efforts. In our first century graduate students have written more than eight hundred theses, and they and our faculty have published a larger, uncounted number of scientific articles. Many of their investigations have focused on the forests, forest products, water, and wildlife of Pennsylvania. Yet they also extend to national issues and international topics and include some rather unusual subjects. Graduate theses are an important part of the publications record. Topics addressed in the publications of our graduate students and faculty have been so extensive and diverse that they can be sampled here only in a superficial way. Some uncommon topics are identified first, before returning to more typical research projects.

Quite a variety of subjects that might be unexpected by those outside the research community have been studied over the early years—for example, range management (1913), rubber production in West Africa (1946), tree planting on strip mines (1948), wood properties of Costa Rican hardwoods (1948), municipal shade trees (1952), herbicides for controlling vegetation under power lines (1952), and marketing Christmas trees (1955). The importance of these subjects became fully apparent only years later.

More recent unusual graduate thesis topics include irrigation with sewage effluent (1964), a seismic study of bedrock (1966), aerial photography of Costa Rican forests (1967), a visitor survey in Yosemite National Park (1968), modeling a wolf-moose predator-prey system (1973), heavy metals in northern fur seals (1977), acoustic energy effects on fluid uptake (1979), repairing failing septic systems (1984), polymer composite theories (1986), parks in Scotland (1987), roost selection by bats (1994), growth of Atlantic sturgeon (1995), carbon storage by utility-compatible trees (1999), artificial wetlands for treating wastewater (2000), climate change effects on wet deposition (2000), and chemical control of Japanese knotweed (2002).

More conventional thesis topics include flakeboard particles (1959), timber versus recreation values (1961), the public image of forestry (1964), predicting demand for forest recreation in the United States (1975), finger jointing in furniture (1970), dendrology instruction in the United States (1978), interfacing remote sensing with geographic information systems (1982), microcomputers as instructional tools (1985), direct mail in extension programming (1986), historic woodlots at Gettysburg (1990), community forestry grants (1994), forest owner associations in the United States (1998), electronic commerce in retail home centers (1999), equilibrium analysis of forest taxation (2000), the impact of public lands on a regional economy (2001), and internet-based forestry extension (2002).

Faculty members are always required to justify their research by explaining to sponsors the scientific and practical benefits. Individual faculty are most knowledgeable about their own fields of expertise, so it was logical to ask each of them which of their publications they believe has produced the greatest impact (Table 14). The titles are indicative of benefits to society, industry, or science in some cases, but not so obvious in others. Rest assured, our faculty will gladly explain their research to anyone who inquires.

Our School has gained a strong reputation in several fields of research, especially in the past five decades, through groups of projects that have continued over extended periods of time. The somewhat arbitrary groupings that follow are for illustrative purposes only. There is some overlap among the topics and the participating faculty. Some projects have involved several participating faculty, while others have been pursued more independently. These fields of research include (1) forest ecology and silviculture, (2) forest management and economic analyses, (3) forest genetics and tree improvement, (4) forest hydrology and watershed management, (5) wood products engineering, (6) wood products marketing and

Table 14 Research Publications of Recent Faculty with the Greatest Scientific or Practical Impact, in the Opinions of the Authors

Abrams, M. D. 1992. Fire and the development of oak forests. *Bioscience* 42: 346–53.

Blankenhorn, P. R., B. D. Blankenhorn, and A. G. Norton. Selected quality characteristics of white ash used in professional baseball bats. *Forest Products Journal* 53 (3): 43–46.

Hoover, J. P., M. C. Brittingham, and L. J. Goodrich. 1995. Effects of forest patch size on nesting success of wood thrushes. *Auk* 112: 146–55.

Carline, R. F., P. M. Barry, and H. G. Ketola. 2004. Dietary uptake of polychlorinated biphenyls (PCBs) by rainbow trout. *North American Journal of Aquaculture* 66: 91–99.

Kirk, T. K., J. E. Carlson, N. Ellstrand, A. R. Kapuscinski, T. A. Lumpkin, D. C. Magnus, D. B. Magraw Jr., E. W. Nester, J. J. Peloquin, M. B. Sticklen, A. A. Snow, and P. E. Turner. 2004. *Biological confinement of genetically engineered organisms*. Washington, D.C.: National Academies Press.

DeWalle, D. R., B. R. Swistock, and W. E. Sharpe. 1988. 3-component tracer model for stormflow on a small Appalachian forested catchment. *Journal of Hydrology* 104 (1–4): 301–10.

Gerhold, H. D., N. L. Lacasse, and W. N. Wandell, eds. 2001. *Landscape tree factsheets*. University Park: Pennsylvania State University, College of Agricultural Sciences.

Jacobson, M. 2002. Factors affecting private forest landowner interest in ecosystem management: Linking spatial and survey data. *Environmental Management* 30: 577–83.

Lynch, J. A., J. W. Grimm, and V. C. Bowersox. 1995. Trends in precipitation chemistry in the United States: A national perspective, 1980–1992. *Atmospheric Environment* 29 (11): 1231–46.

McDill, M., S. Rebain, and J. Braze. 2002. Harvest scheduling with area-based adjacency constraints. *Forest Science* 48 (4): 631–42.

Johnson, G., W. Myers, and G. P. Patil. 2001. Predictability of surface water pollution loading in Pennsylvania using watershed-based landscape measurements. *Journal of American Water Resources Association* 37 (4): 821–35.

Sharpe, W. E., and P. W. Fletcher, eds. 1975. *Proceedings Conference on Water Conservation and Sewage Flow Reduction with Water-Saving Devices*. Information Report 74. University Park: Pennsylvania State University, Institute for Research on Land and Water Resources.

Sherwin, Lysle S. and K. R. Tamminga. 2001. Keystone projects: Service-learning practica in watershed stewardship. *Water Resources Update* (Universities Council on Water Resources) 119: 27–41.

Smith, P. M., and C. D. West. 1994. The globalization of furniture industries/markets. *Journal of Global Marketing* 7 (3): 103–31.

Gould, P. J., K. C. Steiner, J. C. Finley, and M. E. McDill. 2005. Developmental pathways following the harvest of oak-dominated stands. *Forest Science* 51: 76–90.

Strauss, C. H., and S. C. Grado. 1992. Input-output analysis of energy requirements for short rotation intensive culture woody biomass. *Solar Energy* 48 (1): 45–51.

Swistock, B. R., D. R. DeWalle, and W. E. Sharpe. 1989. Sources of acidic storm flow in an Appalachian headwater stream. *Water Resources Research* 25 (10): 2139–47.

Wiant, H. V., M. L. Spangler, and J. E. Baumgras. 2002. Comparison of estimates of hardwood bole volume using importance sampling, the centroid method, and some taper equations. *Northeastern Journal of Applied Forestry* 19: 141–42.

Yahner, R. H. 2000. *Eastern deciduous forest: Ecology and wildlife conservation.* 2d ed. Minneapolis: University of Minnesota Press management, (7) wildlife ecology and management, and (8) fisheries ecology.

Most of these multiproject research efforts have been under way for several decades. The following overviews describe the research topics, their origins, the significance of accomplishments, and the principal project leaders who have been most active in the School's research.

FOREST ECOLOGY AND SILVICULTURE

Studies of the establishment, growth, and ecology of trees were among the first research topics at Mont Alto and at Penn State, but few records of silvicultural research results have been found from the first two decades. Arthur C. McIntire, the first designated research forester at Penn State, conducted research on silviculture and other topics after his appointment in 1927, particularly on oaks and Virginia pine. Ecological investigations by Harold J. Lutz during the 1930s also are noteworthy, as Lutz later became a renowned professor of forest ecology at Yale University. Donald D. Stevenson, who replaced McIntire in 1937, published on coniferous plantations and forest management subjects.

When William C. Bramble was appointed head of forestry research at Penn State in 1945, he continued some of the ecological studies of McIntire and Stevenson, and started new ones as well. He pioneered studies of coal spoils revegetation, Christmas tree production, and most notably utility right-of-way vegetation management and ecology as affected by herbicides. His assistant, W. R. "Dick" Byrnes, worked actively with Bramble on these studies beginning in 1950. After moving to Purdue, they both continued the right-of-way ecology research in Pennsylvania for some forty years, collaborating first with Russell J. Hutnik and later with Richard H. Yahner.

Hutnik and his students expanded research in forest ecology during his tenure from 1956 to 1986, and he continued to publish even after he retired. His interests included pollutant effects on forests, revegetation of strip mine spoil banks, and ecological effects of herbicides on rights-of-way. Other faculty who studied revegetation of spoil banks included William E. Sopper and Larry H. McCormick. The acclaimed 1973 book Hutnik edited, *Ecology and Reclamation of Devastated Land*, included his work and similar projects in other countries. Hutnik established *Research Briefs* in 1966 to facilitate the timely reporting of research results by faculty and graduate students. This in-house publication was a forerunner of the School's annual and later biennial reports, which started in 1984.

Silvicultural research by Wilber W. Ward from 1960 to 1980 was concurrent with Hutnik's and related in some ways. With graduate students Todd W. Bowersox, Larry H. McCormick, and others, Ward studied site evaluation of hardwoods, regeneration, fertilization, flooding tolerance, and strip mine reclamation. Both Bowersox and McCormick became faculty members and developed their own research programs, continuing until both of them retired in 2004. Bowersox was a pioneer in developing biomass plantations of fast-growing trees under short rotations to produce feedstock for the paper, particleboard, energy, and chemical industries. He also was known for his work on solving hardwood regeneration problems and his research for the National Park Service at the Gettysburg National Military Park to ensure restoration of these forests to their 1863 structure. McCormick published a classic paper on the aluminum tolerance of trees planted on surface-mined lands. He also conducted research on establishing woody plants on mine lands amended with municipal biosolids, the effects of herbaceous competition on establishment of oak regeneration, and the control of invasive plants. Robert D. Shipman's silvicultural research during the same time period, 1963 to 1990, focused mainly on the use of herbicides in managing regeneration and on his favorite plantation species, Japanese larch. The Robert D. Shipman Evenaged Management Demonstration Area commemorates his dedication to making research results available to practitioners.

Although Kim C. Steiner was hired as a forest geneticist, much of his research effort migrated toward artificial regeneration in the mid-1980s because the low level of forest tree planting in the state at that time prevented any real progress in the genetic improvement of forest trees. He and his colleagues and students demonstrated that oaks could be planted successfully in clear-cut land with proper care, with the result that attitudes toward planting changed greatly beginning in the 1990s. Early in that decade Steiner began to study natural regeneration with a four-year study of the production and fate of northern red oak acorns. Since 1996 Steiner and James C. Finley have led a large longitudinal study of the regeneration process in mixed-oak forest stands following harvest. The study, made possible by funding from the Bureau of Forestry, is following regeneration in more than fifty stands, from before harvest through, currently, the seventh growing season after harvest. The project has identified several alternative pathways of stand development following harvest, produced models of seed- and sprout-origin oak regeneration, developed the first stocking equations for seedling/sapling populations of upland hardwoods, produced the first practical guidelines for oak regeneration in the Appalachians, and introduced the concept of "aggregate height" as a novel and useful measure of density for seedling populations, analogous to "basal area" as applied to stands of larger trees.

Since 1987 Marc D. Abrams and his students have continued in unique ways the School's long-term interest in the ecology of oak forests. They have focused on how fire, drought, and other disturbances have affected the composition, structure, historical development, species recruitment patterns, and succession of old-growth forests. Employing dendro-ecological analyses and ecophysiology techniques for these studies, they have provided helpful insights into the management of oak forests, particularly involving the use of periodic burning of understory vegetation. For his exemplary work Marc was named the Nancy and John Steimer Professor of Agricultural Sciences, and received the 2002 Alex and Jessie C. Black Award for Excellence in Research. The Steimer professorship has enabled Marc to pursue his research interests and to support graduate students.

In 1997 Kim Steiner, Henry Gerhold, and James Zaczek started a series of experiments aimed at developing silvicultural methods for introducing resistant chestnut varieties into forests. These studies investigated planting methods and ways of controlling competing vegetation. Steiner, with the help of graduate students and research assistant Timothy Phelps, has continued and expanded these studies, and has installed a fifth-generation chestnut seed orchard on the grounds of the Arboretum at Penn State. Sara Fitzsimmons and Tim Phelps have facilitated close collaboration with the Pennsylvania chapter of The American Chestnut Foundation; Phelps is the current president.

FOREST MANAGEMENT AND ECONOMIC ANALYSES

The first professor to specialize in forest management research was H. Arthur Meyer, starting in 1937, although his title did not reflect his management expertise. Victor A. Beede was the first to have "forest management" in his title. Meyer, with his colleagues Donald D. Stevenson and Ronald A. Bartoo, conducted research that incorporated European concepts of growth, yield, stand structure, and the selection method for managing uneven-aged forests. They also prepared management plans for the

FIG. 33   Forest management research. John Bailey measuring trees, 1988. College of Agricultural Sciences photo.

School's forests and collaborated with A. B. Recknagel on two editions (1952 and 1961) of the textbook *Forest Management*.

Meyer made significant conceptual contributions to the management of forests through his books and his articles in the *Journal of Forestry*. He is credited with developing the q factor (the ratio of trees in a diameter-size class to the number of trees in the next-larger diameter class) as a means of quantifying the reverse-J curve for stocking control in uneven-aged stands. His publications *Management Without Rotation* and *Structure, Growth, and Drain in Balanced Uneven-Aged Forests* were classics.

Over the years the focus of forest management gradually shifted from timber management to meeting a variety of the goals of public, private, and corporate landowners. The spatial scope also expanded from individual stands or properties to landscape and regional scales and increasingly beyond the borders of Pennsylvania. The leadership and expertise of F. Yates Borden (1963–77) in remote sensing and biometrics was instrumental in founding the Office of Remote Sensing and Ecological Research in the College of Agriculture. He pioneered some early research on using satellite imagery to understand macroregional phenomena, with support principally from the National Aeronautics and Space Administration. One project was a depiction of the spatial advance of gypsy moth infestations through northeastern forests. Borden also employed remote sensing data for regional critiques of forest types and herbaceous cover, and for evaluating capacities of water resource systems.

Borden's work in remote sensing was conducted in cooperation with a multidisciplinary group at Penn State led by the co-founders of the Office for Remote Sensing of Earth Resources (ORSER), Gary Petersen in Agronomy and George McMurtry in Engineering. ORSER was one of the early centers for analysis of NASA satellite image data from the Landsat and SkyLab programs. Borden worked closely with Brian Turner in the development of software. Wayne Myers joined the faculty of the School in 1978 after the death of Yates Borden, having parallel research interests in multivariate analysis and remote sensing, and became part of the ORSER interest group. Myers worked cooperatively with Brian J. Turner (1969–84) in areas of remote sensing and biometrics. Turner replaced McMurtry as co-director of ORSER when McMurtry became a dean in the College of Engineering, and Myers in turn became co-director when Turner left Penn State to join the faculty of Australian National University at Canberra in his homeland.

Myers was influential in continuing the development of methods for remote sensing analysis, and also was a pioneer in geographic information systems (GIS) at Penn State using the Stone Valley Experimental Forest and the state game lands at the Barrens as test-beds for GIS in natural resources. Myers coordinated the GIS-based work of biodiversity assessment for Pennsylvania under the national GAP analysis program, with Robert Brooks leading the biological team. Most recently, Myers and his graduate students have been developing GIS-based approaches to landscape-level ecological mapping for Pennvania in cooperation with the Bureau of Forestry. Myers became the director of ORSER in 2005, and the name was changed to the Office for Remote Sensing and Spatial Information Resources (ORSSIR) to reflect its broad purview in providing spatial information across the Commonwealth through the Pennsylvania Spatial Data Access web-based spatial data facility.

Quantitative methods in forest management research were advanced further with the appointments of Stephen E. Fairweather (1984–93), Marc E. McDill in 1997, and Harry V. Wiant Jr. in 2002. Fairweather conducted research on analyses and modeling of growth and yield, site index, and timber harvest methods and scheduling. McDill has worked closely with the DCNR Bureau of Forestry to develop and apply forest management planning tools based on linear and integer programming. McDill's research has focused primarily on developing spatially explicit forest management models. These models allow planners to project the spatial layout of management actions and their impact on forest conditions such as habitat connectivity and fragmentation. Wiant continued work on the centroid method of tree and log volume determination that he and co-workers had developed at West Virginia University and Australian National University. He reported on probably the first use of 3P sampling in a timber trespass inventory, and with Dr. John R. Brooks at West Virginia University developed simple techniques for estimating cubic volume yields. He developed MensiTutor, a software program to help students learn the basics of forest measurement and inventory.

Elements of economics research can be traced back to studies of silviculture and wood utilization. For example, faculty members such as Arthur McIntire, Donald Stevenson, and Wilber Ward delved into cost analyses of production systems and allied considerations of rotation length and forest maturity. Similarly, Newell Norton, Orvel Schmidt, Wallace White, Richard Jorgensen, and Wayne Murphey studied the economics of manufacturing and logging systems and the longevity of certain wood products.

Merwin Humphrey and, later, John Muench were the earliest faculty members to focus specifically on forest economics and finance, although this research interest was not evident from their professorial titles. Humphrey's interest in the economics of forest management systems and financial maturity evolved from his liberal arts education, which also explains his interest in classical literature, poetry, and international affairs. Muench directed his research to the financial analysis of forest rotations and the macroeconomics of the national forest system. He left in 1965 to pursue a career as the chief economist of the National Forest Products Association; later he worked on economic development projects with the Agency for International Development and then became a research scientist at Virginia Polytechnic Institute and State University.

Charles Strauss was the first faculty member to have "forest economics" in his title, consistent with his formal training. After joining the faculty in 1966 he conducted research on the market structure of the pulpwood industry. Subsequently he organized a cost analysis of Pennsylvania's Bureau of State Parks, involving more than one hundred parks and a like number of irritated park superintendents whom he coerced into recording monthly costs that eventually spanned ten years. The ensuing econometric models enabled the bureau to predict budget needs and to achieve more efficient operations. Secretary Goddard also used the results for leverage in annual budget hearings.

During the 1980s and 1990s Strauss led a series of regional economic impact studies on recreation systems managed by the Pennsylvania Bureau of State Parks, the Pennsylvania Game Commission, the National Park Service, the U.S. Forest Service, and the Southwestern Pennsylvania Heritage Preservation Association. These first-time measurements of the somewhat elusive recreation industry defined its importance and interdependencies with other economic sectors. More recently, Strauss completed similar economic evaluations of the wood products industry within all regions of the state.

Public recreational systems also were the subject of research by F. Yates Borden, who investigated operational and ecological issues. He was instrumental in persuading the National Park Service (NPS) to establish an office in the School. Borden's contract work with NPS in Grand Canyon National Park and in the Great Smoky Mountain National Park provided operational guidelines for commercial river-running trips on the Colorado River and trail capacities in the Smoky Mountains. Strauss was a member of the three-week "Borden Expedition" that in 1973 floated the entire stretch of the Colorado River through the Grand Canyon and contributed to the team's economic critique of this world-class whitewater system. Subsequently, Strauss conducted similar studies of whitewater rivers for Pennsylvania's Ohiopyle, Lehigh Gorge, and Nockamixon State Parks and for the Delaware Gap National Park; these resulted in new operational regulations and policies.

A research team led by Paul Blankenhorn, Todd Bowersox, and Charles Strauss evaluated economic, biological, and energy aspects of short-rotation biomass plantations from 1980 to 1992, with support from the U.S. Department of Energy. They grew and harvested multiple crops of hybrid poplars using irrigation and fertilization and analyzed silvicultural methods, energy derived from ethanol, and economic potential. Several West Coast corporations adapted the methods to the more arid regions of Oregon solely for fiber production. In the 1990s the ethanol-based systems were not competitive with energy produced from petroleum, but fifteen years later there was renewed national interest in extracting ethanol from woody biomass.

FOREST GENETICS AND TREE IMPROVEMENT

Research aimed at creating improved varieties of trees started formally in 1956, when Henry Gerhold was hired to develop Scotch pines that would not turn yellow-green in the winter for Christmas tree growers. Growers realized that this vexing problem could be solved through genetics. Professors Bramble and Byrnes already had some seed source experiments under way with Scotch pines and Douglas-firs. Gerhold and his students developed effective selection and breeding techniques. Through controlled matings and selection he created four Scotch pine varieties and a Douglas-fir variety, which were formally released by the Agricultural Experiment Station. In 1991 he arranged for the harvesting of cones from seed orchards via formal arrangements with the Pennsylvania Tree Improvement Program (Penn-TIP), a group of nurserymen and tree growers that has distributed the seed for commercial production and participated in cooperative research. Since the 1960s Gerhold's interests turned also to other species and to resistance of trees to pests and air pollutants. He was the principal organizer of the first international symposium, in 1964, on "Genetic Improvement for Disease and Insect Resistance of Forest Trees," and he edited the proceedings, *Breeding Pest-Resistant Trees.* Changing directions somewhat in the 1970s, he has focused more on landscape trees, and was a principal founder of the Metropolitan Tree Improvement Alliance and of the Pennsylvania Urban and Community Forestry Council. The School's research in genetics broadened in scope, particularly after Kim C. Steiner joined the faculty in 1974 and again when John Carlson came on board in 1997.

Steiner's work initially focused on the genetic improvement of trees used in urban landscapes and mine spoil reclamation, with a special emphasis on the genetic control of nutritional problems such as iron chlorosis and aluminum toxicity. In the early 1980s he and his students began studying the genetics of cold tolerance, with studies of green ash, pitch pine, sweetgum, and loblolly pine. In the 1990s he collaborated with the Bureau of Forestry to establish a series of northern red oak progeny tests to guide seed source selection for the bureau's forest nursery. For much of the 1990s he and John Skelly, professor of plant pathology, collaborated on two EPA-funded projects studying the genetics and ecophysiology of ozone injury in the forest canopy. He has also collaborated with The American Chestnut Foundation to establish seed orchards to produce blight-resistant trees, and to determine the conditions required for successful regeneration of American chestnut trees in Pennsylvania forests.

John Carlson has pursued the Christmas tree research theme with a project on micropropagation that will capitalize on the genetic gains achieved in Gerhold's work. Carlson's research on clonal propagation by tissue culture has focused primarily on the improved Douglas-firs and Scotch pines from Gerhold's breeding program. And recently his work has expanded to blue spruce, concolor fir, Fraser fir, and Rhabdocline-resistant Douglas-fir trees from Christmas tree farms in Pennsylvania. The Christmas tree research has been a major focus of the Schatz Center for Tree Molecular Genetics that was established through endowments from the School's alumnus Louis W. Schatz, Mont Alto class of 1934.

The Schatz Center, which Carlson directs, participates in large multi-institutional collaborative projects, a current trend in academic research. Carlson's research emphasizes genomics, the newest approach to genetics research, in which all of the genes in a plant are studied simultaneously for their role in complex traits. Carlson's genomics research has led to interesting collaborations on the genetics of flower formation in tulip-poplar and cottonwood trees, the susceptibility of sugar maples to heavy metals in acidic forest soils, the structure of chromosomes in spruces and other conifers, the development of DNA tools for breeding of blight resistance in the American chestnut, the response of northern red oak to gypsy moths, the dispersal of oak acorns by squirrels in old-growth forest stands, and the genetic basis of different tolerances and susceptibilities to ozone damage among poplar and black cherry genotypes. Carlson's research on ozone damage in trees is in collaboration with the Plant Pathology Department and follows up on Kim Steiner's earlier research, which identified families of black cherry that differed genetically in their susceptibility to ozone.

FOREST HYDROLOGY AND WATERSHED MANAGEMENT

A cooperative program of watershed management research started in 1957 with the Pennsylvania Bureau of Forestry and the USDA Northeastern Forest Experiment Station. The purpose was to study the effects of forest management activities on water resources and to evaluate the effectiveness of best management practices for controlling water pollution related to forest harvesting. Professors Bramble and Byrnes had conducted some previous studies and helped lay the groundwork for this project. William E. Sopper, the lead investigator, then proceeded to have stream-gauging stations and climatic instruments installed on three experimental watersheds in Stone Valley that have sandstone soils, to develop a sound basis for the integrated management of timber and water. In 1961 three more watersheds were similarly equipped, and these had shale soils and irrigation systems that could augment rainfall.

James A. Lynch, having worked together with Sopper since 1967 when he was a graduate student, soon afterward took over in monitoring hydrological and biological data and publishing results from the experimental watersheds. Lynch officially became the lead investigator after he completed his doctoral degree, and continued until 2005. The watersheds have been a focal point for many studies dealing with such diverse topics as the effects of acid rain on episodic and long-term changes in stream chemistry and acidity, the effects of gypsy moth defoliation on water quality, and the potential effect of climate change on water supply.

Bill Sopper's pioneering research in watershed management took a new direction in 1963, when he became the lead investigator in a university-sponsored project on recycling of municipal wastewater and sludge on forests and agricultural lands. He helped to develop the concept of using soil and vegetation as a "living filter" to remove contaminants from municipal wastewater, and later extended the idea to mine spoils. Since 1970 millions of gallons of treated sewage wastewater generated by the university have been sprayed onto forest sites and agricultural crops; recycling through the living filter absorbs wastes and nutrients from the water and recharges groundwater reserves. Perhaps Sopper's most challenging achievement was to revegetate a superfund site, the zinc-contaminated Blue Mountain near Palmerton, Pennsylvania, using sewage sludge and fly ash. His research attracted attention far and wide, as in many places there are huge tracts of disturbed land that could be reclaimed with municipal sludge and wastewater.

Richard Lee was a faculty member in forest hydrology from 1967 to 1969 and then became a professor at his alma mater, West Virginia University. There he wrote two textbooks, *Forest Hydrology* and *Forest Microclimatology*. While at Penn State Lee advised two graduate students who later made significant contributions in the field of forest hydrology, and one of them, William Sharpe, became a faculty member in the School.

David R. DeWalle has conducted several kinds of microclimatic and hydrologic studies related to watershed management since joining the faculty in 1969. To assess effects of atmospheric pollutants on water quality, he has monitored long-term trends and episodic changes in stream chemistry and aquatic biota on five forested watersheds in Pennsylvania. Dave also employed stable isotopes of oxygen, hydrogen, and nitrogen in precipitation, stream flow, soil water, and groundwater to trace the sources and pathways for water and nitrates. He has investigated the magnitude and timing of chemical changes in the soil due to fertilization and acidification by analyzing the chemical element content in annual growth rings of hardwood and coniferous trees on a forested watershed in West Virginia, in cooperation with the U.S. Forest Service. In order to improve snowmelt computations and the prediction of stream flow from snowmelt, DeWalle has used telemetry records of snowpack data from remote, high-elevation stations in Colorado in cooperation with the USDA Agricultural Research Service. He founded Penn State's student chapter of the American Water Resources Association and helped to establish the Graduate Center for Watershed Stewardship.

Starting in 1972, William E. Sharpe and his students and colleagues have studied acid rainfall effects on streams and forests, water conservation measures, and domestic water systems. One of the issues of concern to them has been the decline of sugar maples in various places, including more than a hundred thousand acres of the Allegheny National Forest. They have been evaluating soil acidification as a predisposing stress factor, with emphasis on calcium, magnesium, and potassium nutrition and aluminum toxicity. In recent years the mortality of northern red oak and oak regeneration problems have become evident. Acidic runoff episodes in southwestern Pennsylvania have resulted in the extirpation of all fish from many headwater streams. Studies have indicated that soil acidity is a major factor in both the oak and fish problems, and Sharpe has not been one to shy away from the ensuing controversy. The research should lead to appropriate silvicultural and management schemes to alleviate these problems. It has helped to convince Congress to pass the Clean Air Act Amendments.

Jim Lynch broadened the research on deposition of toxic substances in 1980, when he established a statewide monitoring network to determine the spatial and temporal variations in deposition patterns. The Pennsylvania Acid Deposition Network gained national recognition, and Jim has served as chair of the National Atmospheric Deposition Program. Pennsylvania receives the most acidic deposition in North America, and this adversely affects sensitive ecosystems. The long-term objective of the

FIG. 34   Hydrology research. Bryan Swistock, Extension Associate, taking measurements in a stream. College of Agricultural Sciences photo.

project is to determine the effectiveness of national and state regulations in reversing the long-term acidification of streams that drain forested watersheds. In 2000 Lynch began a study to determine the effectiveness of reductions in sulfur dioxide emissions on precipitation chemistry and atmospheric deposition throughout the United States; sulfur dioxide emissions had dropped an average 2.86 million tons (39 percent) between 1995 and 1997 as a consequence of federal regulations.

These investigators and their graduate students have conducted a wide variety of studies of how climatic conditions, soil properties, vegetation types, and timber harvesting practices affect stream flow and water quality. They also have branched out into other research involving acid rain and other pollutants, as well as applications of sewage effluent and sludge to forest soils and disturbed sites. Applications of the research include integrated watershed management, restoration of watersheds and disturbed lands, improving residential water supplies, and riparian zone management. Their results have contributed immeasurably to the environmental quality that everyone wants.

WOOD PRODUCTS ENGINEERING

The first recorded research project in the Forestry Department was a study of the durability of wooden shingles and shingle nails installed on a barn by instructor R. R. Chaffee in 1909 and later on the rear wing of Fergie's Woodshed; John A. Ferguson published results of the study in 1938. Another early wood durability study was conducted for many years by Wallace E. White, this one on fence posts, with results published in 1954. White employed students to dig holes for the fence posts, this book's author among them. Annually a standard force was applied to the posts to determine how many years went by before they failed. These two topics indicate the agricultural influence on early research.

During the 1950s and 1960s research related to wood products and properties proliferated, at first gradually and then at an accelerating pace. William T. Nearn, a faculty member from 1947 to 1960, studied moisture relationships and extractives of wood. His enthusiasm for research attracted some bright graduate students and excited their interest. At about the same time Richard N. Jorgensen (1949–61 and adjunct professor 1965–73) undertook an interesting but frustrating project trying to determine why pileated woodpeckers were damaging wooden utility poles.

Dick's main research, however, was on the physical and mechanical properties of wood, laminated wood beams, and oak flakeboard. He also had some international positions at the Universidad de los Andes in Venezuela and with the UN Food and Agriculture Organization in Rome. Upon leaving Penn State in 1961 Jorgensen continued his career in wood products at Michigan State University, and then in various positions with the U.S. Forest Service until 1978. A former graduate student of Nearn's and Newell A. Norton's, Wayne K. Murphey, came back as a faculty member in 1960 and conducted research involving wood preservatives, wood anatomy, and lamination. Jorgensen and Murphey collaborated in studies of hardwoods used in structural flakeboard and other reconstituted wood products, and co-wrote *Wood as an Industrial Arts Material*. After leaving in 1978 Murphey's continuing career in wood products research increasingly included more administrative work in academia and with federal agencies.

In the 1970s Robert C. Baldwin specialized in cellulose degradation and bark extractives, and he collaborated with plant pathologists on wood decay mechanisms, although his principal responsibility was teaching. He joined with Wayne Murphey in studying bark extractives, and with Francis C. Beall on wood decay processes and allelopathic effects of bark mulch on plants. In the 1980s Baldwin and Peter Labosky Jr. studied the deterioration of oaks killed by gypsy moths, after this insect reached epidemic proportions throughout Pennsylvania. Labosky's other research dealt with wood chemistry and pulping processes. Baldwin became assistant dean for resident education in the College of Agriculture in 1987, but he continued to teach wood products courses while he was dean and for years after he retired.

Since those early beginnings, wood products research has proliferated into engineered wood products, processing, marketing, and wood products business management. Many of these research projects are highly collaborative and include research teams that are interdepartmental, intercollege, and interuniversity. Paul Blankenhorn in particular has promoted this cooperative approach since 1975.

Blankenhorn and Labosky examined uses of red and white oaks killed by gypsy moths and also collaborated with the Penn State Biotechnology Institute in examining the biopulping of hardwoods. Blankenhorn, Todd Bowersox, and Charles Strauss studied the financial and energy balances in growing hybrid poplar and processing that woody biomass into energy and chemicals. Blankenhorn worked with researchers in the materials research laboratory on the development of wood-cement composites, seeking techniques that enhance their strength and durability. Blankenhorn, Labosky, John J. Janowiak, and agricultural engineer Harvey B. Manbeck collaborated on a major project that developed the engineering standards for hardwood glue-laminated (glulam) timber bridges. These standards also enable hardwood glulam timbers to be designed into structures other than timber bridges. The red maple glulam timbers in the atrium of the new Forest Resources Building were designed using the standards developed by the Penn State research team. Janowiak also investigated the feasibility of producing structural laminated veneer lumber from underutilized red maple resources.

Other collaborative projects by the wood products faculty include the research of Charles Ray and Judd H. Michael with the U.S. Forest Service on lean manufacturing and operations research within the wood products industry, including wood products industrial safety. Janowiak has worked with the USDA Forest Products Lab on the use of recycled wood and treated lumber, and with researchers in the materials research laboratory on phytosanitization of wood, which is essential for exporting certain wood products. Blankenhorn, Ray, and Forest Service researchers are developing new kiln schedules for drying hardwoods and defining lumber yield and quality from processing small-diameter hardwoods. Blankenhorn and Nicole Brown, together with Forest Service researchers, are quantifying the volatile organic emissions during drying of hardwoods and modifying dry kiln schedules to reduce drying defects. Brown and visiting scientist Jeffrey M. Catchmark have launched studies employing the emerging field of nanotechnology to evaluate molecular and atomic structures of wood that could lead to innovative manufacturing systems and new composite products.

WOOD PRODUCTS MARKETING AND MANAGEMENT

Research on the marketing of wood products and management issues in wood industries has been rather restricted until recently. Newell A. Norton and colleagues in another department are credited with the first publication on "Marketing Forest Products in Pennsylvania," dated 1955. Walter W. Johnson, whose time was devoted mainly to extension, conducted limited research involving marketing and management from 1973 to 1992. He studied the particleboard industry, log exports, the pallet industry, and secondary products industries.

FIG. 35 Wood products research. Assistant Professor Nicole Brown using the scanning electron microscope to study wood morphology. College of Agricultural Sciences photo.

Since 1991 Paul M. Smith has been researching domestic and global marketing issues of wood products. Initially he collaborated with the U.S. Forest Service and the American Hardwood Export Council offices in Mexico City, Tokyo, Osaka, and Washington, D.C., to examine value-added opportunities for hardwood products in Mexico and Japan. Smith also has studied global markets for certified forest products, the impact of electronic commerce in channels, international trade show use and effectiveness, customer delivered value, and various topics related to Pennsylvania's hardwood industries. His research in Pennsylvania has primarily involved cooperative studies with the Forest Service laboratory in Princeton, West Virginia, the Pennsylvania Hardwood Development Council, and the Pennsylvania Department of Agriculture. In addition, Smith collaborated with faculty at Virginia Tech on two separate USDA CSREES National Needs Fellowship Ph.D. training grants in forest products marketing.

Smith has continued working on technology-driven product/market development research projects that he started in 1987, before coming to Penn State. These have been funded by the Office for Naval Research to examine wood fiber–plastic composite products in industrial and residential applications. Primary cooperators include Washington State University, the Strandex Corporation, and the Naval Facilities and Engineering Service Center. Other cooperators have included Michigan Technological University, the University of Maine, New Mexico Institute of Mining and Technology, the University of Idaho, the U.S. Forest Service, the University of Tennessee, BP Amoco Company, Honeywell Corporation, and McFarland Cascade Corporation.

Since 2000 Judd H. Michael has expanded on Paul Smith's wood marketing emphasis. Michael's activities include researching business management topics and teaching courses on leadership, communications, teamwork, safety, and managerial finance. Some of his early research at Penn State examined the job-related expectations of new forestry and wood science graduates from programs across the country. The remainder of his research has focused on managerial and competitiveness issues, primarily for value-added hardwood manufacturers. Specific topics have included lean manufacturing as a business strategy and how best to apply it in a wood-based environment, improving the safety performance of wood manufacturers, and how "change management" can be applied in the wood industry. His most recent emphasis has been on increasing retail markets for used building materials and related sustainability issues. Michael's research has been funded by the U.S. Forest Service, the USDA National Research Initiative, and various agencies of Pennsylvania. He also is active in management training and has conducted courses for a variety of corporations.

WILDLIFE ECOLOGY AND MANAGEMENT

John L. George was the first faculty member of the School to devote all of his time to research and teaching of wildlife ecology and management, although a great deal of wildlife research preceded his arrival. Much of the previous research was carried out in conjunction with the Cooperative Wildlife Research Unit, described below. Before 1938 wildlife research was simply considered to be part of the ongoing forestry research.

When he came to Penn State in 1963, George already had published scientific papers on damage to wildlife caused by pesticides. His early research on DDT effects, even before the publication of Rachel Carson's *Silent Spring*, contributed to the ban on this pesticide. After joining the Penn State faculty he found evidence of DDT in Antarctic wildlife species, indicating that this pesticide had spread to the farthest corners of the earth. He also conducted research on deer, turkey, elk, otter, and eastern coyote, and published nine books and more than two hundred scientific and popular articles. He played a major role in advocating, vigorously and tenaciously, wildlife educational programs and research. Before retiring in 1983, George saw the wildlife faculty increase to two in 1967, then to three in 1972, four in 1978, and five in 1981. There also have been some periods of retrenchment.

Research interests proliferated as the wildlife faculty grew and teaching responsibilities increased, culminating with the B.S. degree program begun in 1981. Each wildlife species presented unique problems and opportunities. The second wildlife faculty member, Gene W. Wood (1967–74), taught courses in wildlife research techniques and wildlife ecology. His research focused on the influences of forest practices on wildlife and specifically on the influences of clear-cutting, wildfire, prescribed burning, and wastewater irrigation. He and his students studied an array of species, including songbirds, small mammals, rabbits, and deer. That work resulted in several publications as well as a contribution to the 1984 Forestry Handbook of the Society of American Foresters. The research of Robert G. Anthony (1972–77) and George M. Kelly (1977–83) extended to some of the same and additional habitats and animals, large and small. James S. Wakeley (1976–86), who served as chair of the wildlife program from 1981 to 1984, focused on the ecology and management of game and non-game birds. These were principally the American woodcock, and forest songbirds in habitats subjected to spray irrigation of municipal wastewater. Urban wildlife was another of Wakeley's interests. He and his students studied songbird use of municipal street trees, diets of urban and rural house sparrows, and the extent and cost of blackbird damage to ripening field corn.

Walter M. Tzilkowski joined the wildlife faculty in 1978, adding expertise in wildlife population dynamics and biometry. He developed techniques for sampling animal populations and has concentrated especially on damage caused by white-tailed deer to forest regeneration and agricultural crops. He has shown that the intensity of damage varies by crop type, spatially and temporally. Unbiased estimates of damage by counties for two high-value crops, corn and cabbage, enabled farmers to quantify the extent of their losses. Effects of deer on the regeneration of mixed-oak forests were assessed under three levels of canopy openings. Deer exclosures established on one-half of the inventory plots enabled comparisons of herbaceous plants and woody seedlings before and after treatment.

A major focus of Richard Yahner's work, since he joined the faculty in 1981, has been wildlife diversity in relation to managed forests and landscape changes. Yahner and his students have studied a variety of wildlife, including mammals, birds, reptiles, amphibians, and butterflies in national parks, state game lands, state forests, residential areas, powerline rights-of-way, and agricultural areas. Their research publications have contributed to an understanding of wildlife-habitat relationships and formulation of habitat recommendations to enhance land for wildlife on both public and private lands. The former students are now leaders in wildlife conservation and management at various universities, colleges, and wildlife agencies throughout the nation.

The addition of Robert P. Brooks to the faculty in 1983, with his interest in wetlands, resulted in the founding of the Cooperative Wetlands Center in 1993. Its purpose is to create greater opportunities for training students and to facilitate interaction among governmental agencies that manage wetlands, private industry involved in resource extraction, and Penn State scientists and students. Brooks studied numerous wetland and river systems in the United States, including emergent marshes, peat lands, shrub and forested wetlands, large rivers, and headwater streams.

He has been a consultant on wetlands to the U.S. Environmental Protection Agency since 1987. In 2003 Brooks and the wetlands center moved to the College of Earth and Mineral Sciences. To celebrate his twenty-fifth anniversary as a Penn State faculty member, he and his wife established the Robert P. and Rebecca P. Brooks Endowment for the Cooperative Wetlands Center in 2005. The endowment will help to fund graduate and undergraduate students conducting research through the center.

An avian specialist, Margaret C. Brittingham, alighted in 1988. Her research has included the population dynamics of birds and the ecology of bats. She and her students found that declines in the numbers of area-sensitive, forest-dwelling birds were related to forest fragmentation caused by agriculture and urban/suburban development. Nesting success was higher in extensive areas of forest than in small forest fragments. She also has studied habitat use by neotropical migrants during migration and the effects of acidic deposition on forest birds. Margaret and her students have studied how wildlife enhancement practices and programs such as wetland restoration, stream bank fencing, and the Conservation Reserve Enhancement Program (CREP) affect avian abundance, diversity, and productivity. Because many Pennsylvanians are interested in managing their property for wildlife, Margaret developed an extension program to help landowners enhance wildlife habitat while minimizing nuisance and damage problems, using publications, demonstration areas, and field training.

In 1995 Gary J. San Julian joined the faculty, initially as the southeast regional director for cooperative extension, and in 1998 he moved to University Park to fill a teaching and extension appointment as one of the extension wildlife specialists. While he does not have a research appointment, he has been active on numerous graduate committees and has advised several graduate students in the areas of human dimensions, environmental education, and wildlife management. In order to maintain and increase access to recreational opportunities on private land, his students investigated why landowners post their property. A significant portion of his work relates to extension programming for wildlife damage management at the state, regional, and national levels.

FISHERIES ECOLOGY

The first faculty member in the School to conduct research on fishes was Jay R. Stauffer Jr., starting in 1984. He has pursued the ecology and sys-

tematics of fishes in two locales, the streams and rivers of the Appalachian
region and Lake Malawi in Africa. The habitats of darters were compared
in diverse communities—the Allegheny River, the Susquehanna River, and
the Potomac River. *In situ* and laboratory studies evaluated reproductive
success, food preference, and habitat selection of the darters in these different habitats. Ways and means were then developed for artificially nur-
turing fish species subjected to invasive practices such as highway
construction, and for reintroducing them to their original habitats.

The freshwater resources of Lake Malawi provide some 70 percent of
the animal protein consumed by Malawians. Fewer than five hundred of
the thousand to fifteen hundred species of freshwater fish that live in Lake
Malawi have been described. No doubt this important resource is being
overexploited, but it is virtually impossible to implement effective management strategies to protect this resource when the majority of species
cannot be identified. Jay and his colleagues are searching for congruence
among morphological, genetic, and behavioral data to effectively delimit
and describe these species. They also are investigating strategies that can

protect the people of Malawi from a parasitic disease by using fish to control the intermediate snail species of human schistosomes. Excessive fishing has drastically reduced the snail-eating fishes in the inshore areas of the lake, which in turn has permitted the invasion of bilharzias-vector snails. In 2005 Penn State appointed Stauffer as distinguished professor of ichthyology, in recognition of his high standards of academic excellence and exceptional contributions to teaching, research, and outreach.

A second faculty member, C. Paola Ferreri, extended the fisheries research in 1995. She and her students have worked with quantitative fisheries management and population dynamics of several species. They studied a yellow perch population in the Pymatuning Sanctuary located in Crawford County, Pennsylvania, using trap nets and electrofishing gear. The age and size structures of the population were dramatically different for males and females collected on the spawning grounds. The number of large, older females collected seemed to be unique to unexploited systems.

In another project Paola and colleagues investigated the population dynamics of lake trout in Lake Superior in relation to the presence of sea lampreys. They found that reducing fishing mortality had a greater effect on the population growth rate than reducing mortality by sea lampreys. In a related study they assessed the impact of improved water quality on sea lamprey production by simulating transformer production in a model stream at three levels of habitat availability. They concluded that in order to counteract improved habitats in tributaries, sea lamprey control efforts must be increased to enable lake trout rehabilitation to succeed.

This overview of research in the School of Forest Resources would not be complete without mentioning the valuable support provided by various categories of research assistants. Many technicians and graduate research assistants have temporary funding for one to a few years. Several who have been on continuing, multiple-year appointments have contributed very substantially to the research and teaching within the School.

PENNSYLVANIA COOPERATIVE FISH AND WILDLIFE RESEARCH UNIT

The Pennsylvania Cooperative Wildlife Research Unit was created in 1938, and the Cooperative Fishery Research Unit in 1964. In 1982 these were combined into the Cooperative Fish and Wildlife Research Unit, which was transferred from the Biology Department to the School of Forest Resources. The unit is a joint venture of the Biological Resources Division of the U.S. Geological Survey, Pennsylvania Game Commission, Pennsylvania Fish and Boat Commission, the Penn State School of Forest Resources, and the Wildlife Management Institute. The Game Commission and the Fish and Boat Commission provide annual base funding, which is used to conduct research projects designed in conjunction with the state agencies. The university provides clerical staff and office support, as well as office, laboratory, and storage space for the unit. The Biological Resources Division of the U.S. Geological Survey provides funding for two or three full-time biologists who constitute the permanent unit staff (Table 15). The Wildlife Management Institute works to ensure continued

Table 15 Leaders of the Pennsylvania Cooperative Fish and Wildlife Research Unit, 1938–2005

Leaders	Years
Logan J. Bennett (W)	1938–1948
Ward M. Sharp (W)	1948–1962
James S. Lindzey (W)	1962–1980
Robert L. Butler (F)	1963–1980
Dean E. Arnold (F), Acting Leader	1980–1982
Gerald Storm (W), Acting Leader	1980–1982
Dean E. Arnold (FW), Acting Co-leader	1982–1984
Gerald Storm (FW), Acting Co-leader	1982–1984
Robert F. Carline (FW)	1984–present
Assistant Leaders	
Pennoyer F. English (W)	1938–1958
H. Norton Cope (W)	1958–1959
John L. George (W)	1963–1969
Anthony Bodola (F)	1964–1967
Donald C. Hales (F)	1967–1969
Charles T. Cushwa (W)	1969–1971
Robert F. Raleigh (F)	1970–1972
Gerald L. Storm (W)	1972–1980
Gerald L. Storm (FW)	1984–1997
Dean E. Arnold (F)	1973–1980
Dean E. Arnold (FW)	1984–1999
Duane Diefenbach (FW)	1999–present
Erin Snyder (FW)	2001–2003

W = former wildlife unit
F = former fishery unit
FW = combined unit

national legislative support for the unit program, and the U.S. Fish and Wildlife Service provides support for cooperative research projects on an irregular basis.

The unit's mission is to conduct interdisciplinary applied and basic research in fish and wildlife management and to contribute to graduate education. The research emphasis is on (1) integrating ecology and management of terrestrial and aquatic habitats, (2) evaluating the effects of human activities on wildlife, fish, and their habitats, and (3) providing guidelines for restoring and maintaining important terrestrial and aquatic communities. Unit personnel contribute to graduate education by engaging graduate students in research projects and teaching graduate-level courses. Since 1939 more than 274 graduate students have completed M.S. and Ph.D. degrees under the direction of unit staff. More detailed information appears on the unit's website at http://pacfwru.cas.psu.edu.

The aquatic research program has focused on management and ecology of streams since 1982. Unit staff have a long history of studying the effects of acidic deposition and acid mine drainage on streams. Several studies have examined the effectiveness of different types of mitigation projects aimed at reducing or reversing declines of aquatic communities in acidified streams. The effects of human disturbances on streams, such as agricultural practices and road construction, have been the subject of several long-term studies. These projects have demonstrated that restoration of degraded riparian areas can produce positive results in a relatively short time and that significant reductions in sediment loading can be accomplished economically by installing narrow riparian buffer zones.

Since 1982 the wildlife research program has focused on population-level ecology and management research topics. A long-term cooperative project started in 1975 with the Pennsylvania Game Commission has studied the response of ruffed grouse populations to intensive habitat management. Other research has focused primarily on game species such as woodcock, bobcat, wild turkey, black bear, and white-tailed deer, but has also included use of reclaimed surface mines by grassland songbirds and use of wastewater treatment areas by small mammals. Recently much effort has been devoted to an integrated approach to studying white-tailed deer ecology and management, including fawn survival, yearling male dispersal, deer hunter movements and behavior, hunter satisfaction with buck harvest regulations, harvest rates of female deer, and accuracy of harvest estimates. Results have been used by the Pennsylvania Game Commission to monitor the effects of changes in deer hunting regulations.

NATIONAL PARK SERVICE

The National Park Service (NPS) established an auxiliary scientific unit, a Cooperative Park Studies Unit, within the School in 1972. John Karish, an alumnus of the School (B.S. 1970, M.S. 1973), was assigned by the NPS in 1974 to lead this national effort. The remote sensing systems analyses and ecological research pioneered by F. Yates Borden in the Grand Canyon and Great Smoky Mountains National Parks facilitated the establishment of this national collaborative unit. The NPS transferred the supervision of the unit to its mid-Atlantic regional office in 1976, when Karish took over the responsibilities of coordinating the various natural resource research needs for NPS parks in a five-state area.

Over the years Karish, who became chief scientist for the NPS Northeast region (extending from Maine to Virginia), has supervised numerous projects dealing with ecological and social parameters conducted by faculty and students of Penn State and other universities. In 1993 Michele Batcheller (B.S. 1986) joined the unit with the main responsibility of preparing a white-tailed deer management plan for Gettysburg National Military Park. Research conducted by School faculty supported the successful implementation of a deer management program at the park. Batcheller also coordinates wildlife and endangered species issues in northeastern national parks. Wayne Millington became an NPS member of the unit in 1996 to work with the university's faculty in applying integrated pest management principles for controlling native and exotic plant and animal pests with ecologically sensitive practices. He also supervises the activities of two NPS exotic plant management teams whose goal is to stem the spread of exotic species in the Northeast.

Owing to a new NPS science mandate in 1999, the unit grew again in 2003 when Matt Marshall and Nathan Piekielek were stationed with the School as coordinator and data manager, respectively, of one of the NPS Northeast region's inventory and monitoring networks. Working cooperatively with School and other university faculty, Marshall and Piekielek oversee the inventorying and monitoring of the status and trends of significant riverine and forested resources in nine national parks in Pennsylvania and West Virginia.

MUNICIPAL TREE RESTORATION PROGRAM

The conflict between utility wires and trees has often stirred up emotions, as some people react against pruning that disfigures trees. Not everyone realizes that the pruning of branches around power lines is necessary to assure safe, reliable electrical service. To find the best long-term solution, the Municipal Tree Restoration Program has been conducting research with communities since 1987. The originators of this cooperative program were Walter R. "Dick" Rossman, Penelec forester; Henry D. Gerhold; and Norman L. Lacasse and Patrick M. Lantz, both with the DCNR Bureau of Forestry. They convinced nine electric utility companies and six arboricultural firms to join with the Bureau of Forestry and the School of Forest Resources, and also received support from the U.S. Forest Service for some of the MTRP projects.

The focus of a combined research and demonstration approach has been on removing larger, deteriorating trees and replacing them with low-growing trees that are compatible with overhead utility wires. Utility members of MTRP have provided free, compatible types of trees that do not interfere with wires to seventy-eight municipalities. The replacement trees served as demonstrations of the compatible tree concept, and also for research on tree varieties. Periodic evaluations of sixty-one named, cultivated varieties identified the best trees for planting along streets, resulting in scientifically based planting recommendations. Publications that have been produced through MTRP, *Street Tree Factsheets*, *Compatible Tree Factsheets*, and *Landscape Tree Factsheets*, contain factual information and color photos of all of the commonly planted landscape trees in temperate North America. The *Landscape Tree Factsheets CD* replicated the same information and photos.

To qualify for the free trees, the municipalities had to plant them and pledge to improve their tree-care programs. In 1999 a survey of fifty-four of these communities found that 82 percent of the residents liked the planted replacement trees and 69 percent favored the removal of the large trees. Besides appreciating the replacement trees themselves, 91 percent of the municipalities reported progress toward their pledges by improving their tree programs through ordinances, tree commissions, tree inventories, or management plans.

Resources devoted to research have been redirected gradually since 2001 to a new grant program to help Pennsylvania communities. The Pennsylvania Urban and Community Forestry Council has provided MTRP electric utility grants that pay for the purchase of trees to replace deteriorating trees under utility wires.

RESEARCH

THE AMERICAN CHESTNUT FOUNDATION

A Chestnut Operations and Research Center of the Pennsylvania chapter of the American Chestnut Foundation (TACF) opened in the School's Forest Resources Laboratory in 2005, supported by a $50,000 grant from the Pennsylvania Department of Economic and Community Development. Chapter president Timothy Phelps is located at the center, as is tree-breeding coordinator Sara Fitzsimmons. Tim is a senior research technologist who assists several of the School's faculty with research projects. Faculty became involved with the chapter in 1997 when Kim Steiner initiated silvicultural studies of how best to introduce resistant varieties to forested sites, and Henry Gerhold organized a plantation to test adaptation of advanced generations of the breeding program. Since then Steiner, Phelps, and graduate students have expanded the silvicultural studies. Also, John Carlson started research on developing molecular genetic methods for breeding blight-resistant trees. Since 1998 Steiner has served on the national science board of TACF and has been instrumental in the development of the organization's strategies for testing and deployment of resistant chestnuts, as well as in establishing closer ties between Penn State and TACF.

The most advanced seed orchard, which will produce blight-resistant chestnut trees, was installed at the Penn State Arboretum in 2002. At the dedication ceremony Steiner introduced dignitaries who made brief remarks, including Marshall Case, executive director of TACF; John Oliver, secretary of the Department of Conservation and Natural Resources; Robert Steele, dean of the College of Agricultural Sciences; and Herbert Darling, president of TACF board of directors. Darling added the final signature to a memorandum of understanding that calls for TACF eventually to provide two professional staff to the arboretum to support chestnut research and outreach. Eventually some thirty thousand trees will be added to the first seedlings planted at the dedication ceremony. Through careful selection these will be pared down to about 210 of the very best trees, which will produce improved seeds for reintroducing this valuable species into forests. Financial support for some of this work has been provided by the Robertson Family Endowment.

The Pennsylvania chapter has been very active, and it accomplishes all of its work entirely with volunteers. Sara Fitzsimmons, a research technologist in the School of Forest Resources, manages a database and communi-

139

cation network that assists volunteers in managing the chapter's orchards, including pollination of selected trees, inoculation to test resistance, and pedigree records. The Pennsylvania chapter was the first state chapter to start its own breeding programs with the goal of developing regionally adapted, blight-resistant chestnut varieties.

12

EXTENSION AND OUTREACH

Research-based knowledge, through its transfer and adoption, is the foundation of the extension educational system. Extension faculty in the School of Forest Resources, most of whom are also engaged in research and some in teaching, serve a diverse clientele in the Commonwealth and beyond. They work closely with county extension staff and partner agencies to deliver practical information through workshops, conferences, newsletters, and publications to landowners, forest industries, municipalities, and the public. The information they compile, digest, and present in formats adapted to various audiences comes from sources that extend far beyond the research conducted in the School of Forest Resources.

From the very beginning in 1907, Hugh Baker, John Ferguson, and other faculty of the Forestry Department were engaged in outreach activities. They participated in Farmer's Institutes to discuss tree planting, woodlot management, and timber marketing. Even before the Smith-Lever Act of 1914 had established the extension system, Professors C. R. Anderson and George Green actually handled many external requests for lectures, technical assistance, and information. They assisted farmers with timber estimating and marketing, and the farmers apparently valued their help, as they paid for the travel expenses of these professors.

ACTIVITIES OF EXTENSION FACULTY

The first forestry extension specialist at Penn State, Clarence R. Anderson, an instructor in the Forestry Department, was assigned in 1916 to spend one month per year mainly educating farmers about thinning their woodlots. The School of Agriculture financed his activities and in 1919 appointed him extension forester. Anderson was one of the first forestry extension agents in the country. The only other states known to have provided similar extension services at that time were Maryland, New York, and North Carolina. Anderson's extension assignment was increased in 1921 from one-quarter time to full time. In that year workshops were started jointly with the Department of Forests and Waters on tree planting, and demonstration areas were installed along "major highways." In 1924 the Clark-McNary Act explicitly provided funding for forestry extension specialists. The first portable sawmill school in the country was held in 1925 under the direction of the Department of Farm Forestry of the Pennsylvania State College; 150 sawmill men and some students attended.

In 1923 Frank T. Murphey was hired as Anderson's assistant to handle the increased demand for services. Ira Bull became Anderson's assistant in 1930, and he was replaced by Walter Simonds in 1936. Frank Murphey became head of forestry extension in 1931 upon Anderson's death. The statewide teaching by these men included woodlot management, tree planting, timber estimating and marketing, timber manufacturing, maple syrup production, saw filing, and 4-H forestry activities. After 1940 they also assisted the fledgling Christmas tree industry. By the end of the first decade of formal forestry extension activities, county agents had held six hundred tree-planting meetings, nearly four hundred improvement-cutting meetings, and about eighty timber estimating and marketing meetings, attended by some fourteen thousand people. This was a remarkable increase from the first county meeting, held in Monroe County, where only four adults and a few children from a nearby school showed up.

Fifty years ago there were only two full-time extension foresters at Penn State, but there has been considerable growth in outreach since then. Walter W. Simonds started in 1936, and Edward P. Farrand in 1951. At that time they devoted much of their effort to Christmas trees, helping to make Pennsylvania a national leader in the production of nursery stock and field-grown trees. They also worked with forest landowners and producers of maple products. In 1961 Robert G. Wingard, a wildlife specialist, joined them in the Forestry Building. The same year Charles H. Strauss became an extension specialist in wood products, a new position providing education programs on lumber drying, timber marketing, and capital investments.

School director Peter Fletcher, in order to consolidate and expand forestry-related extension programming, brought these specialists together and named Wingard chair of the group. Wingard actually had been doing extension work in wildlife since 1952 in an office located next door to the

Forestry Building. The group was loosely organized, and their activities, projects, and publications were especially responsive to requests from county agents and state agencies.

Wingard's extension work in wildlife dealt with different audiences, continuing until he retired in 1983. County agents were particularly concerned with problems that wildlife caused for farmers, whereas government agencies concentrated on the concerns of sportsmen and management practices. Bob produced many publications about various species and practices, and the titles of the most important ones that he wrote or contributed to are indicative of his broad interests: *Deer Management in Pennsylvania; Rural Land Use Planning; Conservation—Living in Harmony with Land; Pond Construction and Management in Pennsylvania; Aquatic Plants—Management and Control in Pennsylvania; Woodlands and Wildlife*. To promote greater access for hunters to posted lands, Wingard illustrated his many talks with slides of all kinds of "No Hunting" and "No Trespassing" signs, ranging from the ordinary to the humorous and outrageous. He teamed up with William Carroll, agricultural economics extension specialist, and Stanley Forbes of the Game Commission in holding many meetings throughout the state to "sell" deer management to hunters and landowners alike. Gradually these audiences began to accept the rationale behind doe hunting and greater access to private properties.

When Strauss took up his extension duties in 1961, one of the first of several tasks that confronted him was resurrecting the Keystone Kiln Drying Association. Lumbermen, manufacturers of wood products, and scientists met biannually to learn about the fine art and science of drying lumber. The sawmill industry at that time was engaged in a transition to fewer but larger mills. Selling "green" lumber was no longer standard practice, and the larger mills invested in kilns to improve the quality of their products. Concurrently Pennsylvania's forests were maturing, providing higher-grade logs and more diverse species. Additional pulp and paper mills also had recently entered the state, leading to expanded logging and the need for better specifications for roundwood. Cost analyses and investment considerations, for both lumber drying and logging operations, became topics for forest products extension.

Roe S. Cochran, better known as Sandy, became the next extension agent to have wood industries responsibilities in 1966, when Strauss moved to the forest economics faculty position. But Sandy was stationed in Ridgway, not at University Park. He was the first Penn State extension forester housed in a county office with responsibilities extending to several counties. Having worked previously for the Armstrong Forest Company in forest management and wood procurement, he understood the management needs of private forests as well as those of the logging industry. Cochran built a successful extension education program by focusing on industry-related issues. Some of his more popular workshops focused on mill alignment, better edging and trimming skills, and logger safety training. Working with the U.S. Forest Service Experiment Station in Irvine, he cooperated in developing SILVAH, a computer tool for making silvicultural decisions in hardwood stands of the Allegheny mountain region. This training program remained popular for many years, reaching hundreds of foresters who manage public and private forests. Sandy was an advocate for research and continually besieged various faculty members to consider the information needs of his region. He partnered with Strauss in several projects dealing with the sawmill industry and timber availability.

Several counties hired forestry area extension agents in the 1960s and 1970s. Richard Rodenbaugh was hired in Wyoming County, but he soon took a position at the new Proctor and Gamble mill in Mehoopany. David Taber continued in this post, and before long moved to a similar position at Cornell University. James Philp, who had completed a master's degree in the School and had worked in the South, was the next area agent, but he was assigned to work in Dushore. When Philp left to start Dushore Wood Products, James Finley next filled the Dushore position in 1975.

After the succession of area agents in northeastern counties, Finley's position was changed to focus on private forest landowner concerns. He worked closely with state service foresters and county extension agents to reach out to this diverse, newly designated audience. In the late 1970s and early 1980s Finley helped found the first county associations of forest landowners in the state, which now number more than twenty.

In 1972 the College of Agriculture reorganized the extension system, transferring specialists to departments and the School of Forest Resources. Since then it has become commonplace for extension specialists to allocate part of their time to research, and in some cases to resident education. The 1970s was a time of growth for extension specialists in the School, with increased numbers and new topics.

Water-related programming became part of the School's extension activities in 1972 when William Sharpe joined the faculty. He has worked with acidification of aquatic and terrestrial ecosystems, drinking water quality, and residential water conservation. Pennsylvania is home to more than a million groundwater wells, sixty-five thousand miles of streams, and thousands of ponds, lakes, and reservoirs. Bill Sharpe, Bryan Swistock, and other water resource educators have assisted Pennsylvanians with private water supplies, pond management, droughts, watershed education, and water conservation. They have produced numerous publications and educational materials to help farmers, landowners, and homeowners properly manage their water resources.

Walter Johnson conducted an active extension program related to wood products from 1973 to 1992. His lumber-grading workshops were very popular and so were offered twice in some years and attracted audiences from throughout the region. He also conducted workshops on wood preservative treatments for utility companies. A workshop on timber bridges for highway engineers led to subsequent research on improved construction methods and specifications. For Pennsylvania's bicentennial celebration in 1976, Johnson helped make a video of a log raft floating down the Susquehanna River, commemorating this historic means of transporting tree-length logs.

Terry Rader was a wildlife specialist from 1973 to 1988. Much of his work was concerned with wildlife damage and pond management. Terry also started a long-term series of extension publications, *Pennsylvania Forest Resources*, consisting of ninety issues. This periodical covered a diverse set of topics and was published more or less monthly for nearly eight years.

After Ed Farrand retired in 1978, Mel Baughman came from Minnesota to assume his position in 1981. At the same time, Jim Finley was reassigned to University Park to work with private forest owners, maple producers, and Christmas tree growers. When Baughman left in 1983, James R. Grace returned to Penn State, where he had previously completed his doctoral degree. In the interim Grace had been the extension forester at Rutgers University and had become well known in the northeastern region for his innovative extension programs.

During his tenure at Penn State, Grace led the development of the Pennsylvania Woodlands series. He was chairman of the "Year of the Forest" in 1986, an event that coincided with the hundredth anniversary of the Pennsylvania Forestry Association and celebrated the Commonwealth's forests and all the values they provide. The Pennsylvania Forestry Association honored Jim with the Rothrock Award for Conservation that year for his leadership. Grace left the School of Forest Resources in 1987 to become deputy secretary of the Department of Environmental Resources, and continued in the same position in the new Department of Conservation and Natural Resources. In 1991 Grace became director of the Bureau of Forestry and has led important efforts to have the bureau's lands certified and to implement ecosystem management.

Steve Jones next directed the forest resources extension program, starting in 1988 and continuing until 1997. Jones instituted the Forest Issues Working Group, an important effort to bring resource professionals and environmental stakeholders together to talk about the state's forests. He and Finley worked with state forester James Nelson in 1992 to secure funding for the awareness and information campaign for the forest stewardship program. This has been a very successful partnership with the bureau, the U.S. Forest Service, and the School of Forest Resources. Its quarterly publication, *Forest Leaves*, reaches nearly fifteen thousand forest landowners and stakeholders. One of the most successful outcomes of this effort is the VIP-Coverts program, renamed the Pennsylvania Forest Stewards (PaFS) in 2005. PaFS members work with extension educators and Bureau of Forestry foresters to develop and deliver education programs. Since 1992 more than 350 volunteers have participated in the program, and they have helped to start many of the county forest landowners associations.

FIG. 37 James Finley conducting an extension workshop for forest landowners. Photo by Howard Nuernberger, College of Agricultural Sciences.

An amplified wildlife emphasis on birds resulted when Margaret Brittingham was appointed in 1988. Her special expertise is in ornithology, but her extension work is more broadly based. Margaret's extension program on wildlife management for private landowners recognizes that many Pennsylvanians are interested in managing their property for wildlife, from backyards to woodlots to farms. The program helps landowners enhance wildlife habitats while minimizing nuisance and damage problems through publications, demonstration areas, and classroom and field training.

Another new dimension, urban forestry, appeared in forestry extension programming in 1991. U.S. Forest Service funding enabled the hiring of four extension urban foresters stationed in county extension offices and an instructor at University Park. John Beauchamp was stationed in Crawford County (he was later replaced by Scott Sjolander), Vincent Cotrone in Luzerne County, Julianne Schieffer in Montgomery County, and Mark Remcheck in Washington County. The main objective of their statewide program is to assist municipalities in managing their landscape trees. William Elmendorf and Henry Gerhold at University Park have coordinated their work and provided technical support, including a newsletter, the magazine *Sylvan Communities*, and many practical publications. The Pennsylvania Urban and Community Forestry Council provides guidance and a link with the Bureau of Forestry. The bureau receives Forest Service funding that has been allocated mainly to the extension program, and most of the remainder goes to modest incentive grants awarded to communities.

Jim Finley was appointed assistant director for forestry extension in 1997, when Steve Jones became the director of extension at Auburn University. Jim continued his educational work with forest stewards and county associations of forest landowners, and also had responsibilities for research and teaching. More important, perhaps, he instituted regular meetings of all faculty and county staff who had extension responsibilities, to improve coordination of programming through better communication. Jim also continued to organize the School of Forest Resources issues conferences, which he and Sandy Cochran originated in 1982. These have become biennial events attracting large audiences from the northeast region (Table 16).

Michael Jacobson joined the School's faculty as an extension forester in 1999, focusing on forest economics and nontimber forest products. Mike has been instrumental in starting the Forest Finance series and has been educating private forest owners about taxes, cost-share programs, and the

Table 16 Topics of the School of Forest Resources Issues Conferences

1982	Coping with the Gypsy Moth
1983	Regenerating Hardwood Stands
1984	Forest Management and Water Quality
1985	Forest Management Decisions Based on Future Forest Product Requirements
1987	Economics of Eastern Hardwood Management
1989	Timber Management and Its Effects on Wildlife
1991	Practicing Stewardship and Living a Land Ethic
1993	Penn's Woods: Change and Challenges
1995	Ecosystem Management: Translating Concepts to Practice
1997	Forest Sustainability: What's It All About?
1999	Natural Resources Management: Interactive Opportunities
2001	Conserving Future Forest Productivity
2003	Forestry's Role in Integrated Water Management
2005	Pennsylvania's Forest Resources: Assessing Their Condition

economic benefits of long-term forest management. He also has a strong interest in international forestry and has pursued opportunities in research and extension programming in South Africa and taught related courses in the School.

In 2001 Sanford Smith, an extension agent in Warren County, moved to University Park to help develop a youth education program and to pursue graduate studies. After completing a doctoral program Sandy remained in the School, building a very successful program for the state's youth. One of his most successful efforts is the From the Woods series, consisting of short, colorful publications designed for youths eight to ten years of age, comprising fourteen titles so far.

When Charles Ray joined the faculty in 2002 as an extension specialist in wood products operations, he immediately created a website to communicate with his audience. WoodPro, the Pennsylvania Wood Products Productivity Program, and its website, http://woodpro.cas.psu.edu, ensure that the wood products industries of Pennsylvania receive optimal exposure to relevant, value-adding resources from Penn State and around the world. Industries receive support in best practices, technology trends, and decision support at all phases of wood products manufacture. Ray's interests include operations management, process control, simulation, and optimization; statistical quality control; artificial intelligence; lean manufacturing; and quality management systems.

By 2005 there were nine faculty and two technical staff in the School of Forest Resources, most of whom had part-time extension appointments.

These faculty members develop extension programs and resources in forest resources, wildlife and fishery sciences, and wood products. In addition, in certain county offices, cooperative extension maintains a professional staff of four regional forestry specialists, two water resources agents who serve multiple counties, and four urban foresters who are supervised and financed through the School. These field educators collaborate in program development and delivery with extension faculty specialists at University Park.

Extension methods have changed over the years, incorporating new technology such as computers, videos, PowerPoint presentations, electronic mail, and the internet. The natural resources website, http://rnrext-.cas.psu.edu/, helps people make informed decisions about forest resources that improve their own well-being and ensure clean water, viable populations of native wildlife, recreational opportunities, attractive and safe communities, and the sustainable production of wood and paper products. Furthermore, the natural resources extension program educates youth through 4-H about forest productivity and sustainability, ecology, and the environment.

CURRENT EXTENSION TOPICS

The current cooperative extension program of the School of Forest Resources covers the major resource topics of forest stewardship, urban and community forestry, wood products, wildlife and fisheries management, and watershed management. All extension activities in the College of Agricultural Sciences are now organized according to plans of work. The plans address important issues that have been identified by extension educators and clientele groups in four-year cycles. The School of Forest Resources has principal responsibilities for the following five topics.

Rural Forests: Helping Landowners Plan and Manage Their Properties to Achieve Their Goals for Forestry, Wildlife, Recreation, and Aesthetics

Pennsylvania is the nation's leader in hardwood lumber production and an important supplier of nontimber products sought by many nations. Nearly three-quarters of the state's forestland is in private ownership. The decisions private landowners make have long-term impacts on forest values and productivity. Unfortunately, poorly executed timber harvests are not uncommon. Adoption of best management practices, already established for the state, could improve the future condition of the state's forests. Although recent inventories indicate a tremendous increase of mature saw timber, there are also problems with less desirable species, inadequate regeneration, and more invasive plants.

Extension faculty deliver research-based education programs to stakeholders that address such issues as taxation, land parcelization, estate planning, forest management planning, silviculture, biodiversity, water resources protection, recreational opportunities, marketing, and nontimber forest products. The forest stewardship program and the forestland enhancement program, funded by the U.S. Forest Service and the Pennsylvania Bureau of Forestry, represent a unique partnership, with extension developing and delivering educational materials and programs to reach private forest stakeholders. These stakeholders include landowners, foresters, loggers, industry, and the diverse publics who benefit from long-term forest stewardship. Especially important are the state's youth, the future owners and benefactors of responsible forest resource management.

Community Forests: Helping Towns and Cities Develop and Manage Their Tree Resources for a Wide Range of Benefits, Increasing Citizen Involvement and Support, and Improving the Expertise of Tree-Care Professionals

Pennsylvania's citizens and visitors draw myriad social, economic, and ecological benefits and services from forests. Trees, parks, and open spaces have been an integral part of communities since the first American settlements, and they continue to have important impacts on human health, welfare, and safety. Despite the benefits of natural environments to municipalities, many public and private trees and landscapes continue to be inadequately managed and ignored in ongoing community development.

When Pennsylvania's Extension Urban Forestry Program started in 1991, only 28 percent of municipalities had any kind of tree-care program and many public trees and parks were in poor condition. Many municipalities continue to think that they should not spend their limited resources on trees and parks. As a result, such communities continue to have unattractive business districts, pay storm cleanup costs resulting from poorly maintained trees, endure power outages, suffer property damage and injuries caused by hazardous trees, and experience declining property values and municipal image because of poorly planned and managed parks and open spaces.

The Extension Urban Forestry Program assists municipalities and volunteer groups in developing sustainable community forestry programs through education, technical assistance, publications, and modest incentive grants. Workshops, conferences, publications, and educational and technical assistance cover a wide range of topics. These address the needs of municipal tree commissions and planning commissions, community leaders, volunteer groups, young people and teachers, underserved people, members of the green industries, and the general public.

Funding and planning for this program of education and assistance has been coordinated with the Pennsylvania Bureau of Forestry, the U.S. Forest Service, and the Pennsylvania Urban and Community Forestry Council. The council provides linkages with many partners, including other state agencies, associations of cities, boroughs, and counties, nonprofits, green industries, and utility companies.

Wood Products Processing: Helping Wood Industries Develop, Manufacture, and Market Products Efficiently and Profitably, and Extending Information to the Public on Professional Careers and Consumer Products

More than two thousand wood products-related companies in Pennsylvania have annual sales exceeding $15 billion, and they account for 10 percent of the state's manufacturing employment, with nearly a hundred thousand employees. Nationally, Pennsylvania ranks number one in hardwood production. Products span the spectrum from disposable diapers to wooden cabinets, engineered wood products, and fine furniture. The wood products industry represents a major economic opportunity, spurred by a plentiful supply of timber and unprecedented global demand for many of the select hardwood species that make up Pennsylvania's forests. Wood as an industrial raw material is sustainable and renewable, and many wood products can be recycled.

The wood products industries of Pennsylvania are under intense international competition, however, both for the raw material resource in the Commonwealth and the markets for the products. One-third of the wood-furniture plants in the United States have been closed since 2000, their production shipped overseas. Accordingly, extension has provided assistance by identifying areas of strategic importance that will sustain and increase the competitiveness of the Pennsylvania wood products industries and by providing new, cutting-edge technological training for wood processors.

Managing Wildlife and Fisheries: Educating People About the Value of Fish and Wildlife, Proper Management Practices, and Minimizing Nuisances and Problems That May Affect Human Health or Damage Crops

Fish and wildlife are important economic, aesthetic, scientific, ecological, educational, recreational, and cultural resources. In Pennsylvania $3 billion is spent annually in activities such as hunting and fishing, wildlife watching, feeding, and landscaping for wildlife. Sustaining the health and diversity of fish and wildlife populations involves working with a diverse mix of habitats, owners, and objectives.

Wildlife nuisance and damage problems affect residents throughout the state. In agricultural areas more than $76 million in damage annually is due to wildlife. As suburban sprawl increases, suburban residents, often unfamiliar with wildlife, come into contact with wildlife more frequently, often with negative consequences for both. In Pennsylvania's forests an overabundant deer population has negative effects on tree regeneration, herbaceous plant abundance, wildlife habitat, and species diversity. A key to sustaining fish and wildlife populations within the state is to increase awareness of how development, agriculture, and forestry can affect fish and wildlife populations, and how to minimize the negative effects.

A number of diseases, such as West Nile virus, rabies, and Lyme disease, may be transmitted directly or indirectly from wildlife to humans. Anxiety and the risk of infection can be reduced by understanding these diseases and by implementing methods to reduce risks. Chronic wasting disease, which is affecting deer in western states and in other parts of the country, has the potential to cause economic loss and concern if found in Pennsylvania. Keeping citizens updated and informed about this disease will reduce these risks.

Pennsylvania youths show a strong interest in fish and wildlife programs and outdoor recreational activities such as fishing, hunting, and shooting sports. Large numbers of young people enroll annually in 4-H wildlife, firearm safety, and sport fisheries programs. Many Pennsylvania youths raised in urban or suburban areas have lost the link with the land. Natural resource programs help to reconnect our youth with the natural environment by increasing their knowledge and awareness of the value and sustainability of fish and wildlife resources.

Fish and wildlife are influenced by changing land-use practices, and private landowners have a major impact. Professional land managers and decision makers in state and local governments also strongly influence land-use decisions for private and public lands. Extension wildlife and fisheries programs aim to increase awareness of the importance of these natural resources within the state, encourage individuals and groups to implement sound management practices, and provide the tools and techniques for minimizing conflict between humans and wildlife, enhance wildlife habitats, provide recreational opportunities, and help sustain rural economies.

Environmental Stewardship of Land and Water Resources: Helping Individual Homeowners and Rural Communities Acquire and Manage a Supply of Pure, Abundant Water

Pennsylvania has abundant water resources, but traditionally these have been abused and poorly managed. Rural drinking water supplies frequently do not meet health standards, and improper disposal of household wastewater contributes to groundwater contamination problems. Non-point source pollution from storm water, urban landscapes, private ponds, agriculture, mining, and other land uses continues to be a major threat to surface and groundwater resources of the state. In recent years water quantity has also become an issue in Pennsylvania because of persistent droughts. More than five hundred watershed organizations have formed around the state in response to local water resource and land-use issues, but most are in dire need of education and training on best management practices related to watersheds. Extension programs assist clientele in improving management of water resources and ultimately reduce water pollution and wasteful water use.

PROFESSIONAL DEVELOPMENT AND OTHER OUTREACH

An administrative management program for natural resource managers was initiated in 1960 by Robert McDermott of the School of Forest Resources and Earl Strong, professor in the College of Business Administration. They jointly developed this intensive two-week program for middle-level managers of natural resources in government agencies and industry to improve their managerial skills and decision-making abilities. Participating agencies included the U.S. Forest Service, the U.S. Fish and Wildlife Service, natural resource agencies in various states, and conservancy groups. The program enjoyed an excellent reputation, although the audiences varied according to variability in funding of the agencies. The program's co-directors following McDermott were Ronald Bartoo, Orvel Schmidt, Rex Melton, Ben Twight, and Al Sullivan. After Sullivan left in 1993 the School's role in managing the program was reduced. In 2005 the Smeal College of Business changed the name to the management program for public service leaders.

The School currently provides an annual series of professional development programs to meet the educational needs of various professional audiences. These are typically one-day to three-day fee-based programs, usually at the University Park campus, and involve faculty and other guest professionals as teaching staff. These programs span the various disciplines within forest science, wildlife and fisheries science, and wood products. Typically twenty to thirty different programs are held each year, with enrollments of ten to eighty participants per program. They deal with diverse topics, including GIS/GPS in forestry, forest taxation, and wood products.

The School's website, http://www.sfr.cas.psu.edu/, provides information to students and prospective students, faculty and staff, business and industries, alumni and friends, and the general public. It contains information on educational programs, research, outreach, and current items of interest, including the biennial report.

Forums and Lecture Series

Outreach activities that enable professionals and the public to learn about and discuss natural resource issues include the Goddard forum, the Ibberson forum, the forest issues conference, the community forestry conference, and the Rachel Carson lecture series. The Glatfelter Company sponsored a distinguished lecturer series from 1992 to 2003 (Table 17).

Goddard forums have been offered through the Goddard chair on a variety of topics (Table 18), and they have been co-sponsored by various organizations. This outreach effort focuses on emerging issues in natural resources policy and local solutions to global issues. In 2001 the endowment supporting the Goddard chair was increased to support periodic forums and to support one or more Goddard fellows who enhance the chair's mission.

In 2003 Professor Harry Wiant initiated the Ibberson forestry forum, sponsored by the Pennsylvania Forestry Association and the School of Forest Resources. Financial support from the Pennsylvania Forestry Asso-

Table 17 Speakers and Topics in the Distinguished Lecture Series

1992	W. D. Ticknor, Forestry Consultants: "A Vision of the Future of Forestry"
1993	Ronald J. Slinn, American Paper Institute: "The Pulp and Paper Business: Answers to Questions You Might Never Have Thought to Ask About Some Taken-for-Granted Forest Products"
1994	Stephen G. Thorne, Maurice K. Goddard Chair: "Unfinished Business: Creating the Future Forests of Pennsylvania"
1995	Michael P. Dombeck, USDA Forest Service: "From Commodity to Community: A Common Sense Approach to Understanding Ecosystem Management"
1997	R. Scott Wallinger, Westvaco Corporation: "An Optimistic View of Sustainable Forestry"
1997	Alston Chase, Harvard University's Kennedy School of Government: "Is U.S. Natural Resource Preservation Policy Based on a Mistake?"
1999	Jerry Franklin, College of Forest Resources, University of Washington: "Science and Recent Development of Forest Policies in Western North America"
2003	Claire Schelske, Department of Geological Sciences, Land Use and Environmental Change Institute, University of Florida: "Tracking the History of Eutrophication in the Great Lakes Using Silica Depletion"

Table 18 Topics of the Goddard Forums

2001	Water: A Finite Resource
2002	Global Warming: Causes, Effects, and Mitigation Strategies for States and Localities
2002	Biodiversity: Addressing a Global Issue Locally
2004	Developing Sustainable Communities: State and Local Practices, Technologies, and Policies to Promote Economic Development and Social Equity While Sustaining the Environment
2005	Putting the Market to Work for Conservation: Traditional and Non-Traditional Market-Based Mechanisms for Achieving Environmental Improvement
2006	Opportunities and Challenges of the Pennsylvania Renewable Portfolio Standard: Emerging Technologies, Regulations, and Institutions

ciation comes from its Joseph E. Ibberson and Henry Chauncey endowments. The purpose of the forum is to promote interactions among forest landowners, consultants, wood industries, and government agencies (Table 19).

The outreach program also involves coordination with the College of Agricultural Sciences international programs, alumni relations, and advisory board relations. School director Al Sullivan appointed a broadly based school advisory board in 1991. Its members represented state and federal agencies, several kinds of forestry-related industries, organizations inter-

Table 19   Topics of the Ibberson Forums

Year	Topic
2003	Pennsylvania's Wood Supply and Productivity, Protecting Private Property Rights
2004	Ecoterrorism, Timber Trespass
2005	What You Need to Know Before Selling Timber

FIG. 38   The first Ibberson Forestry Forum was organized by Harry Wiant (*at left*), introduced by Charles Strauss, supported by Joseph Ibberson, and welcomed by Lloyd Casey (*at right*), president of the Pennsylvania Forestry Association. Photo by H. D. Gerhold.

ested in forestry and wildlife, and legislators. Subsequent directors have continued to rely on the advisory board, with changing membership, for evaluating the School's programs and providing advice about teaching, research, extension, development, and the academic role of the School within the university. Many of the board's suggestions have been implemented, and feedback has been a means of keeping members informed about progress.

Nittany Lion Restored

Outreach sometimes takes unusual turns. In 1992 Richard Yahner, professor of wildlife conservation and assistant director for outreach, became aware of a mounted specimen of the eastern mountain lion that had been stored since 1953 at the Carnegie Museum in Pittsburgh. It had been lent to the museum as part of an endangered species exhibit but was never returned. An investigation revealed that it was the Original Nittany Lion, symbol of the Penn State mascot.

The lion had been adopted as Penn State's mascot in 1904. For a time the mascot, which had a decidedly African appearance (Fig. 39), was known as "Old Nittany," and was retired because it reputedly brought bad luck to the football team. The name "Original" refers to the origin of the genuine mascot, as the native lion had already been displayed in Old Main as part of a wildlife exhibit from 1894 to 1929. The mounted lion had also been displayed at the World Columbian Exposition in Chicago in 1893 in an exhibit depicting rare animals. Duane Schlitter, curator of mammals at the Carnegie Museum of Natural History, stated that the Original Nittany Lion "is as unique and significant to the history of the Commonwealth as is William Penn's original deed to Penn's Forest."

Through Yahner's efforts the Original Nittany Lion is now part of a beautiful panorama, depicting a happy valley–Nittany mountain setting in autumn 1856—one year after the founding of Penn State. The panorama, located in Pattee Library, is the product of several years of planning and work by the Original Nittany Lion Committee, chaired by Yahner, the careful touch-up by a nationally known conservator, and the artistic abilities of museum experts.

The Original Nittany Lion, which is the only mounted eastern mountain lion in Pennsylvania, not only was the impetus for Penn State to have a native mountain lion as its mascot but also represents a rich conservation story about the historic demise of large carnivores throughout the United States. The story of the Original Nittany Lion is documented in the book *The Nittany Lion: An Illustrated Tale*, published by Penn State Press.

FIG. 39   Gifford Pinchot encounters the Nittany Lion
mascot, circa 1924. Penn State University Archives,
Pennsylvania State University Libraries.

13

ALUMNI RELATIONS

The Penn State–Mont Alto Forestry Alumni Association was founded in 1939 by a group of alumni who had started meeting in 1936. Members included graduates of the old State Forest School at Mont Alto, prior to its merger in 1929 with Pennsylvania State University, and also the forestry graduates of Penn State together with those who completed the two-year ranger course, as well as anyone who completed graduate work in forestry at Penn State. The avowed purpose was to promote and maintain standards of forestry instruction in Pennsylvania and to provide for professional fellowship and solidarity among the forestry alumni of the two institutions.

Henry Clepper commented on the association's concern about education, "Often to its disadvantage, forestry education at Penn State was in direct competition for funds, facilities, and faculty with other units of the College of Agriculture. It was quite apparent that the staff of the Department of Forestry required the support of an informed and aggressive body of alumni" (1969, 47). At the first general meeting on October 12, 1940, the main subject of discussion was establishing a forestry school rather than a department. Subsequently several attempts were made to exert pressure toward improving the status of forestry within the college. More recently, relationships among alumni, the School, and the college have become much more constructive.

Several alumni reunions have been held, many of them at Mont Alto. The School's alumni association also has been active in organizing and participating in the 50th, 60th, 75th, and 100th anniversary celebrations at University Park. The Mont Alto graduates have held reunions every five years on that campus. Each year the School and alumni sponsors an alumni get-together at the national convention of the Society of American Foresters, and also alumni gatherings at the national meetings of the Forest Products Society, the American Fisheries Society, and the Wildlife Society.

The level and types of our alumni activities have varied over the years. In 1948 alumni dedicated a plaque in the lobby of Ferguson Building to the Penn State forestry students and alumni who lost their lives in World Wars I and II. On the fiftieth anniversary of the School in 1957, alumni completed a memorial tree planting that also commemorates those individuals. A small bronze plaque, originally fastened to a stone near the northeast corner of Wagner Building, now rests at the base of the only memorial trees that remain, the last two oaks at the intersection of Curtin and Porter roads. In 1973 the association installed and dedicated a plaque and stone monument at Mont Alto commemorating the founding of the Pennsylvania State Forest Academy in 1903.

An alumni newsletter is published with assistance from the School and is available on the School's website. Since publishing its first alumni newsletter in 1943, the School has distributed a newsletter once or twice a year to an ever-growing group of alumni. In winter 2001 the alumni newsletter became part of RESOURCES, a new publication for School of Forest Resources alumni and interested friends.

In 1993 the Penn State–Mont Alto Forestry Alumni Association became the School of Forest Resources Alumni Group, an official Affiliate Program Group (APG) within the College of Agricultural Sciences Alumni Society and the Penn State Alumni Association. At the time, the association had only one surviving officer, Al Schutz '53, who had served as secretary-treasurer for the previous thirty-one years. Glenn Haney '51, director Al Sullivan, and an ad hoc alumni committee were instrumental in getting the APG established (Table 20).

The alumni group serves to stimulate the continued interest of all graduates and friends of the School, acts as an informal advisory board to the

Table 20   Officers of the School of Forest Resources Alumni Group (with Class Year)

Term of Office	President	Vice President
1993–1997	Glenn Haney, 1951	Al Schutz, 1953
1997–1999	Paul Shogren, 1951	George Kemp, 1953
1999–2001	George Kemp, 1953	Terry Harrison, 1977
2001–2003	Stan Rapp, 1952	Terry Harrison, 1977
2003–2005	Lowell Underhill, 1956	Ted Jensen, 1950
2005–2007	Tom Yorke, 1964	Mark Webb, 1973

NOTE: Bruce Snyder, class of 1981, served as secretary-treasurer 1993–1999; Marilyn Snyder, class of 1991, served as secretary-treasurer 1999–2002, after which the office of secretary-treasurer was eliminated.

director, and provides a means whereby alumni may join together for the improvement of the School and the College of Agricultural Sciences in its entirety. An alumni and friends banquet is held annually in the spring; in alternate years it is held in conjunction with the School of Forest Resources issues conference. The alumni group presents awards to outstanding alumni and provides other forms of support to the School.

In 1997 the School of Forest Resources Alumni Group created the Alumni Fund for Teaching Excellence, dedicated to providing up-to-date equipment needed to enhance the education of students and prepare them for a changing and challenging future. The alumni fund supports innovative experiences for students in field, laboratory, and other hands-on activities. This endowment has a goal of $100,000, about half of which has been contributed. The earnings may be used for all School programs and classes, including those at University Park, Mont Alto, and DuBois. Examples of purchases made possible by the fund include water quality equipment, specimens for ornithology, mammal track casts, GPS equipment, and GPS software. Proceeds from the sale of *Woodland Notes*, with artwork donated by John Sidelinger ('74 and '78), also benefit the Alumni Fund for Teaching Excellence.

Membership in the School of Forest Resources Alumni Group is open to all graduates of the School, including graduates of intercollege graduate programs who were advised by School of Forest Resources faculty, and to other friends with a special interest in the School's programs. The alumni group relies on contributions to support alumni activities, as no membership dues are charged. In July 2005 membership totaled 5,124 people living in all fifty states and twenty-five countries. Another 453 alumni were inactive (that is, no current address was known), and an additional 1,273 were deceased.

14

ACCOMPLISHMENTS OF ALUMNI AND
FACULTY—LOOKING BACK

Any one person can know only a few of the more than eight thousand graduates and faculty who have been associated with the School of Forest Resources, including the Academy at Mont Alto. But even a small sample is enough to show that they have had a tremendous beneficial impact on the forestry professions, on natural resources, and on the well-being of people. To capture the flavor of their manifold accomplishments, we assembled brief biographies of selected alumni and faculty, soliciting their help whenever possible.

The following biographies are in alphabetical order, organized within eight categories: forest management, wood technology and industry, parks and recreation, hydrology and watershed management, wildlife and fisheries, urban forestry, academia and professional organizations, and entrepreneurial mavericks who ventured into seemingly unrelated fields of endeavor. Some of these specialties have been part of the School's offerings for less time than others, so there are fewer biographies in some of the categories. Furthermore, the careers of some may not fit neatly into a single category.

Biographies were selected somewhat subjectively based on our faculty's knowledge, records of awards made by the School of Forest Resources (Table 21), recommendations of alumni, and availability of biographical information. In some cases one person was selected among several whose careers were similar. For example, Richard Thorpe was selected from nine Penn State alumni among the twelve state foresters who have served Pennsylvania (Table 22). Many of the state foresters of other states also have been Penn State alumni.

Collectively the biographies represent a sampling of alumni and faculty who have achieved professional prominence, or made unique contributions, or pursued unusual careers. Many of the biographies describe alumni or faculty members from the first fifty years of the School's exis-

Table 21 Alumni Achievement Awards Presented by the School of Forest Resources at the 50th, 60th, and 75th Anniversaries, and After 2000 by the Alumni Group

Award Year	Recipient and Year of Graduation
50th Anniversary	
1957	Henry Clepper, 1921
1957	Frank C. Craighead, 1912
1957	George W. Dean, 1926
1957	George L. Drake, 1912
1957	Edmund O. Ehrhart, 1913
1957	Irvine T. Haig, 1923
1957	B. Frank Heintzleman, 1907
1957	Earl W. Loveridge, 1912
1957	Arthur C. McIntyre, 1929
1957	Carl A. Rishell, 1923
1957	Herman Work, 1910
60th Anniversary	
1967	William G. Edwards, 1914
1967	Albert G. Hall, 1933
1967	Durell E. Hess, 1935
1967	Ralph C. Wible, 1927
75th Anniversary	
1982	Arthur L. Bennett, 1940
1982	Samuel S. Cobb, 1939
1982	Edward P. Farrand, 1940
1982	Peter W. Fletcher, 1933
1982	Calvin H. Glattfelder, 1949
1982	John L. Gray, 1941
1982	Edward L. Kozicky, 1942
1982	David A. Marquis, 1955
1982	Louis W. Schatz, 1934
1982	Michael A. Taras, 1942
1982	Wilber W. Ward, 1940
Alumni Group Awards	
2001	William C. Bramble, 1929
2001	Eugene Decker, 1952, M.S. 1955
2001	Pamela J. Edwards, 1981
2001	John C. Good, 1941
2002	Edward F. Kocjancic, 1954
2002	Robert H. Rumpf, 1949
2002	David Spencer, 1937
2003	Joseph E. Ibberson, 1947
2003	Gregory M. Schrum, 1967, M.S. 1969
2003	Mark R. Webb, 1973
2003	Thomas L. Serfass, Ph.D. 1994

Table 21 Continued

Award Year	Recipient and Year of Graduation
2004	James R. Grace, Ph.D. 1978
2004	James C. Nelson, 1952
2004	W. R. Rossman, 1950
2004	A. M. Townsend, 1964
2005	Robert H. Bommer, 1956
2005	Phillip J. Craul, 1954, M.S. 1960
2005	John T. Steimer, 1949
2005	Richard G. Wallace, 1956
2005	James J. Zaczek, Ph.D. 1994
2006	Keith D. Atherholt, 1979
2006	Alex Kirnak, 1937
2006	Robert C. McColly, 1972
2006	Darrel L. Williams, 1973, M.S. 1974

Table 22 The State Foresters of Pennsylvania, Including Nine Penn State Alumni

State Forester	Years in Office
George H. Wirt	1901–1910
Title discontinued	1910–1920
Robert Y. Stuart	1920–1923
*Lewis E. Staley	1923–1927
Joseph S. Illick	1927–1931
*John W. Keller	1931–1936
*R. Lynn Emerick	1936–1946
*O. Ben Gipple	1947–1952
*Ralph C. Wible	1952–1966
*Samuel S. Cobb	1966–1977
*Richard R. Thorpe	1977–1989
*James C. Nelson	1989–1991
*James R. Grace	1991–present

* Penn State alumnus

tence. Their careers can be described thoroughly, as nearly all of them have retired by now and some have been documented in obituaries. Sadly, we were unable to obtain information about some whose accomplishments are known to be substantial.

Just a few of the biographies are about alumni who graduated within the past thirty years. Most of the more recent alumni and faculty are still engaged in their careers, so they are less well represented. Their time for greater recognition is yet to come.

FIG. 40   Many alumni have received awards, this one presented by Coach Joe Paterno to Joseph Ibberson in 2006. College of Agricultural Sciences photo by Stacie Bird.

BIOGRAPHICAL SKETCHES OF ALUMNI AND FACULTY, BY CAREER FIELD

The School of Forest Resources is justifiably proud of the achievements of its graduates. Besides their professional accomplishments, many of the alumni profiled below, as well as many not featured here, also served their country in the various branches of the armed forces. In World War I the 10th Forestry Engineers Regiment and the 20th Forestry Engineers Regiment of the U.S. Army produced all kinds of wood products needed by the army, and in World War II there were smaller forestry units of battalion or company size. The 10th Mountain Division (ski troops) also attracted recruits from forestry. As returning World War II veteran Frank Wawrynovic (class of 1950) put it so well, "We were the generation that had fought and won history's greatest war and had preserved the freedom that Americans enjoy today."

Forest Management

Most of the School's alumni and faculty have pursued careers focusing on, or closely related to, the management of public forests, industrial lands, or privately owned woodlands. They have found employment throughout the nation and abroad. Many of them have played a role in the restoration and improvement of Pennsylvania's forests, which now occupy about 58 percent of its area, having recovered from a low of about 30 percent in 1907. The 2.1-million-acre state forest system is one of the largest in the eastern states, yet 74 percent of the Commonwealth's forests are owned by about half a million private owners. The high quality of Pennsylvania hardwoods is known around the world. The wood products, paper, and furniture industries contribute $15 billion annually to the state's economy and employ nearly one hundred thousand people with a $2.8 billion payroll.

Robert H. "Bob" Bommer (b. 1934)

After completing his B.S. degree in 1956, Bob served for two years in the U.S. Navy, receiving training as an officer and naval aviator. In 1958 he was employed as a CFM forester by the Pennsylvania Department of Forests and Waters. From 1959 to 1961 Bob worked for the M. C. Houseworth Lumber Company in Bedford as a buyer of timber, land, logs, and lumber. He became director of procurement for the Williamson Veneer Company in New Freedom in 1961, where he directed purchase of raw materials, developed a long-range procurement policy for future expansion, and trained and supervised the purchasing staff. During this period he attended night school and in 1965 received the J.D. degree from the University of Baltimore. When the Evans Products Company of Portland, Oregon, purchased Williamson Veneer in 1968, Bommer became the operations assistant to the general manager. His responsibilities included administration, legal activities, procurement of raw materials, and production.

Bommer founded his own consulting service in 1971, R. H. Bommer, Jr. Inc., Forest Consultants. He served clients in the eastern United States, having qualified as a registered surveyor in Pennsylvania, a registered professional forester in Maryland and West Virginia, and as a certified consulting arborist. His specialties included forest management, appraisals, marketing, feasibility studies, legal cases, veneer and specialty log procurement, land acquisition and sales, contract arbitration, real estate and export counseling, land surveying, and shade tree evaluation. His company continued as Bommer-Geesaman & Company, Forestry Consultants, after Bob retired.

Through his professional abilities Bommer made important contributions to various organizations and agencies. In 1959 he received a certificate of appreciation for outstanding work by the American Forest Products Industries. He served as a member of the U.S. secretary of agriculture's Advisory Committee on State and Private Forestry from 1979 to 1981. Bob has spoken frequently at meetings of the Society of American Foresters and the Association of Consulting Foresters, and served as an officer of the latter. As a member of the National Commercial Panel of the American Arbitration Association he used his knowledge to help settle commercial cases through arbitration.

Bob has been a strong supporter of the School of Forest Resources and the College of Agriculture, having contributed time and money to several causes. Furthermore, he helped the Tau Phi Delta forestry fraternity purchase its building and served a term as grand national president. He was named an alumni centennial fellow of Penn State Mont Alto in 2004 and received an Outstanding Alumni Award from the School of Forest Resources in 2005. From the Society of American Foresters he received the Outstanding Service to Forestry Award in 1982.

Ralph Elwood Brock (1883–1959)

Ralph Elwood Brock was born in Pottsville and graduated in the Pennsylvania State Forest Academy's first class of six foresters in 1906. He was the nation's first African American forester. He had been employed previously at the Mont Alto Reserve, now the Michaux State Forest. Following graduation he served for five years as the superintendent of the Mont Alto state forest tree nursery, which had been established in 1902. Brock wrote several technical articles about renewing nursery soils and the effectiveness of various planting practices.

Brock resigned from state service in 1911 to start his own nursery business in the Philadelphia area. His specialties were estate gardens, orchards, and landscaping. He also spent many years working in New York City, where he concluded his career.

Brock was honored by the Department of Conservation and Natural Resources in 2000, when it renamed the South Mountain Seed Orchard at Mont Alto the Ralph E. Brock Seed Orchard. In April 2003 the Pennsylvania Historical and Museum Commission's division of history installed a historical marker to honor Brock near the entrance to the Penn State Mont Alto campus; it stands near another marker that notes the 2003 campus centennial. He was named an alumni centennial fellow in 2004 by Penn State Mont Alto.

B. Frank Heintzleman (1888–1965)

When B. Frank Heintzleman received the B.F. degree from the Pennsylvania State Forest Academy at Mont Alto in 1907, who could have predicted that he would become governor of Alaska? He was one of four in the second graduating class, and like all students at that time he was required to supply his own horse. After earning the M.F. degree at the Yale Forest School in 1910, he entered the U.S. Forest Service at Portland, Oregon, as a forest assistant. He transferred in 1918 to the Tongass National Forest in Alaska, and later became the assistant regional forester for the territory.

From 1934 to 1936 the Forest Service assigned him to cooperative forestry work with the timber industry in Washington, D.C. For one year he was deputy administrator in charge of forest conservation in the lumber division of the National Industrial Recovery Administration.

In 1937 Heintzleman was appointed regional forester for the Alaska region of the Forest Service, with headquarters in Juneau. He negotiated the establishment of two large pulp mills at Ketchikan and Sitka. He also served as commissioner for the Department of Agriculture in the territory, as representative of the Federal Power Commission, and as chairman of the Alaska Planning Council; he played a key part in advocating lakes as a source of hydropower. During World War II he directed the Alaska spruce log program cooperatively with the War Production Board.

In 1953, following his retirement from the Forest Service, Heintzleman was appointed governor of the Territory of Alaska by President Eisenhower. He served four years and resigned in 1957, in anticipation of the passage of the Statehood Enabling Act of 1958.

In recognition of his contributions to the advancement of forestry, he was elected a fellow of the Society of American Foresters in 1951 and was awarded the Sir William Schlich Memorial Medal for distinguished service to forestry in 1958; he had been a member of the society for fifty years.

In 1955 he returned to Mont Alto to visit students and members of his family in Fayetteville. Heintzleman was awarded the Alumni Centennial Award posthumously by Penn State Mont Alto in 2004.

Joseph E. "Joe" Ibberson (b. 1917)

Joseph E. Ibberson retired in 1977 as chief of the Division of Forest Advisory Services in the Bureau of Forestry, in Pennsylvania's Department of Environmental Resources (which subsequently became the Department of Conservation and Natural Resources). In his own quietly effective way, he was the principal leader for thirty years in modernizing the bureau's activities in timber management, pest management, tree nursery production, tree improvement, advice to wood industries, and service to private landowners.

Ibberson completed the ranger program at Mont Alto and State College in 1939, and was the only one in his class who had a job upon graduation. He was employed in the construction of the reservoir that supplies Harrisburg, and was placed in charge of its operation when the dam was completed. His education was interrupted by World War II. Joe served in the U.S. Army from 1942 to 1945, starting in the Seacoast Artillery and advancing to transport commander after completing officer candidate school. While taking more than twenty trips back and forth across the Atlantic, he saw many ships sunk by German U-boats but escaped this danger himself. He returned to Penn State to complete the B.S. degree in forestry in 1947, and then received an M.F. degree from Yale University in 1948.

Working for the Pennsylvania Department of Forests and Waters' Bureau of Forestry, Ibberson was in charge of developing the first forest resource plans for managing some 2 million acres of Pennsylvania state forestland. The huge project started in 1948 with the preparation of a manual to guide the mapping and inventorying of every forest stand by forest type and site class. In 1950 Ibberson hired dozens of foresters to measure trees on sample plots, organize compartment maps, and develop forest resource plans for each of the twenty forest districts. By 1955 the project was finished on schedule. Many of the foresters hired for the project later became district foresters, division chiefs, and even bureau directors. The forest resource plans have been revised at fifteen-year intervals.

The research division Ibberson headed was renamed the Division of

Forest Advisory Services in 1956, after a controversy with Penn State about research responsibilities of the Bureau of Forestry versus those of the university. Ibberson's "Dream Team" expanded the forest resource plans to address more comprehensively the preservation of endangered species and wetlands. Through Ibberson's vision and initiative, the Bureau of Forestry added programs in forest pest management, wood utilization and marketing, and scientific multiple-use management. He started a forest genetics program and implemented improved nursery management practices that enabled the tree nurseries to produce greater quantities of desirable and improved species. He also created a service forester program to aid private citizens in managing their forested land.

In 1962 Joe began buying his own land to create tree farms on which he practiced various forms of forest management, eventually accumulating more than two thousand acres. In 1998 Ibberson gave 350 acres of this land to the state's Department of Conservation and Natural Resources. It became the Joseph E. Ibberson Conservation Area, the first of its kind in the state. His gift stimulated several others that also were made conservation areas.

Through Joe's generosity and astute investments, he endowed two chairs in Penn State's School of Forest Resources. In 1998 he initiated a gift of $1.5 million to establish the Joseph E. Ibberson Chair in Forest Resources Management, currently held by Harry V. Wiant Jr., professor of forest management. Its purpose is to educate students and provide leadership in the professional management of privately owned forests. His second gift, in 2003, committed $2 million from his estate for a chair in urban and community forestry, designed to provide leadership through instruction, research, and public service. He also gave $50,000 to the Pennsylvania Forestry Association to promote wise use of the many resources derived from forests, and has promised an additional $1 million.

Ibberson was elected fellow of the Society of American Foresters, the most prestigious recognition SAF bestows. He has been recognized through numerous awards, including the 1998 Outstanding Tree Farmer in the Northeast, the 1999 Pennsylvania Stewardship Conservation Award, the 2001 Joseph Trimble Rothrock Conservationist of the Year Award, the 2001 Nature Conservancy Landowner of the Year Award, the 2003 Outstanding Alumni Award from Penn State's School of Forest Resources, in 2004 the Penn State Mont Alto Centennial Fellows Award and the Central Pennsylvania Conservancy Conservationist of the Year Award, and the Outstanding Alumni Award of the College of Agricultural Sciences in 2006.

Robert G. "Bob" Kintigh (b. 1922)

Bob Kintigh graduated from Penn State in 1943 with a B.S. degree in forestry. During World War II he fought in several major naval battles in the Pacific as an officer on a destroyer. He received the M.F. degree in 1947 from the University of California. Then he moved to Oregon, where he worked as a forestry consultant and later was employed by the Bureau of Land Management until 1960. Since 1957 Bob has operated a business that produces timber products, Christmas trees, and nursery stock. His rhododendron garden contains more than 650 varieties.

Kintigh served twelve years in the Oregon state senate. He was the only forester to have served there, and also has the distinction of being elected president pro tempore. He focused attention on forestry issues, landowner rights, and sound management practices. In 1995 he introduced landmark legislation giving landowners an incentive to plant trees on land not currently supporting a forest. He also sponsored the Adopt-a-Highway program in Oregon, worked on salmon restoration issues, and served four years on the Western Legislative Forestry Task Force.

In addition to his legislative service, Bob has served as president of the Oregon Small Woodlands Association, as national councilman of the Society of American Foresters, on the board of directors of the Oregon Forest Resources Institute, on the Friends of Paul Bunyan Foundation board of directors, and as president of the Eugene chapter of the American Rhododendron Society. He also has been active in his community and his church.

Kintigh has received many awards, including that of fellow in the Society of American Foresters and the Lifetime Achievement Award from the Oregon chapter. In 1997 he was recognized by the Agriculture and Natural Resources Leaders of Oregon for distinguished service and leadership. Penn State's College of Agricultural Sciences recognized him with a 1999 Outstanding Alumni Award, which provided the opportunity for interaction with students, faculty, and alumni. Bob and his wife (Margaret Kilgore, 1942, botany) were named Oregon Tree Farmers of the Year in 2005.

Edward F. "Ed" Kocjancic (1932–2006)

Edward F. Kocjancic was born and raised in a lumber camp in northern Pennsylvania. His parents started the camp just two days after their marriage, and they operated the camp with a twenty-five-man crew. His mother raised Ed and his three older brothers in the lumber camp after her husband was killed in an auto accident when Ed was just five years old. All four brothers have made their livelihood in wood industries, but Ed was the only one who went to college. By the age of twelve Ed was already a pretty good hand with the double-bit axe, the cross-cut saw, and other tools of the trade. At age seventeen he was competing professionally in woodsmen's shows in Pennsylvania and other northeastern states. He has held national records in cross-cut sawing events, and his three brothers also competed in world-class logging contests.

Ed earned a B.S. in forestry in 1954 and served in the U.S. Army from 1955 to 1957. Most of his career in forestry was as a forest consultant. He was president of Edward F. Kocjancic, Inc., a consulting firm based in Kane, Pennsylvania, that employs a staff of eight and is known internationally for its veneer expertise, especially black cherry. Ed's company offers the gamut of natural resource management services, including aerial and GIS mapping and domestic and international marketing.

Kocjancic demonstrated by example the importance of forest stewardship, sustainability, and multiple use in the management of private forestland. He was a Forest Stewardship Council resource manager. Ed was named a finalist in the 2001 Governor's Export Excellence Award, which recognizes companies and individuals who are leading contributors to Pennsylvania's expanding international markets.

Ed served on the School's advisory board beginning in 1995, and often hosted visits by whole classes of undergraduate students. His company has worked in conjunction with the School to develop the latest computer technology for forest inventory and information gathering. His support of the new Forest Resources Building includes funding for a teaching laboratory, named the Kocjancic Forest Soils and Water Laboratory, which contains twenty-four stations for students taking classes in forest soils, hydrology, and related subjects.

Kocjancic's professional affiliations and awards demonstrate his dedication to forestry and to Penn State. He was a longtime member of the Society of American Foresters, a life member of the Pennsylvania Forestry Association, a director and president of the Allegheny Hardwood Utilization Group, a director of the Pennsylvania Forest Industry Association, a director of the McKean County Conservation District, a director of the Pennsylvania Council of Professional Foresters, and a member of the Pennsylvania Hardwood Development Council. In 2002 he received the School of Forest Resources Outstanding Alumni Award, and in 2004 the Centennial Fellows Award of Penn State Mont Alto. Ed was a very strong supporter of Penn State's Grand Destiny Campaign and also served as a volunteer in that effort. He was a life member of the Penn State Alumni Association, an inductee in 2000 to the Penn State Mount Nittany Society, and a Penn State President's Club member. He was selected as a Penn State alumni fellow for 2005, the highest award given by the alumni association. Three of the four children of Ed and his wife, Patricia, have degrees from Penn State.

His community involvement included serving on the advisory board of Northwest Savings Bank, Kane Branch; serving as a director on the Kane Area Industrial Development Council; and serving as leadership gift director for St. Callistus Church in Kane, Pennsylvania, where he spearheaded the fund-raising of $1 million to help the church meet its building campaign goal. He was honored as Kane's Outstanding Citizen in 2002.

David A. "Dave" Marquis (b. 1934)

David Marquis received his B.S. degree in forestry from Penn State in 1955, and his master's and doctoral degrees in forest ecology and silviculture from Yale University in 1963 and 1973. After graduating from Penn State he served two years as an officer in the army, as an instructor in the Engineering School at Fort Belvoir, Virginia.

Dave was a silviculturist at the USDA Northeastern Forest Experiment Station from 1957 until he retired in 1991. Starting in New Hampshire with studies of regeneration and thinning in northern hardwoods, he next served on the timber and watershed management research staff at the station's headquarters in Pennsylvania. Between 1970 and 1990 Marquis was project leader of the silviculture research unit at Warren, Pennsylvania, studying the regeneration and culture of high-value hardwoods on the Allegheny plateau. He led a station-wide effort to develop a silvicultural decision model for multi-resource management of all major forest types in the northeastern United States.

His pioneering research at the Warren laboratory developed forestry decision-support systems, including a systematic process for analyzing stands and prescribing silvicultural treatments, and the expert-system computer program SILVAH. More than one thousand practicing foresters attended the series of week-long silviculture training sessions and one-day short courses that Marquis developed. The silvicultural procedures in SILVAH have been widely adopted by forest management agencies in the Allegheny region, and they also have been copied for other forest types.

Marquis is the author of more than one hundred scientific papers on all aspects of eastern hardwood ecology and silviculture. He has written extensively about the silvics and natural regeneration of northeastern hardwood tree species, the impact of deer browsing on regeneration, forest and stand development processes, thinning and other stand cultural practices, and the history of northeastern hardwood forests and its implications for forest management. He has presented the results of his research at nearly 150 conferences and professional meetings in the United States, Canada, France, Yugoslavia, Japan, and Great Britain.

He has received numerous awards, including a Forestry Achievement Award from Penn State (1982), the Outstanding Service to Forestry Award from the Allegheny Society of American Foresters (1984), the U.S. Forest Service Award for Outstanding Contributions to National Forest Silviculture (1989), and seven U.S. Forest Service merit awards between 1977 and 1990. Marquis was elected a fellow in the Society of American Foresters in 1989. He received the Northeastern Forest Experiment Station Director's Award for Excellence in 1991, the U.S. Forest Service Science Award in 1991, and awards honoring his research in Allegheny hardwoods upon his retirement from the Pennsylvania Bureau of Forestry, the Pennsylvania Game Commission, the Pennsylvania Senate, and the Pennsylvania House of Representatives. In 1993 he received the Society of American Foresters' highest award for research contributions, the Barrington Moore Award.

Commenting on his college days, Marquis began by paraphrasing a book title, writing, "Everything I Needed to Know About Forestry and a Career, I Learned at Penn State. This is not to belittle the graduate education or experience I gained later, but my education at Penn State was remarkable in providing both the basic science knowledge and the learning and social skills that I needed later on to undertake advanced studies and a successful career in research."

Victor C. Mastro (b. 1947)

Victor Mastro completed his associate degree in forestry in 1968 at the Penn State, Mont Alto campus. In 1970 he received a B.S. in forestry from Stephen F. Austin University, Nacogdoches, Texas; and in 1973 the M.S. in entomology from Texas A&M University. From 1974 to 1977 Vic was a research assistant for the Department of Entomology at Penn State. His work there was focused on developing new trapping and control techniques for the gypsy moth and the hemlock looper.

Mastro began his federal career in 1977 as an entomologist for the Otis Methods Development Laboratory. He advanced to director of the Otis Plant Protection Center, which works with states, local and foreign governments, universities, industry, and federal agencies to develop regulatory treatments, detection and survey technology, and management strategies for exotic pests that threaten the United States' agricultural and natural systems. These pests currently include the Asian longhorned beetle, gypsy moth, emerald ash borer, Sirex wood wasp, and approximately twenty additional species.

Mastro has written more than sixty publications and has a patent for a controlled-release pheromone dispenser. His research has been focused on insect behavior, identification of pheromones, and other semiochemicals that can be used for monitoring or controlling insect populations. He serves as chairman of three national science panels and served for a number of years on the National Gypsy Moth Management Board's executive committee.

The U.S. Forest Service presented him with the Chief's International Forestry Award in 1995 for development of the Russian Far East Port Monitoring Program. The Entomological Society of America presented the Distinguished Achievement Award to him in 1996. APHIS has presented him with seven internal awards. He was also named an alumni centennial fellow by Penn State Mont Alto in 2004.

Richard R. "Dick" Thorpe (1929–1996)

Dick grew up in a small community near the Allegheny National Forest and served in the U.S. Army Signal Corps from 1946 to 1948 before earning a B.S. degree in forestry from Penn State in 1952. He then joined the former Department of Forests and Waters and continued there for his entire professional career. Dick started as a service forester, providing technical assistance to private forest landowners. Next he worked on the development of timber management plans for the state forests, later implementing timber plans on several state forests while advancing from staff forester to district forester. From 1970 to 1977 he held administrative positions in Harrisburg, putting into place the latest forest resources plan for the 2 million acres of state forests.

Thorpe was promoted to the position of state forester and director of the Bureau of Forestry in 1977, a position he held until his retirement in 1988. His responsibilities included the administration of the state forest system, statewide forest fire protection, insect and disease programs, technical assistance to the private forest landowners, urban and community forestry, and the flora section of the Wild Resource Conservation Act. He presided over a five-year $15 million state forest rehabilitation project and the relocation of district offices from rental properties to state-owned buildings. Another highlight was the building of new offices and other buildings by the Pennsylvania Conservation Corps.

During Thorpe's tenure there were major increases in the Oil and Gas Fund and the Land and Water Conservation Fund, and both the Harrisburg and the field staffs were increased with the addition of biometricians, wood utilization specialists, resource planners, a botanist, and additional field foresters and technical positions. The Wild Resource Conservation Act was implemented, as was "Project 20," a project to evaluate various species of trees and shrubs for strip mine spoils revegetation. An information and education initiative also was launched.

Dick remained very active in forestry affairs during his retirement. He served as an advisor on forestry matters to Congressman Tom Ridge during his campaign for governor and also served on his transition team. He served with Maurice Goddard on the Pennsylvania Forestry Association's Policy and Legislative Committee, which shepherded very important legislation through the General Assembly. The most treasured event during his retirement was the creation of the new Department of Conservation and Natural Resources, resulting from the breakup of the Department of Environmental Resources.

Thorpe was a member and a strong supporter of several organizations, among them the Pennsylvania Forestry Association, which he served as president and as a board member; the Pennsylvania Wildlife Federation (board member); the Pennsylvania Federation of Sportsmen's Club; the Society of American Foresters (elected fellow in 1993); the Safari Club International; the Keystone Trails Association (life member); and the National Rifle Association.

Thorpe received many awards, including the Conservation Professional from the Pennsylvania Federation of Sportsmen's Club in 1986; the Outstanding Service to Forestry Award from the Society of American Foresters, Allegheny section, in 1986; the Annual Service Award from the Nature Conservancy in 1986; the Wildlife Conservation Award from the Pennsylvania Game Commission in 1988; the Service Award from the National Association of State Foresters in 1988; and the Rothrock Conservationist of the Year Award from the Pennsylvania Forestry Association in 1993.

Mark R. Webb (b. 1951)

After Mark Webb completed a B.S. in forest science in 1973, he worked for a year as a sales trainee for Blanchard Lumber Company in New Jersey and New York. Next he was a senior forester and land manager for Fisher and Young Lumber Company in Titusville, Pennsylvania, where he spent six years. Following a year as general manager for the Endeavor Lumber Company in Ashville, New York, he became a consulting forester and partner in Nagy and Webb at Titusville, Pennsylvania.

In 1993 he started his own consulting business in Union City, Pennsylvania, and has been the owner of Mark R. Webb & Co. since then. His company offers forest management services for both private and industrial clients, including complete timber sale management, appraisals and inventories, erosion and sedimentation control plans, forest stewardship plans, and American Tree Farm inspections. His company's work has been featured in *Forbes* magazine and the *Case Study for Sustainable Forestry* by the MacArthur Foundation.

Webb was elected a fellow of the Society of American Foresters in 2000, and he has been a certified forester since 1996. He has served SAF in various leadership positions in the Plateau chapter, the Pennsylvania division, the Allegheny Society, and the House of Society Delegates. Mark is a member of the Association of Consulting Foresters; he has been a regional director and chapter chair in that organization as well and has served on the editorial board of *Consultant* magazine. He is a charter member of the Pennsylvania Council of Professional Foresters and served as chairman for two years. His other state-level activities include the Pennsylvania State Committee–Sustainable Forestry Initiative, the Pennsylvania Rural Development Council Committee on Forest Taxation, the Penn State Forest Issues Working Group, and the Best Management Practices for Silviculture Working Group.

Mark served Penn State's College of Agricultural Sciences Alumni Association as director and as financial secretary, and as a student mentor in the alumni society's mentoring program. He is a member of the School of Forest Resources advisory board. Webb is also a member of Tau Phi Delta and has served in several capacities in that fraternity, including board member and president. He is a life member of the Penn State Alumni Association. In 2004 he was named a Penn State Mont Alto centennial fellow.

Wood Technology and Industry

Graduates who have found employment in the wood industries at first came from the forestry major and more recently also from the wood utilization major and its subsequent revisions. They have worked not only in Pennsylvania and nearby states but also in the West, the South, and other countries.

Pennsylvania's timber and forest products industry currently produces $15 billion of consumer goods and commodities each year for both domes-. tic and international markets. Currently the state's fourth-largest manufacturing sector, the forest products industry boasts one of the nation's largest wood-related workforces, with nearly a hundred thousand Pennsylvanian workers at more than three thousand locations.

Keith Atherholt (b. 1957)

After starting at Mont Alto in 1975 as a forest science major, Keith changed his major to forest products and received his B.S. in 1979. He was employed in sales by the Rex Lumber Company, one of the largest hardwood distribution companies in the nation. For eleven years he covered most of Pennsylvania and New York, calling on woodworking companies, furniture manufacturers, and cabinetmakers to sell kiln-dried hardwood lumber and moldings.

In 1991 Keith joined Dwight Lewis Lumber Company, a hardwood sawmill and timber management company located in Sullivan County. Dwight's son, Marc Lewis, and he had become friends while attending Mont Alto. In the 1980s the Lewis family had purchased a hardwood lumber concentration business, and in 1995 they spun off a separate corporation to concentrate on the distribution of hardwood lumber, ripped blanks, architectural moldings, and chopped parts. Atherholt became the president of Lewis Lumber Products, Inc. What started with five employees grew to forty-five, and sales have grown sixteenfold. Keith, Dwight, and Marc have been very appreciative of their success.

The two companies have remained very close. Dwight Lewis Lumber Co. is a timber-growing and harvesting company that processes about 7 million board feet of hardwood per year. Its main species are cherry, red oak, white oak, hard maple, and soft maple, with a smaller percentage of other hardwoods. Lewis Lumber Products processes 7.5 million board feet of more than thirty different types of hardwoods, including some exotic woods. Half of the raw material comes from the Dwight Lewis sister company, thus conferring quite an advantage for a steady supply of high-quality hardwood. Lewis Lumber Products actively sells into a regional market that extends to a 250-mile radius of Williamsport. Internet sales have had a steady growth, and the most dramatic growth in the company has been in the expansion of its dimension mill.

Atherholt has been a loyal supporter of Penn State and has been involved in various civic activities. He is a past president of the Kiwanis Club of Williamsport and a member of the Montoursville Club. He has been very involved in church activities such as youth programs, Bible study fellowship, and chairing the Central Pennsylvania Kairos Prison Ministry. Keith served on the advisory board of the School of Forest Resources. He coordinated the hardwood millwork interior donation through the Pennsylvania Forest Products Association for both the General Aviation Building at the University Park airport and for the new Forest Resources Building.

Keith commented, "I consider myself blessed to be in this position of leadership and to be surrounded by such great co-workers. I often tell people, 'We have the privilege of marketing and working with the high quality renewable natural resource of hardwood lumber, but our greatest resource is actually the people that work at Lewis Lumber!' My major in Wood Products was critical to my original employment. I owe quite a bit to Penn State and the School of Forest Resources for my position and career. I am very grateful for the years of training and knowledge that helped position me for a great opportunity in life."

Bruce B. Brenneman (b. 1938)

Bruce retired from MeadWestvaco in 2002 after a thirty-six-year career with the company. He started as a research forester in Summerville, South Carolina, where he spent six years, and then became research center leader and research associate in Rupert, West Virginia, for thirty years. After earning a B.S. degree at Penn State in 1960, he was employed by the U.S. Department of Interior's Bureau of Land Management in California, and by the U.S. Forest Service in Boise, Idaho. He served in the U.S. Army from 1962 to 1964.

His research included pine plantation culture; silviculture and protection of Appalachian hardwoods; testing of cold-hardy loblolly, Virginia pine, and pitch x loblolly hybrids; and protection of Appalachian stream quality during land management activities. He established Westvaco's Appalachian Research Center in 1973, conducting innovative research in water quality monitoring and precommercial thinning of hardwoods. Bruce produced about a hundred publications and served as reviewer for the *Northern Journal of Applied Forestry.*

He has served on several Society of American Foresters committees, as secretary and president of the West Virginia Board of Registration for Foresters, as a member of AF&PA's Forest Science and Technology Committee, as a member of the advisory committee for the Hardwood Tree Improvement and Regeneration Center at Purdue University, and on the advisory board for the West Virginia Agriculture and Forestry Experiment Station. He is also active in church and civic organizations. Bruce was named a fellow by the Society of American Foresters in 2003.

In retrospect Bruce commented, "My days at Penn State prepared me for a rewarding and enjoyable 42-year career in forestry."

Franklin Marshall Case (1917–2005)

Marshall received his B.S. degree in forestry in 1938. As a boy he had traveled across the country with his parents in a Model A Ford, in the days when there were few highways. During World War II he served in the armed forces and drove a tank in Italy. A lifelong resident of Troy, Pennsylvania, he operated a sawmill there for some years. When his father retired, he became president of F. P. Case & Sons, a general contracting and hardware firm.

Case took a keen interest in the history of early American industries, especially logging and lumbering. He was one of fourteen charter members of the Penn-York Lumbermen's Club, founded in 1949 for the professional and social purposes of members in northern Pennsylvania and southern New York. For many years he served as master of ceremonies for the annual Woodsmen's Carnival in Cherry Springs, and was a contractor for the Lumbermen's Museum in Denton Hill, Pennsylvania. The Smithsonian Institution invited him to organize a logging and lumbering exhibit on the Washington Mall for the nation's bicentennial celebration. He also traveled to Idaho to interview loggers for the Smithsonian's oral history program.

Marshall was active in many civic activities and organizations. He served on the board of directors of the Bradford County Heritage Association and Farm Museum, the Alan F. Pierce Memorial Library, the Robert Packer Hospital, and the First Bank of Troy. He and his wife hosted many foreign exchange students through his membership in Rotary International. He was a member of the Armenia Mountain Debating Society and the Genealogical Society.

There were overtones of forestry even in his funeral arrangements, at which the Reverend Kenneth Maple officiated. Interment was at the Glenwood Cemetery, after which there was a time of fellowship at the Olde Covert Church on Armenia Mountain.

John Clyde Davies (b. 1929)

John Davies earned a B.S. degree in wood utilization in 1952. He served in the U.S. Air Force for two years during the Korean War and then in the Air National Guard for ten years. He returned to Penn State in 1954 and completed a master's degree in 1957, specializing in wood utilization. He began his career in forest products sales, being employed first by a plywood company for three years.

Then Davies worked as a salesman for a small brokerage firm that specialized in selling various types of forest products, including hardwood lumber, high-grade hardwood plywood, hardwood dimension materials, panels, and parts to manufacturers of kitchen cabinets, furniture, and other items. He joined that firm as a partner in 1963 and in 1974 became the sole owner of the Mell-Davies Lumber Company, a wholesaler of hardwood forest products throughout the eastern United States and Europe. He found it to be a very interesting and challenging business, resulting in many more successes than disappointments. John retired in 1992 and sold the business to one of his sons, who had joined him in 1987 after being in banking for nine years.

Reflecting on his college days, John commented, "I don't believe I can adequately express my deep appreciation for the Penn State experience and the dedication and patience of the faculty and staff, particularly Drs. Norton and Nearn. Throughout my professional career the technical knowledge that I acquired in the School of Forest Resources was invaluable. It was a great asset in being able to understand the problems and concerns of both sides, the supplier and the customer, and speak intelligently about them."

John and his wife, Esther, and their three sons lived for many years in suburban Philadelphia and were very active in their community and local church. John held leadership positions with the local YMCA, the Boy Scouts, and on the board of the Methodist Hospital in South Philadelphia.

The Davies family and friends endowed the Keith A. Davies Memorial Scholarship in the College of Agricultural Sciences in 1990, in memory of their son. It is intended for undergraduate students enrolled or planning to enroll in the School of Forest Resources, selected according to promise of superior academic achievement, demonstration of outstanding qualities of citizenship, and participation in extracurricular activities within the school. First consideration is given to wood products majors, and then to residents of southeastern Pennsylvania. In Davies's words, "Support of the university is, to us, the most appropriate means of service. Penn State has played an invaluable role in my involvement in the forest industry, and we hope to help future industry enthusiasts take advantage of the tremendous opportunities available there."

George L. Drake (1889–1979)

To earn money for college George Drake and his college roommate, Frank Craighead, milked rattlesnakes in the summer and sold the venom for antidotes. They lived in a cabin in Clinton County, separated from the snakes only by a wire mesh fence. When Drake graduated with a degree in forestry in 1912 he immediately went to the Pacific Northwest. His career with the Forest Service started in Oregon, and for four years he was assistant supervisor of the Tongass National Forest in Alaska. During his forty-two-year career, first with the U.S. Forest Service and then the Simpson Logging Company, he became an international figure in forestry and conservation. He had broad experience as a logging engineer and in forest fire control, timber appraisals, and sales management. After retiring from Simpson in 1954, he stayed active as a forestry consultant.

In 1930 Drake was hired as assistant to the president of the Simpson Logging Company and became general superintendent of logging in 1932. Besides directing the production of some 200 million feet of logs a year, he developed a sustained-yield program for the company. The Simpson tree farm was enlarged to 170,000 acres, and up to a million seedlings were planted per year. His regeneration methods after logging virgin timber became the silvicultural basis of the West Coast's conservation code and later were written into the Washington Conservation Act of 1945.

Drake became vice president of Simpson Logging in 1945. An important part of his job was to devise ways that new kinds of logging equipment could be organized as the company kept pace with expanding use of raw material. He helped to design logging trucks that "could get places you couldn't dream of getting with a railroad." During World War II smaller and low-grade timber was harvested. Fiberboard was produced from wastes from sawmills, thinnings, and material that formerly was wasted in the woods.

Drake was credited with the first and only application of the Cooperative Sustained Yield Agreement under Public Law 273, the Sustained Yield Forest Management Act of 1944. This notable event in 1946 stabilized forestry employment and the economy of towns in Washington. He opened Camp Griswold, which he wanted to be a true forest community that would be attractive to logging families. It featured an "undressing room" where a man could strip off his wet clothes before entering his house—a big hit with the housewives. Drake believed that "to keep a good man, you've got to please his wife."

George Drake was a leader in national and West Coast forestry organizations. He served as president of the Society of American Foresters from 1952 to 1954 and was awarded the Gifford Pinchot Medal in 1967. Drake was active in the Pacific Logging Congress, the Loyal Legion of Loggers and Lumbermen, the Western Forestry and Conservation Association, and the National Lumber Manufacturers Association. He was elected to the World Forestry Center's Hall of Pioneers.

Calvin H. "Cal" Glattfelder (1924–2004)

Cal received his B.S. degree in forestry from Penn State in 1949. The story of his thirty-six-year career at the Glatfelter Pulp Wood Company would be incomplete without also commenting on the many Penn State foresters associated with him. The following information was compiled by alumni Bob Rumpf and Art Oplinger.

Cal's college education had started at Iowa State University in 1942 but was interrupted by World War II. In the navy's V-12 program he was assigned to Penn State, and then served as an ensign on torpedo boats and minesweepers until 1947. After graduation in 1949 he started his career as a farm forester with the Pennsylvania Department of Forests and Waters and soon was at work on the first of the state forest management plans organized by Joe Ibberson. Cal helped to develop the procedures in this pioneering project for acquiring and compiling data and preparing the final plan.

In 1952 Cal joined the Glatfelter Pulp Wood Company, which had been formed in 1918 to handle procurement for the P. H. Glatfelter pulp mill at Spring Grove, Pennsylvania. As a forester in Virginia Cal promoted tree farming and acquired pulpwood for the company. He became manager of the southern division in 1956 and vice president in 1965. From

1973 to 1988 he served as vice president and general manager and as director of woodlands. His major responsibility was to assure an adequate wood supply for the P. H. Glatfelter Company, a leading manufacturer of high-quality papers. He supervised industrial forest management on the company's lands and a public information and technical forestry assistance program for private woodland owners. Under his leadership the company greatly increased its woodland acreage and planting of conifers.

Cal actively promoted good forestry and the pulpwood industry in various ways. He was a member and chairman of the American Pulpwood Association. In this capacity he traveled extensively, carrying the message of environmentally sound forest management. He served on the USDA Advisory Committee on State and Private Forestry, Pennsylvania's Department of Environmental Resources Citizen's Advisory Council and Forest Resources Advisory Committee, and Penn State's Forest Resources advisory board and its advisory committee for the M. K. Goddard chair.

Glattfelder received the 1982 Forestry Achievement Award from Penn State, the 1988 Outstanding Leadership in the Industry Award from the Northeastern Loggers Association, and the 1988 Rothrock Conservationist of the Year Award from the Pennsylvania Forestry Association, in which he was active as member, director, and chairman of the Legislative and Policy Committee. He was a golden member of the Society of American Foresters and was elected a fellow in 1990.

A postscript to Cal's career is appropriate, in recognition of the contributions of his many Penn State colleagues to the Glatfelter Company's success. They often worked together as a team, in various combinations, and include:

Name	B.S. Year	Year Employed
Durell E. Hess	1935	1946
Harold W. Geiger ·	1944	1951
Ray O. Brooks	1938	1952
Calvin F. Glattfelder	1949	1952
Robert H. Rumpf	1949	1954
Howard W. Sheffer Jr.	1953	1956
Samuel H. Dyke	1954	1957
Wilbur E. Wolf	1959	1959
Thomas N. Reeder	1961	1961
Arthur J. Oplinger	1962	1962
Peter P. Alexander	1963	1963

The first Penn State forester hired by the company in 1946 was Durell E. Hess, known by all as Hessie. He was gregarious and ideally suited to the public relations aspects of wood procurement, and established an assistance program for woodland owners. Hessie also was a tried and true Penn Stater who hired forestry graduates and was active in the School of Forestry Alumni Association. All of these men felt a great sense of loyalty to the School of Forest Resources and often talked about their college experiences. Many maintained close contacts by serving on the School's advisory board, the Goddard chair committee, the alumni group, the forest issues group, or the Mont Alto advisory board. Several attained positions of leadership within the company. They took pride in their accomplishments, believing that much of their success was made possible by their excellent forestry education.

Several of the Penn State foresters have served the company as vice president and general manager besides Cal Glattfelder—D. E. "Hessie" Hess (class of 1935), Arthur J. "Art" Oplinger (1962), and Robert H. "Bob" Rumpf (1949). Individually and collectively they have been proponents of industrial forestry and articulate spokesmen for responsible stewardship on industrial and private woodlands.

Alex W. Kirnak (b. 1916)

Alex Kirnak graduated from Penn State with a B.S. degree in forestry in 1937. Lacking the money for train fare, he hitchhiked to Longview, Washington, wanting to be part of the timber industry. But he soon realized that thousands of loggers and mill workers were unemployed and that his chances of finding work at the unemployment office were zero.

So for several days he pounded on the door of Roy Morse, vice president of the Long-Bell Lumber Company. Finally Morse phoned one of his logging operations and said, "I'm sending a big green kid up. Put him to work. If he doesn't learn fast and work hard, run him off!"

For the next five years Alex worked at all the jobs in the woods and was exposed to several innovations. He operated one of the first power saws used in the Northwest, a two-man saw that weighed 140 pounds. That led to his lifetime interest in power saws. He worked on Long-Bell's first truck logging operation; previously all had been railroad shows.

His logging career was interrupted by three years in the U.S. Navy during World War II in the Pacific theater. As staff engineering officer in a flotilla of rocket-firing gunboats, he narrowly escaped death on the flagship before it was sunk by a Japanese mine. He had been invited by the captain to a Thanksgiving turkey dinner but at the last minute had been called away to repair an electrical problem on another ship.

He returned to Long-Bell after the war, and later worked for several other lumber companies. His interest in innovations continued. He had two-way radios installed, became involved in building and operating a large sawmill that salvaged timber from the Tillamook Burn, and introduced export cutting to many Oregon mills. He pioneered the packaging of lumber for export, which previously had been stowed in ships one piece at a time. When he retired from corporate life in 1971, he had exported half a billion feet of clear lumber.

As time went on, Alex became more involved in conservation efforts. Through much of his career and afterward, Alex has been critical of the ways federal agencies have mishandled insect control, fire control, and silvicultural practices. He refuted certain inaccurate claims of both the Forest Service and industry about the proposals to create the Olympic National Park and the North Cascades National Park.

Since his retirement Alex has been a consultant to the chainsaw and forest products industries. He served as an expert witness for six chainsaw manufacturers involved in many liability lawsuits. He also has been active in community service and advisor to Oregon State University, and has maintained an interest in his Penn State alma mater. The Portland, Oregon, Wholesale Lumberman Association awarded him the 1994 Lumberman of the Year Award for fifty years of leadership in the industry.

Thinking back on his school days, Alex commented, "Mont Alto was a hands-on, common sense, close contact with the trees and environment, introduction to forestry. The staff was superb. I often wonder if I ever would have succeeded in getting a foothold in the rough and tumble lumber industry of the Northwest without Mont Alto. Probably not."

William T. "Bill" Nearn (b. 1920)

Before Bill could complete his B.S. degree (1943) at the New York State College of Forestry at Syracuse University, the Japanese attack on Pearl Harbor changed his plans for the immediate future. Enlisting in the Army Signal Corps, he completed officer training school, and as a second lieutenant went to Harvard for advanced technology classes. He was then sent to New Guinea, where he became commander of the motor pool, loaded vehicles and tractors on landing boats, and then moved to the Philippines to prepare for a landing in Japan. After Japan surrendered, Nearn's unit was ordered to Tokyo to set up communication and transportation networks.

He found an opportunity to transfer to the army's forestry division, which General MacArthur had established, gathering data throughout Japan on timber resources and forest industries and compiling these in a report.

Instead of staying on in Japan to work as a civilian, Bill enrolled at Yale and completed the master of forestry degree in 1947. He was hired as an instructor at Penn State and was thrown into teaching two or three courses a semester with a minimum of coaching on how or what to teach. During 1950–51 Nearn returned to Yale on a leave of absence to undertake doctoral studies. He devised pioneering methods to study moisture relationships and extractives of wood, then returned to Penn State to continue laboratory experiments while resuming his teaching duties. He completed the doctor of forestry degree in 1954 and was enjoying research with faculty colleagues and some sharp, determined graduate students. Undergraduate students regarded him as an excellent teacher, and he achieved tenure and promotion to associate professor of wood utilization. But Nearn's outlook on his career was about to change.

By 1959 Bill had become dissatisfied with the process of the College of Agriculture in seeking a replacement for M. K. Goddard, director of the School of Forestry, though he worked diligently as a member of the faculty search committee. He informed the dean that he would like the job but was told this was not going to happen. So he accepted an opportunity in 1960 to become a senior scientist in the research division of the Weyerhaeuser Company in Seattle, Washington. In the pioneering research laboratory he initiated the wood morphology group, working on microanalysis of wood and wood products. In 1968 Nearn shifted to a series of managerial positions, supervising some hundred scientists and technicians employed with wood sciences, scientific services, and control technology. He thoroughly enjoyed his career at Weyerhaeuser, and retired in 1984.

Bill then returned to academia for three years as associate director of the Mississippi Forest Products Laboratory. The lab is recognized as a leader in the application of wood science and technology in the South, owing in part to Nearn's leadership. Through his industrial experience he strengthened its research and academic programs.

Nearn has been active in professional organizations, chairing the editorial board of the periodical *Wood and Fiber* and serving as secretary-treasurer, vice president, and president of the Society of Wood Science and Technology. He has written more than thirty scientific publications and many technical reports. In 1994 his achievements were recognized by the Society of Wood Science and Technology Distinguished Service Award.

Frank Schrey III (b. 1931)

Frank Schrey III received a B.S. degree in forestry in 1953 and the master of forestry in 1957 for his work on forest products marketing with Newell Norton and William Nearn. In between he served on active duty in the armed forces during the Korean War. After a short stint as service forester, he became the first wood utilization advisor in the Bureau of Forestry in 1957. In 1966 he moved to the Pennsylvania Department of Commerce, where he started as a research analyst, progressed to chief of the research division, next to industrial development representative, and after several other positions became manager of data services.

In the Bureau of Forestry Schrey took over the *Pennsylvania Marketing Bulletin*, making major changes that made it a success. Through efficiency studies he provided technical advice to many industries. He created a sawmill directory and conducted a study of timber drain from Pennsylvania forests. Frank designed a large manufacturing facility at Penn Nursery for making picnic tables and signs for state forests and parks that greatly improved their durability and appearance. After moving to the Department of Commerce he continued his work to attract new wood-using industries to Pennsylvania. These included a Proctor & Gamble mill at Mehoopany, a Masonite plant at Towanda, veneer mills near Williamsport and at Sheffield, a particleboard plant at Mount Jewett, a sawmill at Emporium, and several others. He helped to plan the governor's timber conference and served on many task forces and committees that dealt with timber, forest resources, water resources, wood energy, gypsy moths, and other issues of concern to the Commonwealth.

Besides being dedicated to professional excellence, Schrey has served as advisor simultaneously to two Boy Scout troops, one of them for handicapped scouts. He maintains an active interest in the School of Forest Resources, having collaborated years ago with Charles Strauss on wood utilization extension activities.

Michael A. "Mike" Taras (b. 1921)

Mike Taras earned two degrees from Penn State, a B.S. in forestry in 1942 and an M.F. in wood utilization in 1948. In between he served in the U.S. Army Air Corps (1943–46) as a twin-engine pilot in the 442d Troop Carrier Group in the European theater. Upon returning to Penn State he conducted research on mechanical and physical properties of twenty-three Costa Rican hardwoods. Professor H. Arthur Meyer had collected these specimens while working on chincona production for the treatment of malaria during World War II. In 1965 Taras received a Ph.D. in wood science and technology from North Carolina State University.

His first position in 1948 was at the forest products laboratory of the U.S. Forest Service in Madison, Wisconsin. There he conducted research on the effects of silvicultural treatments on wood properties, wood identification, wood preservation, and packaging. In 1954 Taras transferred to the Southeastern Forest Experiment Station in Asheville, North Carolina, serving as a liaison between wood industries in the southeast and the forest products laboratory. He also assisted in developing a wood products research program at the southeastern station. Mike served as principal wood scientist and project leader, studying the relationship of wood properties and wood quality to environment, genetics, and tree volume. His research on biomass of southern yellow pine contributed significantly to the development of scaling timber on a weight basis, a method for purchasing timber that was adopted throughout the United States.

Taras retired from the Forest Service in 1979 and joined the forestry faculty of Clemson University as the Robert Adger Bowen Distinguished Professor. He continued his biomass research and taught courses in wood properties, drying, wood preservation, and wood identification. He wrote sixty-five publications during his career. In 1981 he became head of the Department of Forestry at Clemson and served in that capacity until his retirement in 1991.

In recognition of his accomplishments Taras received a certificate of merit from the U.S. Forest Service in 1975 for his outstanding performance. Penn State's School of Forestry gave him the Forestry Achievement Award in 1982, at its seventy-fifth anniversary celebration. The Forest Products Society recognized him in 1955, 1967, and 1974 for outstanding and distinguished service. He served as president of the international Forest Products Society in 1989, and also was a member of the Society of American Foresters, the International Association of Wood Anatomists, and the honor societies of Sigma Xi, Xi Sigma Pi, and Gamma Sigma Delta.

Taras wrote that his "most memorable times at Penn State, as is probably with all graduates of my vintage, were Mont Alto and Blue Jay summer camp experiences, which we will never forget. I do want to thank the School of Forestry for their foresight in 1941 to start the Wood Utilization

Program. Had this program not started, I may not have enjoyed the two careers that I was able to pursue. Thank you Newell Norton, my mentor, and Penn State, from one of the first wood utilization graduates."

Thomas G. "Tom" Wright (b. 1916)

Tom Wright obtained the B.S. degree in forestry from Penn State in 1937, having supported himself by washing dishes and grading wood technology exams. While studying for his master's degree (1939) at Duke University, he cruised timber for the U.S. Forest Service in California during summers.

Wright was then employed as a forest economist at the University of British Columbia until 1943, and also taught courses in forest policy, forest history, mensuration, fire protection, and surveying. During summers he worked as a consultant for a major logging company, evaluating forest practices and fire effects on regeneration. He used a "rocks on stumps" technique to establish reference points for plots, noting that "nothing will ever happen to a rock on a stump"—in fact, all of them were found forty years later. He prepared the first sustained-yield forest management plan for an industrial company in British Columbia.

After serving in the 796th Engineer Forestry Battalion from 1943 to 1946 with action in Europe, Tom returned to UBC for two years, then became chief forester of Canadian Forest Products Ltd. (Canfor) until 1962. He managed their timberlands and applied his research interests toward improving the efficiency of company operations.

In 1962 Wright returned to the University of British Columbia as dean of the faculty of forestry. And two years later he returned to Canfor as general manager of coast logging and forestry. After retiring in 1972 Tom spent much of his time managing the forestlands he had acquired, along with his son, who is the full-time manager.

Wright has been a longtime member of the Society of American Foresters and the Canadian Institute of Forestry, which made him an honorary member. He received the Association of B.C. Professional Forester's Distinguished Forester Award in 1986, recognizing his significant contributions to forestry in British Columbia. In 2004 he received the Alumni Centennial Award from Penn State Mont Alto.

Parks and Recreation

The segment of the forestry profession that deals with parks and outdoor recreation was originally considered a subset of forestry. Later, especially after World War II, forest recreation became a professional field in its own right. Tourism has become a major economic force in Pennsylvania, and natural resources are a vital part of it. People engage in all sorts of outdoor recreational activities in the state's parks and forests.

In 1962 the Pennsylvania Bureau of State Parks was created by M. K. Goddard, who elevated it from a division within the Bureau of Forestry. So it is appropriate to continue next with the second part of Goddard's biography, after he moved from Penn State to Harrisburg. The first part of his biography is found in Chapter 4.

Maurice K. Goddard (1912–1995)

In 1955 incoming governor George Leader persuaded Goddard to leave Penn State and appointed him secretary of the Department of Forests and Waters. He continued in this post until 1971, when he was named secretary of the new Department of Environmental Resources, with much broader responsibilities. Goddard served under five governors, three Democrats and two Republicans; he was registered as an Independent.

One of his first actions in Harrisburg was to extend the civil service system to all professional positions in the Department of Forests and Waters. This was part of a broader executive order designed to replace political appointees with professionals and thus to improve state services; in 1963 civil service for foresters was solidified through legislation. Goddard also devised a way to gain access through legislation to revenues from oil and gas royalties for conservation, recreation, dams, and flood control. He created the department's Division of Minerals to manage revenues that amounted to more than $28 million in the next twenty years. But most of his time was spent on building new state parks and coping with water-related problems.

Soon after taking office, Goddard helped in forging cooperation among officials of Delaware, New Jersey, New York, Pennsylvania, and federal agencies toward solving flooding and water-use problems of the Delaware River. Having withstood some twenty years of bickering, they formed the Delaware River Basin Commission, which developed plans for water use, flood control, and low-water augmentation. Despite this spirit of cooperation among the states, battles ensued about a Corps of Engineers plan to build a dam at Tocks Island. They also fought about water use during a protracted drought, and about augmentation of flow to prevent salination at Philadelphia's intake. President Lyndon Johnson and Secretary of the Interior Stewart Udall had to intervene and arrange a compromise. In

1958 Goddard gave a prophetic speech titled "Water Is Pennsylvania's Future" to the Pennsylvania Electric Association.

In 1957 Goddard started implementing a plan to have a state park within twenty-five miles of every resident of the Commonwealth, including a ring of parks around Philadelphia and Pittsburgh. In 1962 he elevated the Division of State Parks within the Bureau of Forestry to a separate Bureau of State Parks. Two projects that he worked on for years were the Independence Mall State Park in Philadelphia and Point State Park in Pittsburgh. The number of state parks nearly doubled by the time Goddard left state government; forty-eight opened while he was in office and four more afterward. By 1995 Pennsylvania had 283,000 acres in state park land, much of it purchased through Project 70, Project 500, and the Oil and Gas Lease Fund. The parks fulfilled Goddard's vision to save such scenic beauty and recreational amenities for future generations.

Goddard's vision led to the crafting of Project 70, a plan announced in 1961 for building a network of parks, open space, and other recreational facilities. Voters approved a referendum for a $70 million bond measure in 1963. For each proposed park, Goddard and staff members William Forrey and John Rex presented park plans at a public meeting. Some of the meetings were acrimonious, but Goddard's openness and common sense were persuasive and always prevailed. For thirty-two years Bill Forrey was with the Pennsylvania Bureau of State Parks, starting in 1960 as a landscape architect, then chief of state park planning, assistant director, and director. As director (1973–92) he supervised the operation, maintenance and development of the 114 state parks, retiring in 1992.

In 1964 President Lyndon Johnson appointed Goddard to the Land Law Review Commission, which met with officials in many states to review laws and procedures pertaining to all sorts of natural and mineral resources. President Richard Nixon, in accepting the final report in 1970, said that "it will have without question a very great effect on the policy of this country. It is essential to plan now for the use of the land."

Goddard persuaded Governor Scranton to hold the Governor's Conference on Natural Beauty in 1966. Goddard had organized the Federal-State-Local Partnership Panel for President Lyndon Johnson's White House Conference on Natural Beauty the previous year. The conference led to the Highway Beautification Act, the President's Council on Recreation and Natural Beauty, and the Intergovernmental Cooperation Act of 1968.

The Pennsylvania legislature, with admonitions by Goddard and others, in 1966 approved a Project 500 bond issue via the Land and Water Conservation and Reclamation Act. Its purpose was to develop recreation areas on lands acquired under Project 70 ($125 million), to acquire or develop additional county and municipal parks ($75 million), to eliminate land scars and water pollution ($200 million), and to build new or improved municipal sewage facilities ($100 million). Forests and Waters used the money to develop facilities for day use, swimming, boating, hiking, nature education, and administrative needs in state parks.

A distinguishing feature of Goddard's stewardship of Pennsylvania forests was the Forest Resource Plan for 1970–85, prepared under the supervision of Joseph E. Ibberson. The plan incorporated multiple-use principles—for timber, water, recreation, minerals, and less tangible benefits—that were less evident in the previous more timber-oriented plan of 1955. Foresters in Pennsylvania and elsewhere had been practicing multiple-use principles for several decades before they became a national mandate in 1960 through the Multiple Use Act (PL 86517). Furnishing timber, protecting the water supply, and providing recreation areas had already been established as legislative objectives in 1897. The department also completed a water resources planning inventory that catalogued all the dams, reservoirs, and natural lakes in the Commonwealth. These two plans were monumental accomplishments under Goddard's direction of the Department of Forests and Waters.

Two events in 1969 profoundly influenced the next phase of Goddard's career. A new superagency including forests and waters, mineral industries, and pollution-control functions—the Department of Environmental Resources—was established over Goddard's objections to combining regulatory and conservation responsibilities. And the Declaration of Rights article was added to the Pennsylvania constitution, asserting "that people have a right to clean air, pure water, and to the preservation of the natural scenic, historic, and esthetic values of the environment." Goddard was appointed to head DER in 1971 and was confirmed months later despite the opposition of the Sierra Club and other groups. Goddard quickly completed the daunting tasks of reorganization, staffing, and developing programs.

After his retirement from DER in 1979, Goddard stayed active professionally. A campaign was launched to endow the Maurice K. Goddard Chair in the School of Forest Resources, which would honor his educational achievements and dedicated service to the people of the Commonwealth. His periodic campaigning to split DER into two agencies finally came to fruition in 1995, when the DER was replaced by the Department of Conservation and Natural Resources and the Department of Environmental Protection.

Goddard's enigmatic death in 1995 was ruled a suicide. This was so contrary to his character that no one could understand or explain it, though he had been ill briefly and was taking a new medication. Those who knew him well remember his hardworking dedication to forestry, and his deeply held convictions and practical pronouncements, which he uttered in a deep, booming voice, sometimes with somewhat ungainly gestures, but always with great sincerity and enthusiasm.

Conrad R. "Connie" Lickel (1921–2003)

Connie graduated in 1942 from the two-year forestry ranger course. He served in the U.S. Army during World War II, was wounded on D-Day, became disabled, and received a Purple Heart. He received the M.S. degree in horticulture from Penn State in 1950.

His M.S. thesis was a thorough study of the relationship between recreation and education in Pennsylvania state parks. He discussed how education was related to park objectives and how it could contribute to park ideals, objectives, and policies. Lickel clearly believed that if more young people could participate and learn in outdoor recreational programs, they would be more understanding of the world about them, enjoy natural landscape elements, and thus contribute to the stabilization of our society. Accordingly, he proposed that nearly every problem of the state parks could be addressed by education about the conservation of human and natural resources.

In 1950 Lickel was employed as an administrative officer in the Division of Recreation, Pennsylvania Department of Forests and Waters. He served as director of state parks from 1964 until 1973, when he was appointed special assistant in the deputy's office for resources management to oversee both parks and forestry operations. In 1962 Lickel was instrumental in the establishment of the four state park regional offices. This was an important prerequisite for the major acquisition and development program that was to follow over the next two decades. One of his major accomplishments was creating the standard for handicapped accessibility in Pennsylvania state parks, long before the Americans with Disabilities Act, and other states followed his lead. He encouraged his staff to visit the parks in a wheelchair or blindfolded, so they could experience firsthand the obstacles a person with disabilities would encounter.

Conrad's solid leadership and direction in the development of the Pennsylvania state park system remain important contributions toward today's state parks. He retired from the Department of Environmental Resources in 1977, after twenty-eight years of service to the citizens of the Commonwealth of Pennsylvania.

Gregory M. "Greg" Schrum (b. 1945)

Gregory M. Schrum started his forestry studies at the Mont Alto campus in 1963 and completed a B.S. in forest technology in 1967 and an M.S. in forest resources in 1969. His graduate thesis work on the genetic characteristics of Scotch pine Christmas trees was under the direction of Henry Gerhold. After serving in Vietnam as a first lieutenant in the army and being awarded the Bronze Star, he worked for the Pennsylvania Bureau of State Parks in various management positions.

Schrum began his state park career in 1972 as the first assistant park superintendent hired for Presque Isle State Park. There he initiated the start of environmental education programming at this major state park, hiring the park's first seasonal environmental interpretive technician. He moved on to become the first park superintendent at the Memorial Lake/Swatara State Park complex, where he initiated a major building demolition program on newly acquired properties in preparation for the developments at the park.

In various staff positions in state park regions 3 and 4, he was responsible for budget allocations to the state parks in his region; transitioned park management into a work environment covered by a collective bargaining contract for the first time; implemented a necessary but difficult furlough process; and implemented a pilot bill-paying method. As an assistant regional superintendent, Schrum improved the efficiency of operations by downsizing office functions, improving concession contracts, and creating the first computer-generated ordering system for all uniformed personnel in the bureau. He supervised the first regional environment education specialist and the development of a program to oversee environmental education activities in the region's parks. He was especially involved in changes that delegated the responsibility for supervising park superintendents to the assistant regional superintendents.

Schrum's forestry background came to good use in his next assignment—environmental management section chief for the Bureau of State Parks. He led the development of the bureau's first resource management plan for each state park, using a committee of intradepartmental experts.

The drafted plans concentrated on mapping, describing, and proscribing natural resource management features and objectives. These plans were then presented for comment at public meetings for each park, thus helping to refine the plans. The most contentious plan that resulted in the greatest improvement to the environment was the 1993 Presque Isle State Park plan. Schrum chaired public meetings that pitted boaters against birders when the draft plan called for the closure of a significant area of the park to human use in order to protect shorebirds during migration and nesting. The plan also called for the prohibition of outboard motor use in interior waterways. This plan is still being followed. During this time, he started the switch to geographic information system technology for the plans. As a result of this effort, his unit has been charged with handling the bureau's Geographic Information System (GIS) and Geographic Positioning System (GPS) needs.

Another major effort that Schrum led as section chief was the implementation of a deer management program for several state parks in southeastern Pennsylvania. Aerial deer counts and determination of the park's deer carrying capacity based on vegetative types identified the magnitude of an overpopulation of deer that required immediate attention. A controlled deer hunt was developed that accounted for safety factors, game law requirements, and the sufficient reduction of animals. At public meetings that were attended mainly by opponents of hunting and animal rights activists, he answered numerous press inquires, letters, petitions, and legislative inquires that addressed this resource issue. The first hunts, held in 1984 at Ridley Creek State Park and in 1987 at Tyler State Park, were conducted safely, were highly successful, and dealt with opposition protesters in a proper and professional manner. The methods developed at these two parks were used to implement controlled hunts for managing deer populations at six other state parks.

Schrum became chief of the recently created Resource Management and Planning Division. The new unit is responsible for directing the management of the natural resources and facility development in the Commonwealth's 117 state parks and three conservation areas. One of the first goals was to implement the recommendations of the bureau's strategic plan—State Parks 2000. The resulting park management plans for each state park incorporated various aspects of park management into one document. The plans include such topics as the parks' architectural styles, future development projects, environmental education recommendations, standards for appropriate recreation, species of special concern, environmental problems, and attendance methodology. But of even greater value was the requirement to have periodic reviews and updates. This gives the park manager an opportunity to meet with all the state park executive staff to discuss issues pertaining to their individual parks. It is the only time the manager has all of these leaders and their undivided attention at one time.

Schrum was instrumental in the creation of a new program in the Pennsylvania Bureau of State Parks called "conservation areas." This program provides for land donated to the bureau to be managed for preserving open space, conserving natural resources, outdoor recreation, and environmental education. A conservation area differs from a typical state park because the land is donated and only passive forms of recreation such as hiking, hunting, and bird watching are permitted. He developed and defended policy language to create this program. The 350-acre Joseph E. Ibberson Conservation Area, located in Dauphin County, became the first conservation area in the Pennsylvania Bureau of State Parks in 1998. Two other conservation areas have since been established and more are expected to follow. Schrum has devoted personal attention to each prospective donor in order to understand the donor's wishes and then incorporate those acceptable to the bureau in appropriate language for inclusion in the property deeds.

Schrum has guided the development of a recreational master plan for Swatara State Park. After years of attempting to remove obstacles that prevented the issuance of a permit to construct a dam and reservoir in the park, the bureau opted to withdraw that consideration and look for alternate facilities for the future park. The process included hiring a consulting firm and embarking on a planning effort that maximized public participation and remained sensitive to the natural resources found in the park. The final plan resulted in a proposal that balanced facility development with resource protection that both the public and the bureau found acceptable. Implementation of the plan is imminent.

Schrum is a member of the Xi Sigma Pi honorary forestry fraternity and Tau Phi Delta professional social fraternity, of which he was treasurer and president. He is a member of the Society of American Foresters, the Pennsylvania Forestry Association (where he is a member of the Communications Committee), and the Pennsylvania Park and Recreation Society. He serves on the School of Forest Resources Advisory Board and the alumni board of directors. He was named Pennsylvania State University School of Forest Resources Outstanding Alumnus in 2003. In 2005 he received the Joseph Trimble Rothrock Conservationist of the Year Award from the Pennsylvania Forestry Association for his work on the conservation area program. He is active in his church, serving on the parish council, as lector, and as extraordinary minister. He is a member of the Lower Paxton Township Lions Club.

Hydrology and Watershed Management

Watershed management and the underlying sciences of hydrology and meteorology first became part of the curricula at the graduate level in the 1960s, and then at the baccalaureate level in 1996 when the watershed management option was instituted. Yet the vital functions of forests in protecting and stabilizing flows of streams, rivers, and underground water supplies were recognized even when forestry was in its infancy, and afterward as management of forests for multiple benefits included water along with timber, recreation, wildlife, and grazing. The Department of Conservation and Natural Resources was previously named the Department of Forests and Waters, sometimes nicknamed Sticks and Cricks (creeks).

George H. Leavesley (b. 1942)

George Leavesley received the B.S. degree in forestry from Penn State in 1964 and the M.S. in 1967. His graduate studies were interrupted by the Vietnam War. Entering the U.S. Air Force officer training program in 1966, he left the service with the rank of captain in 1970. He earned a Ph.D. in watershed sciences at Colorado State University in 1973.

Leavesley joined the Water Resources Division of the U.S. Geological Survey (USGS) in Denver, Colorado, in 1973 as a hydrologist, and worked on a variety of projects in the western United States. In 1978 he joined the National Research Program of the USGS as a research hydrologist and leader of the precipitation-runoff modeling project. His research included hydrologic modeling, simulation of the processes of snow accumulation and melt, estimation of model parameters using physical measures from digital databases and remotely sensed data, and coupling of atmospheric and hydrologic models. He developed the USGS precipitation-runoff modeling system (PRMS), a distributed, parameter, physical-process watershed model to evaluate the effects of various combinations of precipitation, climate, and land use on watershed response. PRMS has been used nationally and internationally on every continent in the world for a wide range of research and operational modeling applications.

In the course of his research, George recognized that one of the impediments to advancing the science of hydrologic modeling was the lack of a common modeling framework that would enable all modelers to share model components and tools, develop and evaluate alternative modeling approaches, and build on the results of others. So he developed the USGS modular modeling system (MMS) to facilitate interdisciplinary and multi-disciplinary research and analysis and enable the transfer of research results directly to operational applications. MMS has been used nationally and internationally to support modeling research and to develop operational decision-support systems for use in the management of water and other environmental resources.

While employed by the USGS, Leavesley also has been an affiliate faculty member of the Department of Earth Resources at Colorado State University since 1978, and of both the Department of Geography and the Department of Civil, Environmental, and Architectural Engineering at the University of Colorado since 1992. He has written or co-written more than eighty scientific publications, including journal articles, book chapters, and USGS investigation reports, and has made formal presentations at numerous scientific meetings and conferences. He has served as a member on two committees of the National Research Council, and as an associate editor for the scientific journals *Water Resources Research* and the ASCE *Journal of Hydrologic Engineering*. He has taught a two-week accredited course in hydrologic modeling at the Friedrich Schiller University in Jena, Germany, since 1996. Other international research and training activities include travels to Austria, China, India, Inner Mongolia, Italy, Japan, Mexico, South Korea, Spain, and Uzbekistan.

George wrote, "My educational experience at Penn State has been invaluable to me both professionally and personally. The choice of forestry for my undergraduate training and forest hydrology for my Masters work provided a broad background in a wide range of natural resources areas. This exposure has provided the foundation on which I have been able to build a rewarding career in exploring and integrating scientific concepts and understanding into models and tools for use in a variety of multidisciplinary research projects. Personally it has provided a network of scientific colleagues, fraternity brothers through Tau Phi Delta, and friends with whom I have maintained contact and shared a rewarding amount of time."

Wade L. Nutter (b. 1938)

Wade L. Nutter received the B.S. degree in forestry from Penn State in 1960. After working for several years in Philadelphia in the imported and domestic lumber and veneer business, he returned to Penn State in 1964 for an M.S. degree in forest hydrology. He earned a Ph.D. degree in forest hydrology and soils in 1968 at Michigan State University and was appointed an instructor there for one year.

Wade joined the faculty of the University of Georgia's School of Forest Resources in 1968 to teach and conduct research in forest hydrology, and retired in 1997 as professor emeritus. He had the good fortune of a supporting educational and research program at the University of Georgia that attracted students to the expanding field of forest hydrology. Although the principal engineering programs then were at Georgia Tech, the School of Forest Resources hydrology program served interdisciplinary interests across the Georgia campus. It provided the opportunity to develop a variety of hydrology-related courses and to interact with graduate students from many disciplines.

Building on his experience at Penn State, Wade started a research program in land application of wastes that led to implementation of scientific-based state and federal guidance not only in the United States but also internationally. He has published widely on the subject, and his research and experience contributed to the design and operation of the three largest forestland application systems in the United States. Other research focused on the hydrology of forested landscapes due to changes in land use, movement of pesticides, erosion and sediment control, and wetland hydrology.

The U.S. Agency for International Development appointed Nutter home campus coordinator in 1982 for a watershed management project in Sri Lanka. His responsibilities included establishing a forest training school, watershed research on degraded tea lands, community firewood programs, and training forest technicians and M.S. degree students in the United States and abroad. It is gratifying that in spite of the civil strife that has plagued Sri Lanka in recent years, many of the students trained in the United States have carried on, bringing modern forestry techniques to Sri Lanka.

In the 1990s Nutter served as a member of the core team that developed the Corps of Engineers' methodology for the hydrogeomorphic functional assessment of wetlands. In recognition of his expertise in hydrology and soils he was appointed by the governor to the Georgia Hazardous Waste Management Authority, and he chaired the site selection group. He also served on the legislature-mandated scientific panel on water quality standards for sediment and turbidity, and the task force for revising the forestry best-management practices manual. In 1994 he was appointed to the governor's Environmental Education Council. He was elected to serve three terms as vice president for working groups of the American Water Resources Association, and in various capacities served other professional organizations at the national and local levels as well.

Today Nutter is president of Nutter & Associates, a ten-employee international environmental consulting firm focusing on water, soil, and waste management issues based in Athens, Georgia. In addition to the usual consulting work, he has served as an expert witness on hydrologic issues for the U.S. Department of Justice, U.S. Environmental Protection Agency, and other federal and state agencies.

Upon reflecting about his educational experience at Penn State, Wade believes his freshman year at Mont Alto was pivotal in guiding his future. It was an opportunity in a unique setting to focus on studies and to develop educational and professional goals. The Mont Alto professors set an example that Wade often recalled in his own teaching career.

William E. "Bill" Sopper (b. 1928)

William E. Sopper received the B.S. degree in forestry from Penn State in 1954 and the M.S. in 1955. His undergraduate studies were interrupted by service as a master sergeant in the Korean War. He earned the Ph.D. in forest hydrology at Yale University in 1960.

Bill joined the School of Forest Resources faculty at Mont Alto in 1955, then moved to University Park in 1958 and retired as professor emeritus of forest hydrology in 1993. In his truly distinguished career he conducted pioneering research with his graduate students on watershed management and on recycling of municipal wastewater and sludge on forests, agricultural lands, and mine spoils. He helped to develop and extend the concept of using soil and vegetation as a "living filter" to remove contaminants from municipal wastewater. Perhaps his most challenging achievement was to revegetate a superfund site, the zinc-contaminated Blue Mountain near Palmerton, Pennsylvania, using sewage sludge and fly ash. His success was publicized by movies called *City's Waste/Country's Wealth* and *The Greening of Appalachia*. He wrote *Municipal Sludge Use in Land Reclamation* to record his methods for others, as "nationwide and worldwide there are huge tracts of disturbed land that could be reclaimed with municipal sludge."

Altogether he wrote or edited five books and published more than two hundred scientific papers, book reviews, and popular articles. He served as a scientific editor for the *Journal of Forestry, Water Resources Research*, and the *Journal of Environmental Quality*. He presented many papers at national and international meetings and served as advisor or consultant to various organizations and government agencies, including those of other nations. His travels included visits to Australia, Brazil, England, Germany, Hungary, Japan, Korea, New Zealand, Portugal, Russia, Scotland, Spain, and Yugoslavia.

Among his many awards and honors are Penn State's Gamma Sigma Delta Award (1975), the 1977 Karl M. Mason Award for Creativity in Environmental Management, the outstanding technical paper award at the 1987 National Symposium on Mining, Hydrology, Sedimentology and Reclamation, and the William T. Plass Award of the American Society for Surface Mining and Reclamation (1992) in recognition of a preeminent research career.

Thomas H. Yorke (b. 1942)

Thomas H. Yorke received the B.S. degree in forestry from Penn State in 1964 and the M.S. in 1967. After completing the course work for his M.S. degree, Tom joined the Water Resources Division of the U. S. Geological Survey in College Park, Maryland, in 1965 as a hydrologist. The hydrologist series was a new classification and Tom, along with fellow graduate students Harold Schindel, Ronald Shields, and George Leavesley, was among the first hydrologists hired by the USGS.

In Tom's first assignment in the hydrologic data collection and analysis section he collected river stage and discharge data and groundwater levels in Maryland. In 1967 he was assigned to a research project that evaluated the effects of urban development in the Washington, D.C., metropolitan area on the runoff and sediment transport characteristics of Piedmont streams. Tom became chief of the project in 1973 and remained in Maryland until the project was completed in 1976. Tom's nine articles and reports on the research were used by the Soil Conservation Service and government agencies to design standards for controlling runoff and sediment from urban construction sites. Tom also helped to document the record drought in 1966 and the record 1969 and 1972 floods during Hurricanes Camille and Agnes.

In 1976 Tom accepted an interagency assignment with the U.S. Fish and Wildlife Service in Columbia, Missouri. His multidisciplinary team was responsible for developing a research program to assess the effects of stream channel alterations activities on biota and the habitat of rivers and their floodplains. He also consulted on numerous water development projects, including the Kissimmee River in Florida, the Atchafalaya River in Louisiana, and the Teton Dam failure in Idaho.

Tom returned to Pennsylvania in 1978 to participate in a river quality assessment of the Schuylkill River. The research project analyzed the occurrence, transport, and fate of trace metals and organic compounds in the river from the headwaters to Philadelphia. The project was a forerunner of the USGS's National Water Quality Assessment Program.

Tom's career changed course in 1980 when he moved from research to management. He managed the field operations and research activities of the USGS in the Susquehanna River basin from 1980 to 1985. He performed similar duties in southwest Florida as chief of the USGS office in Tampa, Florida, from 1985 to 1990. He then moved to the headquarters of the USGS in Reston, Virginia, in 1990 as chief of the national water information system. This program was responsible for maintaining the national databases for stream flow, groundwater and water quality data, and for developing new data management systems.

In 1995 Yorke was named the senior science advisor for surface water and chief of the office of surface water. The office of surface water supported the national network of stream flow-, reservoir-, sediment-, and precipitation-monitoring stations and was responsible for assuring the quality of all river stage, water discharge, and sediment data collected by the USGS. Tom represented the United States in the development and review of national and international standards related to the collection and analysis of surface water and sediment transport data. He also administered programs that supported the development of watershed, hydraulic, and statistical models and other technology for effectively managing the nation's water resources.

During his career with the USGS, Tom wrote thirty research reports and journal articles and made numerous presentations at scientific and management meetings. He was awarded the Superior Service Award by the director of the USGS and the Meritorious Service Award by the secretary of the interior. He also was active in professional organizations. He has been a certified professional hydrologist with the American Institute of Hydrology since 1983, a member of the American Geophysical Union since 1967, and a member of the American Water Resources Association since 1969. He served as president of the Pennsylvania section of AWRA in 1984 and 1985 and treasurer of the Florida sections in 1988 and 1989.

Tom retired from the USGS in 2001, but he has continued water resources management activities as a private consultant. He currently serves as chairman of the U.S. Technical Advisory Group to the International Standards Organization (ISO) Technical Committee on Hydrometry. He also is chairman of the ISO Subcommittee on Instrumentation and Data Management.

Throughout his career, Tom continued his association with Penn State. Tom and his wife, Jeannie, have been life members of the Penn State Alumni Association (PSAA) and Nittany Lion Club members for more than twenty-five years. He and Jeannie represented Penn State at college nights throughout central Florida in the late 1980s. Tom also was on the board of directors and president of the Tampa chapter of the PSAA. They have been members of the Greater Washington chapter of the PSAA since moving to the Washington, D.C., area in 1990. Tom currently serves as the editor of the alumni newsletter of the Tau Phi Delta fraternity. In 2004 Tom was elected to the board of directors of the School of Forest Resources Alumni Group, and he was elected president in 2005. He also serves on the centennial planning committee of the School of Forest Resources.

Wildlife and Fisheries

Foresters and others who hunt and fish have always understood that forests are an essential part of the environments that support animal life. Therefore it is not surprising that wildlife interests have been represented in the teaching, research, and outreach of the School from its beginning. Graduate degrees in forestry enabled students to specialize in wildlife management, yet the undergraduate curriculum in wildlife science did not begin until 1981; it was broadened to Wildlife and Fisheries Science in 1988. The first B.S. degrees in wildlife were awarded in 1983.

Hunting and fishing represent more than outdoor recreation; they are also important commercially. According to the 2001 national survey of fishing, hunting, and wildlife-associated recreation, 4.6 million people spent $3 billion to fish, hunt, and watch wildlife in Pennsylvania that year. The School's graduates have made significant impacts related to wildlife and fisheries, though their degrees have been clearly identified with these fields only recently.

Gary Alt (b. 1952)

Gary Alt earned an associate degree in wildlife technology (1972) from Penn State University's DuBois Campus, a bachelor's degree in wildlife science from Utah State University (1974), an M.S. in wildlife management from Penn State University (1977), and a doctorate in forest resources science from West Virginia University (1989).

Gary first made his mark in wildlife management through his nationally known studies of bear biology. Then "the bearman" was placed in charge of deer. In August 1999 Alt accepted an appointment to head the Pennsylvania Game Commission's new deer management section in the Bureau of Wildlife Management. He worked to build a consensus among deer management stakeholders on a new deer management program, attempting to reduce deer density and improve the health of the herd as well as other wildlife. To bring the deer herd into balance with its forest habitat, Alt instituted two-tiered antler restrictions, concurrent buck and doe seasons, and higher antlerless permit allocations. These measures were designed to increase the number of large bucks and harvest more does.

Alt retired from a twenty-seven-year career with the Game Commission in 2004. Alt said he was leaving because of his frustration with a "broken system." PGC president Russ Schleiden said, "He was a great orator and I have the utmost respect for the great effort that he has put forth on behalf of the deer, our forests and future generations of hunters."

Alt is now a freelance nature photographer and lecturer. He has filmed and photographed deer in the wild and in captivity to organize a "Natural History of White-Tailed Deer" slide lecture, which he has presented at numerous sports shows and public events. During his free time, he has led natural history and photographic tours in Canada, Alaska, the western United States, and Africa. He has narrated and hosted an award-winning video documentary and presented more than a thousand lectures on bear, deer, and other wildlife management topics.

Alt has received numerous honors and awards recognizing his professional achievements. Among the awards are an honorary doctor of science degree from Wilkes University; Pennsylvania Wildlife Federation's Outstanding Conservation Professional; an Alumni Fellow Award (2000) from the Penn State University Alumni Association; the Pennsylvania Forestry Association's Roe S. Cochran Award for natural resource education; the first-ever Pennsylvania Wildlife Federation and Audubon Pennsylvania Lenny Green/Inky Moore Conservation Educator Award (2001); a Northeast Environmental Partnership Award from the Pennsylvania Environmental Council for his efforts to conserve and protect the environment; *Outdoor Life* magazine's Public Service Conservation Award for his work in deer management; and the Safari Club International Conservation

Award, the highest recognition an individual can receive from SCI for service in the field of wildlife conservation and hunters' rights.

Gary, a member of the DuBois program's 1972 inaugural wildlife technology class, credits his educational experience for laying the groundwork for his continued success. When he received the Penn State Alumni Fellow Award in 2000 he commented, "Over the past twenty-five years I have had the career of my dreams, and I owe it all to Penn State."

Frank C. Craighead Sr. (1890–1982)

Frank Craighead received his forestry degree from Penn State in 1912 and his Ph.D. from George Washington University. Besides some wildlife interests of his own, he had a profound effect on the wildlife profession through his children. He spent many hours with them along the Potomac River, teaching them all about the plants and animals. It is his twin sons, Frank Jr. and John, who are so well known for their twelve-year study of grizzly bears using radio transmitters (see www.grizzlybear.org). They both graduated in 1939 from Penn State with A.B. degrees in science. His daughter Jean, also a Penn Stater, won prestigious awards for her books *Julie of the Wolves* and *My Side of the Mountain*. She wrote more than a hundred books, and some sold millions of copies. She also has written many popular articles about wildlife for children and is regarded as something of a legend in the world of children's literature. Jean was the first wife of John L. George, former faculty member of the School of Forest Resources.

Frank Sr.'s career was as a forest entomologist and ecologist working for the U.S. Department of Agriculture in the Bureau of Entomology and Plant Quarantine. Daughter Jean recalled a favorite saying of his: "Study an insect and you are soon studying the whole forest. Study the forest and you are soon studying the insect." Craighead is the author of numerous scientific publications, many of them dealing with forest insects. In 1949 he published a large and definitive book titled *Insect Enemies of Eastern Forests*, USDA miscellaneous publication no. 657. Among other diverse topics are *Orchids and Other Air Plants of the Everglades National Park*, *Trees of South Florida*, and *The Role of the Alligator in Shaping Plant Communities and Maintaining Wildlife in the Southern Everglades*.

After retiring in 1950 as chief of the USDA's Bureau of Forest Entomology, Craighead directed his enthusiasm and scientific training to understanding the biological problems of Florida. He soon became an expert on the rapidly disappearing native plants, the ecological role of hurricanes,

and the environmental problems associated with the area's water resources. As an honorary scientific consultant for the Everglades National
Park, his knowledge of the intricate ecology of the wetlands influenced
decisions of government officials and eventually city and county planners.
Craighead's work in Florida contributed to national concern for our marshes and coastal areas and led to rational and scientific programs for the
conservation of the Everglades and south Florida wetlands.

During the 1950s Craighead and his wife, Carolyn J. Craighead, lived
on a farm near Carlisle for several years. At that time he was employed by
Joe Ibberson in the Bureau of Forestry to work on insect transmission of
oak wilt disease. Their encounters with rattlesnakes, while searching for
diseased trees, led Ibberson to a discovery about Craighead's past. Frank
Sr. and his college roommate, George L. Drake, had earned money for
college by milking rattlesnakes and selling the venom for antidotes. They
lived in a cabin in Clinton County, separated from the snakes only by a
wire mesh fence. Throughout his life Frank captured rattlesnakes, killed
them, and had belts made from them.

Eugene "Gene" Decker (b. 1930)

Gene earned a B.S. in forestry in 1952 and an M.S. in forestry (wildlife
management) at Penn State in 1955. He came from the town of Emlenton,
and Robert Krear (see his biography) was his scoutmaster there. After various positions in Pennsylvania, New York, Georgia, Montana, and California, Decker joined the College of Natural Resources at Colorado State
University in 1967. He was professor of wildlife biology for more than
thirty-one years in the Department of Fishery and Wildlife Biology at
CSU. There he taught courses in natural resources public relations, wildlife
management, and international wildlife resources. He retired from Colorado State in 1999 and was honored with emeritus status.

Professor Decker spent a considerable amount of time serving as a
mentor to international graduate and undergraduate students from Egypt
and other African countries, Iran, Indonesia, Australia, and Nepal. His
international efforts in wildlife conservation included work in Iran and
Africa. He has led many wildlife safaris to Africa, and also some to New
Zealand, Tasmania, and Patagonia.

Decker has received many awards, including the Wildlife Society Conservation Education Award in 1983 for the Colorado wildlife education
program developed under his direction, and the Best Teacher Award from
the CSU student chapter of the Wildlife Society in 1999. He spent exten-

sive time developing, coordinating, and conducting training programs in conservation and in communications/public relations. This includes the well-known week-long wildlife management short course at CSU, ecology study tours of east, central, and southern Africa, and a course in effective personal presentations offered annually for the Wildlife Society.

Gene's community service includes being the founding director, in 1977, of the Rocky Mountain Bighorn Society, a citizen conservation group. He also served as member and chairman of the City of Loveland Parks and Recreation Advisory Board. His military service includes active duty in 1952 and active reserve duty from 1953 to 1960; he was honorably discharged as captain in 1962.

John L. George (1916–1999)

John L. George was professor of wildlife management in the School of Forest Resources from 1963 to 1981. Through his creativity and tenacity, the B.S. major in wildlife science and the associate degree in wildlife technology were initiated. He conducted research on deer, turkey, elk, otter, and eastern coyote, and published nine books and more than two hundred scientific and popular articles. A few of these were co-written by his first wife, Jean Craighead, daughter of Frank C. Craighead Sr. and sister of Frank Jr. and John Craighead.

George received all his degrees—a B.S. in forestry (1939), an M.S. in zoology (1941), and two doctorates in 1952, one in wildlife biology and the other in ornithology—from the University of Michigan. In between he served in the navy from 1942 to 1946 as a combat information officer and saw action in both the Atlantic and Pacific theaters.

He began his professional career at Vassar College, teaching there from 1950 to 1957. Then for a year he was the associate curator of mammals for the New York Bronx Zoo. While assistant chief of wildlife biology at the Patuxent Wildlife Research Center (1958–63), George published scientific papers on damage to wildlife caused by pesticides. His papers preceded the publication of *Silent Spring* by Rachel Carson. His early research on DDT effects contributed to the ban of this pesticide. Later he found evidence of DDT in Antarctic wildlife species, indicating that this pesticide had spread to the farthest corners of the earth.

George was the first president of the Rachel Carson Council, from 1966 to 1974, during its formative years. He served as trustee (1953–84) of the National Parks and Conservation Association; as chairman of the Committee on Ecological Effects of Chemical Controls in the International Union for the Conservation of Nature and Natural Resources in Switzerland (1959–72); and a congressional advisor (1964–80) for the ad hoc committee on the environment. His testimony helped to formulate the National Environment Policy Act, the Endangered Species Act, the Marine Mammal Act, and the Federal Insecticide, Fungicide and Rodenticide Act.

John transmitted his sensitive feelings for nature to many young scientists while a professor at both Vassar College and Penn State. A devoted gardener, his house in State College was surrounded by lush, natural plantings for wildlife, especially birds. He and his second wife, Janice, took great pleasure in these and in visits by his two daughters, three sons, and seven grandchildren. He was an ardent tennis player and continued playing weekly into his eighties.

H. Robert "Bob" Krear (b. 1922)

Bob Krear grew up in rural western Pennsylvania, where he trapped, hunted, fished, roamed the forests, and developed a strong love for nature. To save money for college he worked cutting timber, servicing gas fields, and driving a semitanker truck for the Quaker State Oil Refinery. He enrolled at Mont Alto in 1942 and, after World War II interrupted his studies, completed his B.S. degree in forestry in 1949. Having been a member of the Penn State ski team, Bob found a way to serve in the ski troop division just being formed, the 86th Mountain Infantry of the Tenth Mountain Division. He turned down an opportunity for officer candidate school. Amazingly, he survived the arduous battles of the Italian campaign without any physical wounds.

Krear continued his education at the University of Wyoming, receiving the M.S. degree in zoology in 1953. He was employed in fur seal research by the U.S. Fish and Wildlife Service on the Pribilof Islands in the Bering Sea of Alaska. Then Bob joined the Montana Game and Fish Department as a wapiti biologist, and in 1954 became a seasonal naturalist with the U.S. National Park Service. In 1956 Krear was invited to join the Olaus Murie Brooks Range expedition in a summer of exploration and research that contributed to the establishment of the Arctic Wildlife Range, later renamed the Arctic National Wildlife Refuge, more commonly known as ANWR.

He started work on his doctoral degree in 1956 but interrupted his studies to rejoin the U.S. Fish and Wildlife Service to collaborate in research on sea otters in the western Aleutian Islands. Krear completed his

Ph.D. in animal behavior and ecology at the University of Colorado in 1965. He was honored by being elected to the National Scientific Honorary Society, Sigma Xi, and the National Biological Honorary Society, Phi Sigma; and he received the Phi Sigma Outstanding Graduate Student Award in Biology in 1965.

Dr. Krear taught biology courses at the university level from 1960 to 1984, sequentially at the University of Colorado, Mankato State College, Colorado Alpine College, and Michigan Technological University. At the University of Colorado he specialized in alpine research with the Institute of Arctic and Alpine Research. During his teaching career he also served as a professional seasonal ranger-naturalist in eight national parks. During his academic career, and also after retiring, he engaged in extensive travels, visiting nature preserves, national parks, and tropical reefs in many parts of the world. He joined several of the safaris in foreign countries led by Gene Decker (see his biography).

Bob explains his retirement to Estes Park, Colorado, this way: "I was an Appalachian mountain boy before coming to Penn State, then I became an army alpine trooper, then a university professor, and now I've reverted happily to being a mountain man again who lives a very simple life here on Rams Horn Mountain." In commenting on his education at three universities, Bob commented, "Penn State is and always will be my 'special' university!"

Thomas L. "Tom" Serfass (b. 1956)

Tom is the first recipient of the School of Forest Resources Outstanding Recent Alumni Award, created to honor alumni who graduated in the previous ten years. He completed his doctoral degree in wildlife and fisheries science in 1994 under the direction of Robert Brooks, professor of wildlife and wetlands. His B.S. and M.S. degrees are from East Stroudsburg University.

After several years in a postdoctoral position with the Penn State Cooperative Wetlands Center, Serfass secured a faculty appointment in the Department of Biology at Frostburg State University. He advanced to professor of wildlife ecology and in 2005 was awarded the Wilson H. Elkins professorship, an endowed university-wide professorship at the University of Maryland. His research focuses on development, implementation, and evaluation of carnivore and ungulate reintroduction projects. He coordinated all aspects of the Pennsylvania river otter reintroduction projects since 1982. More recently he has coordinated the reintroduction of fishers in northern Pennsylvania. His graduate students have evaluated the fates and habitat use of elk translocated in north-central Pennsylvania, and river otters reintroduced in western New York. Financial support for these projects has been provided by the Pennsylvania Game Commission, Pennsylvania Wild Resource Conservation Fund, United States Forest Service, National Forest Foundation, New York River Otter Project, and U.S. Army Corps of Engineers.

Tom has devoted his professional career to increasing our knowledge about wildlife and has worked diligently to protect and restore threatened populations. He began his work with otters while still an undergraduate student at East Stroudsburg University. His innovative approaches to carnivore restoration, and his dissertation, "Conservation Genetics and Reintroduction Strategies for River Otters," have led to numerous publications that have redefined reintroduction projects for wildlife. He has always insisted that the utmost consideration be given to the animal, whether it is an otter, fisher, or elk. This has led to the development of protocols for site selection, project evaluation, genetic considerations for the founding members of the reintroduced populations, animal handling, and care involving veterinarians.

Serfass also has implemented well-conceived education and outreach programs for the public. His attention to detail has led to the safe reintroduction of hundreds of individual animals and opportunities for thousands of citizens of all ages to observe seldom-seen species as they were released. He has written numerous popular articles for lay audiences, and has delivered more than two hundred informative and entertaining presentations to children, sportsmen, professionals, and citizens from all walks of life.

Serfass has received national and international recognition for his work. He presented papers in Costa Rica, the Czech Republic, and Chile. Currently he is serving as an advisor to the National Park Service on the potential reintroduction of river otters into the Grand Canyon. He is also the North American coordinator of the International Union for the Conservation of Nature and Natural Resources otter specialist group.

Tom is a member of the Wildlife Society and the American Society of Mammalogists; he has served as president of the Pennsylvania chapter of the Wildlife Society. In 1993, while still a graduate student, Serfass was recognized as the Pennsylvania Conservation Professional of the Year by the Pennsylvania Wildlife Federation, and in 1997 he received the Three Rivers Environmental Award. Now, as a faculty member at Frostburg State University, he continues to advance the science and conservation of wildlife species, while educating the next generation of wildlife biologists and conservationists.

David L. "Dave" Spencer (1915–2000)

After completing his forestry degree in 1937, Dave worked for a few years with the Civilian Conservation Corps, and then as a logger in northwestern Pennsylvania. Next Dave completed an M.S. degree at the University of Michigan in the new field of wildlife management, and began a job with the Missouri State Game Commission in 1942. In 1943 he enlisted in the Naval Air Corps and became a naval flight instructor in multiengine seaplanes at Corpus Christi, Texas.

Dave was discharged from the navy in 1945 and soon began working with Starker Leopold, the son of Aldo Leopold, conducting bird studies in Mexico. Dave then began doctoral studies at the University of Wisconsin, and it was there that he came to know Aldo Leopold. But he soon realized that research was not his preferred vocation, so he entered the U.S. Fish and Wildlife Service in 1946. He flew duck surveys in Mexico, Guatemala, Florida, and Canada, as well as flying to remote areas of Alaska in the late 1940s and 1950s.

In 1948 Spencer became refuge manager of the Kenai National Moose Range. In 1950 his duties were expanded when he became supervisor of all the national wildlife refuges in Alaska. He fought for and guided the Alaskan National Wildlife Refuge System through the turbulent years of poachers and squatters, oil development, statehood, emerging wilderness and environmental ethics, conflicting demands for use of wildlife and their habitats, and the selection of lands to be added to the refuges for the Alaska National Interest Lands Conservation Act. He was instrumental in bringing the Aleutian goose back from the brink of extinction. He retired from the U.S. Fish and Wildlife Service in 1976 and then worked an additional eight years for the University of Alaska.

Dave's professional recognitions are numerous and include the highest honor of the Department of Interior, the Distinguished Service Award, in 1973; the Alaska Conservationist of the Year award from the National Audubon Society in 1981; and the Professional Service Award from the University of Alaska in 1985. In 1997 a unit of the Kenai Wilderness was named in David Spencer's honor.

John Craighead once wrote, "I know of no other who has done as much as Dave to preserve and manage wildlife and its habitat in Alaska. He was a humble and soft-spoken man but resolute in his husbandry of the land

and its wildlife. His integrity was of the highest order and this was matched with a passion for the land and its diversity of life. It is my opinion that he, more than anyone else, set the pattern for natural resource management in Alaska."

Steven A. "Steve" Williams (b. 1957)

Steven A. Williams earned his B.S. (1979) in environmental resource management and his Ph.D. (1986) in forest resources at Penn State. His M.S. (1981) was from the University of North Dakota. He is a member of the International Association of Fish and Wildlife Agencies, the Wildlife Society, and other professional and conservation organizations.

In 2002 Williams was confirmed by the Senate as director of the U.S. Fish and Wildlife Service, and he was formally sworn in by Secretary of the Interior Gale Norton. As director he oversaw the operations of the nation's primary wildlife conservation agency, with more than 7,500 employees and a budget of about $2 billion. His responsibilities included management of the ninety-four-million acre National Wildlife Refuge System, administering the Endangered Species Act, and enforcing federal wildlife laws. In 2005 he resigned as director and became president of the Wildlife Management Institute, a nonprofit organization dedicated to scientific wildlife management. Williams said, "The past three years . . . have been the most rewarding of my 20 years in fish and wildlife conservation."

Williams served previously as secretary of the Kansas Department of Wildlife and Parks from 1995 through 2002. Other former positions include deputy executive director of the Pennsylvania Game Commission (1992–95); assistant director for wildlife for the Massachusetts Division of Fisheries and Wildlife (1989–92); and wildlife biologist specializing in research and management for white-tailed deer for the Massachusetts Division of Fisheries and Wildlife (1985–89).

Commenting on his student days, Steve said, "In college I used to think it was worthless to learn how to write impact statements; I just wanted to go out and count twigs and deer, but little did I know how much my Penn State education would help me."

Urban Forestry

City forestry was an option in the curriculum during the 1920s and was changed to private forestry in 1930. When urban forestry became an option in forest science in 1996, the faculty was not aware of the earlier existence of city forestry but did realize that forestry graduates had found their way into this field for decades. In fact, Ralph Brock, a graduate in the first Mont Alto class, specialized in landscape trees for most of his career after working for a few years in forest management (see his biography). Whether this field is called urban forestry, city forestry, community forestry, or arboriculture, its commercial expenditures are in the billions of dollars and its value to municipalities and residents is practically incalculable.

Phillip J. "Phil" Craul (b. 1932)

Phil received the B.S. (1954) and M.S. (1960) degrees in forestry, and the Ph.D. (1964) in agronomy, all from Penn State. He was employed by the Pennsylvania Bureau of Forestry from 1956 to 1958 and as a soil scientist at the Southern Forest Experiment Station of the U.S. Forest Service from 1964 to 1967. For eleven years he served in the U.S. Army on active duty and in the reserves, and was honorably discharged as captain in 1965.

After teaching forestry and soils courses at Mont Alto (1959–60) and at Delaware Valley College (1967–68), Craul spent most of his career at the State University of New York College of Environmental Science and Forestry at Syracuse (1968–94), retiring as professor emeritus of soil science. He taught courses in soils, soil physics, classification and survey, and geographic information systems, and chaired nearly every faculty administrative committee over his twenty-six years there. For thirteen years he was also senior lecturer in landscape architecture in the Graduate School of Design at Harvard University.

Phillip Craul is the preeminent U.S. expert on urban soils and their effects on landscape trees. For many years he educated generations of students, foresters, landscape architects, engineers, and others about the effects of soils on trees. He is perhaps best known for his books, *Urban Soil in Landscape Design* (1992) and *Urban Soils: Applications and Practices* (1999). Phil has written thirty-five publications and several books, presented papers at sixteen national and international conferences, and served on editorial boards of several national periodicals. Phil reminds his audiences that "it is *not dirt*, it is *soil*, the elixir of life."

He has shared his expertise with many agencies, including the national capitol region of the National Park Service, the U.S. Forest Service, the New York City Department of Parks and Recreation, the State of New York, and several New York municipalities and conservation districts. In

1987 he was invited by English Nature to help develop solutions for soils problems in England, Wales, and Scotland. As a consultant he designed and supervised installation of planting soils for some forty landscape architecture projects. These included the Allegheny Riverfront Park in Pittsburgh, the J. Paul Getty Fine Arts Center in Los Angeles, the Commons Parade and Spectacle Island in Boston, Teardrop Park and the East Lawn of Central Park in New York City, and 1600 Pennsylvania Avenue in Washington, D.C.

A strong supporter of Penn State Mont Alto, Phil was instrumental in activating the Maurice K. and Ethel C. Goddard Scholarship in Forestry, and he established the Joanne M. Craul Scholarship in Nursing in memory of his wife. He served on the board of directors of the Penn State Mont Alto Constituent Society from 1996 to 2001, and helped to organize and support the centennial celebration in 2003.

Craul was elected to several scientific, forestry, and agricultural honorary societies, including Sigma Xi, Xi Sigma Pi, and Gamma Sigma Delta. He was a Bullard fellow for forestry research at Harvard University from 1976 to 1977 and was elected to honorary membership in Sigma Lambda Alpha, the Landscape Architecture honorary society. In 2003 Penn State Mont Alto named him an alumni centennial fellow.

Commenting on what Penn State meant to him, Craul said "I learned the concept of an instructor being tough but fair as a student right here at Mont Alto in 1950 and 1951. . . . I think it has 'paid off' for the students as well as myself." His recollections of the faculty include Maurice K. Goddard (on rainy days he said, "your skin doesn't leak"), Shorty Pflueger (standing on a stump to be heard), Rex Melton (infamous dendrology specimens), Wilbur Ward (giving us the low down on the Waynesboro Watershed), Harold Jarrett (doing his best to get math across to us), John Lotz (in chemistry, "watch me very closely as this may blow up at any time"), and Chester Corson (trying to get us to write in proper style).

John C. "Jack" Good (b. 1918)

Jack Good graduated in 1941 with a B.S. in forestry and an ROTC commission as second lieutenant in the infantry. He immediately served in the U.S. Army as an officer of the 10th Mountain Division (ski troops) and 8th Infantry Division in Europe during World War II. After combat duty in France, Belgium, and Germany, Good was wounded in the Battle of Huertgen Forest. The doctors had grave doubts that he would survive.

His recovery in the army hospital system took many months, ending with disability retirement in 1945 as a full lieutenant and company commander.

Jack began his forestry career in the summer of 1945 as a farm forester in the Virginia Forest Service. In 1946 he joined Bartlett Tree Experts as a trainee and later that year was sent to Chambersburg to open a new market. As the only local company to offer quality scientific tree care, the business grew rapidly and soon was serving clients in three counties. Good was promoted to district manager, then division manager, and later was made vice president of the company and a member of the board of directors. In 1988, serving as senior vice president, he was active in opening new company offices in Texas and the southeast.

Good persuaded the Bartlett company in 1985 to establish scholarships for students interested in careers in urban forestry or arboriculture. The Bartlett Foundation, which he serves as executive director, awards generous scholarships through twenty-seven forestry schools and horticulture departments throughout the United States. This has resulted in the training and recruitment of many summer interns and graduates, not only by Bartlett but for the entire industry. Jack regards his work with the foundation as his greatest contribution to the profession.

Jack Good has served for many years on the advisory boards at Penn State and Penn State Mont Alto. His extensive community services include the Boy Scouts, his church, the Chambersburg Hospital, and many other groups. One of his great loves has been harmonizing in the barbershop quartet Friends-In-A-Chord.

He is also an active member of the International Society of Arboriculture and other arborist organizations. In 1991 he received the Distinguished Alumni Award from the Mont Alto campus, in 2001 the Outstanding Alumni Award of the Penn State School of Forest Resources, and in 2003 he was honored with the Penn State Mont Alto Centennial Fellows Award.

People in all walks of professional and personal life consider Jack a man of the highest integrity, professionalism, and community spirit. He sometimes speaks of his Scottish frugality, but this belies his generosity as a benefactor to his favorite causes.

Jack recalls his freshman year at Mont Alto as having had the greatest impact on his adult life. "The camaraderie enjoyed by the students and teachers was unmatched. H. Norton Cope, a fatherly, wise and firm Christian man, gently led the school in that formative year."

Walter R. "Dick" Rossman (b. 1927)

In his youth Dick Rossman had learned about tree species and wood quality while gathering firewood for the family. His parents and their five children had been evicted from their home during the Depression in the 1930s, and so they moved temporarily to a summer cottage offered by some friends along the Susquehanna River. There Dick explored the woods and the river.

Rossman received a B.S. degree in forestry at Penn State in 1950, after a two-year interruption for service in the U.S. Army Air Force. The GI Bill financed his education, and he found odd jobs to pay for incidental expenses. He worked for Professor Wallace White in the wood technology lab, for Professor Merwin Humphrey at Blue Jay summer camp, and for Professor William Bramble on research projects. "Each of these job opportunities proved to be a learning experience at least equal to my classroom experiences" he wrote later. The research on controlling woody vegetation by herbicides led to his first employment.

Dick's thirty-eight-year career as a utility forester started in 1950 as a system forester in Maryland, and he soon advanced to forest manager for the Pennsylvania Electric Company. He supervised eight Penelec division foresters, managed several thousand acres of forestland, inspected transmission power lines by helicopter, pioneered a replacement tree-planting program, and administered a twenty-five-year research project studying the effect of pollution on trees.

Rossman pioneered standards and methods for chemical treatment of vegetation on powerline rights-of-way and gained permission from the Pennsylvania Game Commission to use chemical herbicides by installing demonstration plots on state game lands. He also established a method of "natural pruning" of street trees for clearance of electric distribution lines. He initiated the first competitive bidding for line clearance contracts, and other major utilities throughout the United States soon picked up his methods. Dick developed the first erosion and sediment control manual for line construction, and also a manual for controlling vegetation on utility rights-of-way, both of which were adopted by utilities throughout the eastern United States. He helped establish the line clearance and forestry committee of the Pennsylvania Electric Association and served as its first chair.

Dick promoted the right tree–right place concept for years before other utility companies started using it in many parts of the country. This led to the founding of the Municipal Tree Restoration Program with Penn State and the Bureau of Forestry, and later Pennsylvania's involvement in the America the Beautiful Program of the U.S. Forest Service. Through a Forest Service grant, Dick helped to develop an arboretum at the Penn Cambria Elementary School that demonstrates to students and communities how different tree varieties look and how to select trees for various landscape sites.

Many awards, leadership positions, and professional memberships attest to Dick's other achievements beyond utility forestry: School of Forest Resources Outstanding Alumnus 2004, fellow of the Society of American Foresters, president of the Pennsylvania Association of Conservation District Directors (1984–86), president of the Pennsylvania Forestry Association, co-founder and chair of the Stony Creek Conemaugh River Improvement Program, Samuel S. Cobb/Bureau of Forestry Award 1988, State Conservation Commission member (1984–91), Pennsylvania Hardwoods Council member (1989–1991), Penn State Agriculture Advisory Council (1990–96), PFA Conservationist of the Year 1994, certificates of recognition by Pennsylvania's State Conservation Committee and by Southern Alleghenies RC&D Area (1995), Cambria County Conservation District Director Service Award (1973–95), president of the Western Pennsylvania Coalition for Abandoned Mine Reclamation, and vice chair of the Pennsylvania Organization for Watersheds and Rivers (1997–98).

Dick's high personal and professional standards are well known to the many people with whom he has interacted, as evidenced by his manifold professional and service contributions. He reminisced, "I believe the leadership, professional character and stature of the professors we encountered at Penn State contributed more to the professional maturity of students . . . than all the facts and theories provided in the classroom." His wife, Mary, described him well in an interview, "He was born to supervise and is tenacious. When he gets an idea, he won't let go of it 'til it is accomplished. We have been fortunate to live in the U.S.A. and feel obliged to give something back to preserve it."

Alden M. "Denny" Townsend (b. 1942)

Denny Townsend graduated in forest science at Penn State in 1964, received the M.F. degree from Yale University in 1966, and earned a Ph.D. in forest genetics and plant breeding at Michigan State University in 1969. From 1970 until 2005 he was employed as a research geneticist by the

USDA Agricultural Research Service, first at Delaware, Ohio, then at the U.S. National Arboretum in Washington, D.C.

His main emphasis has been on increasing disease and insect resistance in elms, maples, and other landscape tree species. He has written more than a hundred scientific and popular publications. These publications described for various tree genera the results of studies on the variation, inheritance, and genetic control of disease and insect resistance, tolerance to environmental stresses, and landscape characteristics such as stem straightness, crown form, growth rate, and autumn leaf color.

Through selection, testing, and breeding, Townsend developed nine improved elm varieties resistant to Dutch elm disease and six red maple varieties resistant to insects and drought. The elms include the two new disease-tolerant American elm cultivars 'Valley Forge' and 'New Harmony,' and seven disease-tolerant non-American cultivars: 'Frontier,' 'Homestead,' 'Ohio,' 'Pathfinder,' 'Patriot,' 'Pioneer,' and 'Prospector.' The red maples he developed are 'Brandywine,' 'Cumberland,' 'New World,' 'Red Rocket,' 'Somerset,' and 'Sun Valley.' All of these have been released for commercial production. Elm enthusiasts have been especially excited by the prospects for restoring this beloved street tree species.

Denny has been active in many professional organizations, including the Ohio chapter of the International Society of Arboriculture, the Metropolitan Tree Improvement Alliance, the Central States Forest Tree Improvement Conference, the USDA Woody Landscape Plants Germplasm Crop Advisory Committee, and the Save the Elms Task Force of Washington, D.C. The outstanding success of his research has been recognized by the School of Forest Resources Outstanding Alumni Award of 2004, the Luther Burbank Award of the American Horticultural Society, the 1982 Award for Arboricultural Research from the International Society of Arboriculture, a USDA-ARS Certificate of Merit in 1996, the Jackson Dawson Memorial Medal from the Massachusetts Horticultural Society, and a 1999 Honor Award from the USDA secretary of agriculture.

Commenting about his education, Denny wrote, "The four years I spent at Penn State resulted in a fine education that has profoundly influenced my life. The curriculum in Forest Science enabled me to receive a very well-rounded 'science' education, and included such diverse university courses as agronomy, botany, biochemistry, chemistry, entomology, geology, physics, plant pathology, and zoology—all providing scientific training and knowledge which I relied upon during graduate studies and throughout my research career. Of equal importance were the School of

Forest Resources forestry courses, which gave me a strong forest biology and forest management foundation and perspective as I moved on to graduate work and a career in forest genetics and plant breeding. But perhaps the greatest influence came from the forestry professors, all of whom were dedicated, approachable, supportive, and enthusiastic about teaching, forestry, and the forestry profession. Classes in the School of Forest Resources were small enough to get well acquainted with the professors and fellow students, fostering a camaraderie that was perhaps unmatched in the wider university community. I also have good memories of the student-led 'Forestry Society,' the weekly forestry seminar, and the summer camp at Mont Alto. I now realize how privileged I was to receive such a superb forestry education."

Academia and Professional Organizations

Graduates who pursue careers in universities or professional organizations exert a strong influence on the lives of other people, and also on the reputation of their own alma maters. Several such graduates have already appeared in the preceding categories. The following additional biographies include our own graduates and also some Penn State faculty members whose degrees are from other institutions.

Our examples begin with one who had a profound effect on the profession of forestry, Henry Clepper. He also is remembered for chronicling the first fifty years of the School's history, and for helping to heal the rift between Mont Alto and Penn State graduates.

Henry E. Clepper (1901–1987)

In forestry circles, for many years, probably the best-known graduate of the Pennsylvania State Forest Academy was Henry E. Clepper. He served as secretary of the Society of American Foresters for twenty-eight years and as the managing editor of its publication, *Journal of Forestry*. He was editor and co-author of *Forestry Education in Pennsylvania*, a book that not only describes the history of forest education but also contains a listing and information about each of the alumni who studied forestry at both the Academy and the university until 1957. Henry was one of the founders of the Penn State–Mont Alto Forestry Alumni Association and was elected its chair, continuing to serve in that capacity until 1946.

Clepper received the bachelor of forestry degree from the Pennsylvania State Forest Academy in 1921 at the age of twenty, having started when

Joseph S. Illick was acting director. When Henry first arrived, Illick instructed him to change his clothes in the dormitory and then report in the field to pick potatoes. His class was the last one whose graduates all found positions waiting for them with the state forest department.

After graduating he worked for Pennsylvania's commissioner of forestry, Gifford Pinchot, for a year, and continued with the Division of Forestry after Pinchot was elected governor of Pennsylvania. Clepper greatly admired Pinchot, "but he was devilish hard to satisfy." For fifteen years following graduation he worked for the Pennsylvania Department of Forests and Waters, first as field forester and later as assistant chief of the Bureau of Research and Education. Following this he joined the U.S. Forest Service and for a year was an information specialist in the Washington, D.C., office.

Clepper's main career as writer and editor got under way in 1922, with articles for the *New York Times*, the *Christian Science Monitor*, and other newspapers. His first article for *American Forests* appeared in 1924, and there were many others over the next fifty years. He became associate editor of the *Journal of Forestry* in 1935, advanced to editor, and served as executive secretary of the Society of American Foresters until he retired in 1966. Among his well-known books are *Origins of American Conservation* (1966), *America's Natural Resources* (1967), *Professional Forestry in the United States* (1971), *Leaders of American Conservation* (1971), and *Crusade for Conservation* (1975). Clepper wrote, co-wrote, or co-edited more than a hundred articles and bulletins on forestry and more than twenty books.

Clepper did much to advance the status of the forestry profession and to keep it in the forefront of natural resources matters in the nation's capital. He helped to organize the Natural Resources Council in 1946, bringing together various conservation groups as the profession of forestry was becoming more sophisticated, and served as chairman in 1950–51.

In 1957 the Society of American Foresters presented Clepper with the Gifford Pinchot Medal for outstanding achievement. The American Forest Products Industries gave him an award for distinguished service to forestry in 1965, and in 1970 he received the Distinguished Service Award from the American Forestry Association. He was one of three Pennsylvania State Forest Academy graduates to receive the Pennsylvania State University Achievement Award in 1957 from university president Eric A. Walker. This award was made for outstanding accomplishments in the forestry profession and continued interest in the School of Forestry. He was named an alumni centennial fellow in 2003 by Penn State Mont Alto.

John L. Gray (b. 1920)

Like many others whose careers have been spent mainly at universities, John Gray also had a variety of other experiences. He earned a B.S. at Penn State in 1941, the M.F. at Yale University in 1942, and the D.F. at Duke University in 1969. He was employed by the Crossett Lumber Company in Arkansas in 1942 and by a paper company in Wisconsin from 1944 to 1945. In between he served as a fighter communications officer in the U.S. Army Air Corps for two years.

Gray was employed from 1945 to 1963 as an extension forester in the North Carolina Agricultural Extension Service. He advanced to professor and head of the Extension Forestry Department, the largest in the nation with a staff of eleven. He reoriented the program from a timber-marketing service to extension education in forestry and wood industries, employing 4-H forestry awards, demonstration, and leader training.

From 1963 to 1977 Gray was director of the School of Forest Resources and Conservation and professor of forest resources policy at the University of Florida. He transformed a small teaching program with under-funded research and inadequate facilities into a modernized curriculum and oversaw a fivefold increase in enrollment and construction of a new building. The innovative curriculum featured integrated instruction, culminating in a capstone resource management course; this approach subsequently gained favor in other forestry schools. His efforts to broaden the school's offerings to include wildlife, range sciences, and fisheries led to changing the school's name. He strengthened relationships with industry, professional groups, and government agencies to form new research cooperatives working on fertilizers and management practices, patterned after the cooperative forest genetics research program.

In 1977 Gray joined the programs and policy staff of the U.S. Forest Service, and then became the first director of the Pinchot Institute for Conservation from 1978 to 1982. There at Grey Towers, the former home of Gifford Pinchot, he completed a master plan for development of Grey Towers, served as advisor to President Carter's Natural Resources/Environment Task Force, and analyzed the role of the Forest Service in environmental education.

The John Gray Fund for Excellence, established in 1991 in honor of his contributions at the University of Florida, sponsors a distinguished lecture series. An introductory speaker at one of these lectures noted that "John has been an actor all of his life, but in the last several years he has become a thespian and is getting paid for his performances." He appeared in the films *Mars Attacks*, *The Rainmaker*, and as Abraham Lincoln in *John Brown's Body*.

Many professional honors have been bestowed on Gray. The Florida division of the Society of American Foresters gave him the Outstanding Forester Award in 1965 and 1976; he was inducted into the Arkansas SAF Hall of Fame in 1994 and the Florida SAF Hall of Fame in 2003; and he was elected an SAF fellow in 1983. He received the Distinguished Service Award in 1977 from the Florida Forestry Association. The School of Forestry and Environmental Studies at Duke University, named him a distinguished alumnus at its fiftieth anniversary in 1988. Penn State's School of Forestry gave him the Forestry Achievement Award in 1982 at its seventy-fifth anniversary.

John has managed to maintain ties with Penn State while moving to different parts of the country. He was master of ceremonies at the School's seventy-fifth anniversary banquet, and served on the advisory committee of the Goddard Chair in Forestry and Environmental Resources Conservation. He often returned for deer-hunting season as a member of a hunting club near Bear Meadows. In commenting on his experiences at Penn State, John stated, "I felt that the freshman 'How To' year at Mont Alto plus the end of the sophomore year summer camp on the Allegheny Forest at Marienville, coupled with courses on the State College campus, provided a good balance between the 'Why's' and the 'How To's' of professional forestry practice needed by foresters of my generation. . . . I think I can truthfully say that I got my parents' money's worth out of my 1937 to 1941 years as a major in forestry at Penn State!"

Hans M. Gregersen (b. 1938)

Hans Gregersen earned a B.S. in forestry at Penn State in 1961. He also holds an M.S. in forestry from the University of Washington (1963) and a Ph.D. in natural resources economics from the University of Michigan (1970).

His career includes two years with the U.S. Forest Service at the Pacific Northwest Forest and Range Experiment Station, four years in Rome with the Food and Agriculture Organization (FAO) of the United Nations, and thirty years as a professor at the University of Minnesota, where he held a joint appointment in the Department of Forest Resources and the Department of Applied Economics. He took early retirement from the University of Minnesota in 2000, partly to pursue his interests in international development work with the Consultative Group on International Agricultural Research (CGIAR), a consortium of sixteen research centers around the world dedicated to sustainable food security and poverty alleviation in the developing regions. The CGIAR is chaired by the World Bank and has some sixty institutional members who provide the resources to carry out the programs of the centers. Hans currently is a member of the CGIAR's Science Council and chairs its Standing Panel on Impact Assessment.

Hans has worked internationally for more than forty years on such topics as natural resources policy and economics, watershed management economics, and assessment of impacts of agricultural and forestry research. He has worked on project design and appraisal, country-level forestry sector studies, policy design and implementation, and related topics. In addition to the FAO and the World Bank, he has worked with the United Nations Environment Programme, the Carter Center, the Inter-American Development Bank, the U.S. Agency for International Development, the Organization for Economic Cooperation and Development in Paris, and many other international groups. He served for a number of years on the advisory board of the forest economics program of Resources for the Future, and has served on various other boards.

Gregersen has written more than 190 publications, including two textbooks and a number of other book-length publications and training manuals dealing with natural resources economics, policy, and planning, focusing on forestry and watershed management. His multidisciplinary work has helped to shape modern concepts of sustainability and natural resources assessment and management.

Commenting on his experience at Penn State, Hans wrote, "Penn State certainly helped me to form my ideas and beliefs that have guided my work and career since college. Also, in between my junior and senior years, I took off for a year and went to the jungles of Guatemala to help map the Mayan ruins of Tikal. That experience, combined with the broad-based natural resources management education at Penn State, helped to shape my interest in international issues related to natural resources policy and the role of forestry in poverty alleviation. Work with Bill Sopper shaped my interest in, and understanding of, watershed management as an integrated land and water use model that productively could be applied in developing countries to help conservation efforts. The integrated watershed management approach is now used in many countries.

"From a more personal perspective, Penn State provided an ideal environment in which to learn and grow. Hiking the mountains and forests around State College on the weekends gave me a chance to reflect on the values that ended up guiding my life so far. Although big even in the late fifties, the campus was friendly and provided a good learning environment."

Lee M. James (1916–2003)

Lee James received his B.S. from Penn State in 1937, when he was class valedictorian. He earned his master's degree in 1943 and the Ph.D. in 1945 at the University of Michigan, both in forest economics. Born in Brooklyn, New York, he spent much of his youth in Philadelphia close to the Appalachian Trail and the mountains that contributed to his love of forests.

Lee started his forestry career as an instructor at Penn State but soon moved on to forestry research with the Northern Rocky Mountain Forest and Range Experiment Station and the Appalachian Forest Experiment Station. After completing his Ph.D., he became forest economist in charge of resource analysis with the Southern Research Station in New Orleans from 1946 to 1951.

James joined the faculty of the Department of Forestry at Michigan State University in 1951 and served as department chairman from 1966 to 1978. He was the major professor for some hundred master's students and thirty-five doctoral students, many with international ties. He introduced a course in international forestry and taught it for more than thirty years. As a pioneering forest economist, he published more than eighty journal articles and research publications. He received the Alpha Zeta Award for excellence in teaching in 1956 and the John L. Arend Research Recognition Award for outstanding forestry research achievements in 1985. He retired as professor emeritus in 1986.

Throughout his career he was an active consultant to numerous agencies of the U.S. government, including the Public Land Law Review Commission, the Water Resources Policy Commission, the Council on Environmental Quality, the U.S. Senate's Committee on Public Works, the secretary of interior's resources program staff, and the Departments of Commerce and Agriculture. James was also a consultant to the forest industry regarding domestic and international forestry, and was involved in projects in the Dominican Republic, Belize, Brazil, Thailand, and Indonesia. He joined the Society of American Foresters in 1937 and was elected fellow in 1973; he held a variety of leadership positions in the SAF spanning four decades.

His colleagues in Michigan remembered him as being "a proud Penn State alumnus."

H. Arthur Meyer (1908–1955)

H. Arthur Meyer was professor of forestry in the Department of Forestry at Penn State from 1937 to 1955. During World War II he assisted the war effort by working in Costa Rica on chincona production. Quinine derived from chincona bark was needed for the treatment of malaria, which threatened our troops in tropical climates. When he returned to Penn State he brought back many specimens of Costa Rican tree species that could be used to study wood properties.

Professor Meyer received his formal education in his native country of Switzerland at the Federal Institute of Technology, earning the forest engineer degree in 1930 and the doctor of technical science in 1934. He emigrated to America and was employed briefly in research by the U.S. Forest Service, and then by the National Department of Forestry in Mexico. He did not insist on being addressed as Professor Doctor Meyer, as was the custom in Europe. But students and faculty did address him typically as either Professor or Doctor.

Professor Meyer played an important role in "Plenterung" (single-stem selective cutting and uneven-aged management) by evaluating and calculating q or k factors for the "de Liocourt's Curve." Switzerland has been known worldwide for uneven-aged management techniques for more than a century. Through his research Meyer was a pioneer because he was one of the first who adapted the Liocourt curve to manage northeastern hardwood forests.

When Dr. Meyer joined the Department of Forestry he was fluent in German, French, Spanish, and English. Some students wished his language proficiency had been in the reverse order when he lectured, and when his Germanic-script writing continued past the edge of the blackboard. When he spoke of the gross growth of the volume, it sounded like "gross gross of zee wolume." In teaching mensuration and forest management he insisted on punctuality, accuracy, and proper interpretation of data. Dismayed by the lack of statistical background of students and some faculty, Meyer tried to remedy the situation by haranguing classes, giving seminars, and engaging colleagues in the Mathematics Department.

Meyer improved the scientific rigor of forestry instruction and research. His studies of forest inventory, growth determination, and regulation of harvests were the basis for research publications and two textbooks used by many schools. *Forest Management*, co-written with his faculty colleague Bartoo and industrial foresters A. B. Recknagel and Donald Stevenson, appeared in 1952, and *Forest Mensuration* was published in 1953. He also worked with other faculty members on management plans for the university woodlands and Stone Valley Experimental Forest.

Arthur was coach of the Penn State fencing team for some years, and also was an ardent skier. He even attempted to play chess while driving an automobile. At least once he nearly scared his passenger-opponent to death.

Professor Meyer deserves credit for inspiring and promoting the first thorough inventory of some 2 million acres of Pennsylvania state forests, the construction of volume tables, and the writing of management plans for each of the twenty forest districts. This tremendous project was carried out by Joseph E. Ibberson, Meyer's former student and part-time employee. While employed by the Pennsylvania Department of Forests and Waters, Ibberson used political connections to secure support for the project. Meyer recognized Ibberson's abilities and political relationships, and actively encouraged him to use his talents to prepare management plans for the state forests. Thus silvicultural and forest management practices were greatly improved, following excessive logging during World War II.

Meyer was at his peak of intellectual productivity when he suddenly succumbed to a heart attack in 1955. Students and faculty alike mourned this great loss of intellectual talent and a fine friend. A *Picea abies* tree was planted in his memory south of Ferguson Building.

Wayne K. "Murph" Murphey (b. 1927)

Murph grew up in Folcroft, a small suburb of Philadelphia near the Tinicum Swamp. After graduating from Ridley Park High School, he served in the U.S. Navy Air Corps from 1945 to 1948. At Penn State he earned a B.S. degree in forestry in 1952 and an M.S. in 1953. He was in residence at the University of Michigan from 1959 to 1960, during which time he taught several courses in wood technology, and he received a Ph.D. in 1961.

Murphey's professional career started in 1953 as an engineer in the technical department laboratory of the Koppers Company wood-preserving division in Orrville, Ohio. In 1955 he became a researcher in forest products at the Ohio Agricultural Experiment Station. After completing his residence requirements at Michigan, he came to Penn State in 1960 as an assistant professor and over the years advanced to professor. In 1978 he moved to College Station, Texas, to head the Department of Forest Science at Texas A&M University. Four years later he moved to Washington, D.C., as principal wood technologist in the USDA Cooperative State Research Service. After retiring in 1998 he volunteered as a member of the Anne Arundel County Forestry Commission.

An active researcher and teacher throughout his career, Murphey published sixty-three refereed papers dealing with various aspects of wood technology, and also co-wrote a book. He taught many of the courses that deal with uses of wood as a renewable material, worked with graduate students, and supported extension activities. At Texas A&M he taught forest policy, wood technology, and introduction to forestry. He believed that the introductory course should be taught by a "grey-haired professor," and he was the only one in the department who fit that description. After retiring he taught a course for one semester at West Virginia University, commuting from Annapolis every week; it snowed fourteen of the sixteen weekends during his commute.

As a "fed" in Washington Murphey entered the world of academic program reviews and research grants and contracts. He led teams that reviewed the McIntire-Stennis research and extension activities and accomplishments in many of the forestry and wood technology programs at educational institutions, and several of the Hatch-funded agricultural engineering programs. He was responsible for grants in the areas of forestry, natural resources, and alternative energy to the 1890 institutions.

Murphey also worked with programs dealing with alternative energy through the Agency for International Development, U.S. State Department, and the governments of the Philippines and Morocco. In the Dominican Republic he reviewed forest management plans for the island nation. In addition, he aided the state of Rio Grande De Sol in Brazil in establishing a program of research and extension, and lectured in the Republic of South Africa on American hardwoods as replacements for woods extracted from rain forests. He served in the courts of eleven states as an expert witness in litigation concerning wood.

Murphey was active in the Forest Products Society and the Society of Wood Science. He also belonged to the Society of American Foresters, American Forests, Sigma Xi, Xi Sigma Pi, and Alpha Lamda Chi.

Larry W. Tombaugh (b. 1939)

Larry Tombaugh earned his B.S. in forestry at Penn State (1960), his M.S. degree at Colorado State (1962), and his Ph.D. in resource economics at the University of Michigan (1969). Tombaugh had a prestigious career in academia, culminating in his appointment as dean of the College of Natural Resources at North Carolina State University from 1989 to 2001. Before that he was chairman and professor in the Department of Forestry at Michigan State University from 1978 to 1989. He held several senior executive positions at the National Science Foundation from 1971 to 1978. During that period he served on various White House task forces dealing with science policy issues. When he left the agency, he was deputy assistant director for research applications. Prior to being in Washington, D.C., he was an economist with the Southeastern and the North Central Research Stations of the U.S. Forest Service. He began his career in 1960 as a junior forester on the Gifford Pinchot National Forest in Washington.

Tombaugh is a fellow of the American Association for the Advancement of Science and a fellow of the Society of American Foresters. He was awarded the silver medal for meritorious achievement by the National Science Foundation, Outstanding Alumnus Award by the Penn State College of Agricultural Sciences, the Professional Achievement Award by Colorado State University, and the Distinguished Service Award by the North Carolina Forestry Association. Over his career he served as an official delegate to the Tenth World Forestry Congress in Paris, as the U.S. representative to the International Council of the International Union of Forestry Research Organizations, and as president of the National Association of Professional Forestry Schools and Colleges. Tombaugh served as an advisor to industries, universities, and governments in South America, Central America, Africa, Asia, and Europe.

Upon retirement from academic life, Tombaugh established Sylvan Advisory Services and currently serves as its president. He is president-elect of the North Carolina Forestry Association and chairman of the board of the Forest History Society. Much of his time is spent as a volunteer guardian *ad litem*. In this capacity, he advocates in the court system for children who have been removed from their homes for abuse or neglect. He is also an incurable fly fisherman.

Larry looks upon his freshman year at Mont Alto, as one of the best of his life. The studies and the weekends spent hiking in the woods convinced him that forestry was the right career for him. He believes that Penn State and the School of Forest Resources provided him with an education in the best sense of the word. "It gave me technical tools needed for my career and, even more importantly, it provided a milieu that enabled me to build important social skills. Indeed, at times I focused more on the socialization process than on my studies. But I particularly cherish the sense of self-confidence that the intellectual and social environment at Penn State nurtured and that has proven so valuable to me over the years."

Laurence C. "Larry" Walker (1924–1999)

Although Larry grew up in the inner city of Washington, D.C., his Boy Scout activities created in him an intense love of the forest. He enrolled at Mont Alto in 1942 and completed the freshman year in 1943 at State College because the Mont Alto campus had been closed for the duration of World War II. He served with the U.S. Army during World War II in the European theater, seeing action in France and the Black Forest and Bavarian forests of Germany. After completing his B.S. at Penn State in 1948, Larry went to Yale for his M.F. degree (1949), and to the New York State College of Forestry at Syracuse for the Ph.D. (1953).

Larry was employed by the U.S. Forest Service from 1948 to 1954 in Texas and Alabama, during intervals bracketing his graduate studies. He was a faculty member at the University of Georgia from 1954 to 1963, advancing to associate professor. Then he joined the faculty of Stephen F. Austin State University, serving as forestry dean from 1963 to 1976. He worked energetically and successfully to improve the quality and reputation of the Forestry Department. Within five years enrollments increased fourfold, the faculty grew from six to fifteen, and the department became the School of Forestry and gained accreditation by the Society of American Foresters. Larry continued as Lacy Hunt Professor until he retired with emeritus status in 1988, though he continued to teach courses and write books.

For the 1986 reunion at Mont Alto, Larry wrote of colorful memories, including blowing up a farmer's outhouse and rebuilding it, collecting skunks, and placing limburger cheese on a dorm radiator. Despite these antics, or maybe because of them, he became a Presbyterian minister along the way. After stepping down as dean in 1976, he provided ministerial services to three congregations that had lost their preachers. At the Mont Alto reunion, Larry also inspired participants with a favorite saying, "*Excelsior:* The higher good."

Walker was a prolific writer, producing more than 250 scientific and popular articles, books, and book reviews about many aspects of forestry. He is the author of *Ecology and Our Forests* (1973), *Trees: An Introduction to Trees and Forest Ecology for the Amateur Naturalist* (1984), *Farming the Small Forest: A Guide for the Landowner* (1988), *The Southern Forest: A Chronicle* (1991), *Excelsior: Memoir of a Forester* (1995), *Forests: A Naturalist's Guide to Woodland Trees* (1997), *The North American Forests: Geography, Ecology, and Silviculture* (1998), and co-wrote *The Southern Forest: Geography, Ecology, and Silviculture* (1999).

Walker received the Distinguished Service Award from the Texas Society of American Foresters in 1968; in 1999 this award was renamed the Laurence C. Walker Distinguished Service Award. He was elected a fellow of the Society of American Foresters in 1971. For many years he was active in SAF and the Texas Forestry Association.

Harry V. Wiant Jr. (b. 1932)

Harry Wiant was selected as the first occupant of the newly endowed Joseph E. Ibberson Chair in Forest Resources Management in 2002. Since coming to Penn State he has taught courses in consulting forestry, forest policy, and forest measurements. Wiant and Professor John Brooks at West Virginia University have written a book titled *Introduction to Consulting Forestry*, a first on this topic. Wiant has also continued research in forest inventory techniques, taught short courses for foresters on that topic, and organized the annual Ibberson Forum for forest landowners and foresters. Harry also served as advisor to the Penn State student chapter of the Society of American Foresters; during that time the chapter was recognized as the Most Outstanding Student Chapter in 2002–3, winning second place for the same award the next year, and placed second for best website for two years. He has been active in the Pennsylvania Forestry Association, serving as vice president in 2005–6.

Wiant had a long and distinguished career of teaching and leadership in the forestry profession before coming to Penn State. For twenty-four years he had been a professor of forestry at West Virginia University, where he received a B.S.F. degree in 1954. He has an M.F. degree (1959) from the University of Georgia, and a Ph.D. (1963) from Yale University. He served in the U.S. Army from 1954 to 1956. He also was employed as a faculty member at Humboldt State University (1961–65) and at Stephen F. Austin University (1965–72). He has published more than two hundred professional articles and two books dealing mainly with forest inventory and silviculture.

Practical experience has been very important to him. Wiant is a registered forester in West Virginia and has served on the West Virginia State Board of Registration for Foresters. Besides his years of experience in the redwood region, the piney woods of Texas, and Appalachian hardwoods, Harry also is familiar with the tropical forests of Honduras and the eucalypts of Australia. He has served as a consultant in silviculture, forest mensuration, software development, and applied statistics.

Wiant was the elected vice president of the Society of American Foresters in 1996 and president in 1997; he had served as chair of the Allegheny section of SAF in 1990. In those years timber interests were under assault by those who exploited the northern spotted owl and politically correct terms such as "ecosystem management" in attempting to return forests to some presettlement condition. In his election campaign he posed the question, "Should we do the same for agricultural land so we can all starve?" and continued, "I truly fear for the future of the profession and SAF. A vote for me is a call to battle." During his presidency he was a strong proponent of science-based forest management.

Previously Wiant held many positions of professional leadership, starting in his student days. He was an officer in Sigma Xi at West Virginia and also in the Stephen F. Austin Club and the Yale Forestry Club. He served on various Society of American Foresters committees, as chair of the SAF Allegheny Society, and as editor of the *Northern Journal of Applied Forestry*. He is listed in many biographical publications, including *Who's Who in American Education, American Men of Science, Outstanding Educators of America*, and *International Directory of Distinguished Leadership*.

Entrepreneurial Mavericks

Some alumni and faculty found their way into rewarding careers in fields quite different from those for which they had prepared. Their reasons for switching are best known to them, and probably are as varied as the paths they followed. In some cases their interests may have evolved, or employment possibilities in their preferred field may have been limited when they graduated. Jobs related to natural resources have been cyclical, so in down periods graduates have had to be resourceful. Their broad forestry education certainly enabled them to seize opportunities that they had the vision to recognize.

Max Dercum (b. 1912)

Skiing has always been imperative to Max Dercum, even while he was on the Penn State forestry faculty from 1935 to 1942. He came to Penn State after graduating in 1934 with a forestry degree from Cornell University. In 1936 Professor John Ferguson suggested that Max attend the third conference on outdoor recreation in Massachusetts, which led to his heightened interest in the development of outdoor winter recreation. Max started the Penn State ski club in the days when wooden skis were seven feet long, poles were bamboo, ski boots were laced like hiking boots, and the bear-trap bindings had no safety releases. His Penn State ski team was the only official varsity ski team in Pennsylvania, and he saw to it that they had local skiing facilities. He organized forestry students to lay out ski trails and clear trees on Bald Top Mountain. The site was made available by Colonel Boal of Boalsburg, northwest of today's Tussey Mountain ski resort. Max and his students built ski trails and slalom glades, a rope tow, a thirty-meter ski jump, six miles of cross-country trails, and two Adirondack lean-to shelters.

In 1937 and 1938 Max and his wife, Edna, a 1936 Penn State graduate in education, engaged in recreational and competitive skiing in California and Oregon. Edna was in charge of the first Pennsylvania ski race state championships held near Boalsburg in 1940 and again in 1941. Their travels and dedication to skiing led to a new career. In 1942 Max decided to move out west with his wife and baby, having secured employment with the U.S. Forest Service in Colorado. He became involved in logging, mining, ranching, and the ski world of Colorado. But mostly he had the vision to realize that a renaissance in recreational skiing was under way.

Max and Edna worked with ski area developers and investors to found the Arapahoe Basin Ski Area, which opened in December 1946. Max recalled "That first year, I was building during the day, cutting logs, and working in the Dillon Garage overnight pumping gas and changing tires, and sleeping on a cot." About twelve hundred people skied the mountain in the first winter, compared to some 250,000 who visited the resort in 2004.

Arapahoe was so successful by the 1950s that Max started developing Keystone Mountain to the south. In the next years he explored the mountain to envision ski trails, and struggled to secure permits and funding. Max and other investors formed Keystone International, Inc., in 1969 and opened the Keystone Resort in 1970. Their proposal to the U.S. Forest

Service stated their intention to develop Keystone Mountain as a world-class ski area. Thirty years later it was attracting more than a million visitors a year from around the world.

Edna Strand Dercum recounted their adventures in her book, *It's Easy, Edna, It's Downhill All the Way*. For years they lived in the mountains above Keystone at Ski Tip Lodge, an 1870s stagecoach stop they had renovated after opening Arapahoe. They were still skiing into their nineties, and enjoying visits with their two children, grandchildren, and great-grandchildren.

Max was the first inductee into the National Standard Race (NASTAR) Hall of Fame of Skiers in 1983. Edna won seventy-five gold medals as a competitive racer between 1938 and 1989. They are the only Penn Staters in the NASTAR Hall of Fame. Both Max and Edna are honored members of the Colorado Ski Hall of Fame. They were honored at Keystone Resort's founders·day celebration in 2004, and immortalized there by the naming of Dercum Mountain.

Albert M. Kligman (b. 1916)

Albert Kligman began his educational career at Penn State Mont Alto, where he enrolled in the forestry program but did not graduate in forestry. He received a bachelor's degree in botany from Penn State in 1939. While a Penn State student, Albert was an accomplished varsity gymnast and a member of Phi Beta Kappa. He earned a Ph.D. in botany in 1942 and a doctor of medicine degree in 1947, both from the University of Pennsylvania. Dr. Kligman is professor emeritus of dermatology at the University of Pennsylvania's School of Medicine.

Commenting on his admission to Mont Alto, Kligman stated, "my parents were immigrants from Russia and . . . I could never have been admitted to Yale, Harvard or Penn. . . . Admission to these schools was based on your wealth and your family occupation. There were also quotas for Jewish students. Penn State had none of these restrictions. . . . Penn State was looking for students with talent and intelligence; they tapped into the gene pool and were way ahead in diversity and plurality. This policy transformed Penn State from an agricultural school to a top university. . . . Mont Alto put me on the track to a successful career that opened up a world totally unknown to my family."

Albert and Lorraine Kligman have helped unlock many of the mysteries of skin physiology and aging, including the development of Retin A, an "anti-wrinkle" cream widely used for acne and photo-aged skin. The recipients of numerous professional awards and citations, they are both widely known as eminent scholars and articulate spokespersons for the scientific process. He was a professor of dermatology at the University of Pennsylvania School of Medicine for some fifty years. Dr. Kligman wrote more than three hundred medical papers and is the author of numerous books. He is proud of his many students who have become distinguished leaders in dermatology in countries all over the world. "Having such an extended family is far more rewarding than getting rich, famous or powerful."

In his personal life Kligman sought adventure, excitement, and joy in diverse activities. Once, while piloting a private plane down the Hudson River in a fog, he flew under the George Washington Bridge and missed a collision by two to three feet, completely forgetting such obstacles. He pondered, "Is there a God?" Some time later, as a balloonist, he achieved local notoriety by landing in a tall tree in Mount Holly, New Jersey, and was rescued by the local fire department. He concluded then, "I guess there is a God."

"The Kligmans' own lives demonstrate the highest levels of achievement in scholarship, research and education, with major discoveries and accomplishments impacting science, gerontology and medical care," according to Penn State University president Graham Spanier. The Philadelphia couple has established an endowment valued at $2 million to create the Albert M. Kligman Graduate Fellowship. In 2004 Dr. Kligman was honored with the Penn State Mont Alto Centennial Fellows Award.

Charles E. Morrison (1927–2004)

Morrison began a thirty-three-year career with the U.S Geological Survey a year after receiving his forestry degree in 1951. Before that he had enlisted in the U.S. Navy and spent two years in the Pacific on a wooden minesweeper.

In the early part of his Geological Survey career Morrison made topographic maps from field surveys in many of the states east of the Mississippi River. His assignments were in the North during the summer and in the South in winter. Later he worked in the research office in McLean, Virginia, and then in the USGS branch of international activities, which led to assignments in Antarctica, Saudi Arabia, and Yemen.

He spent four summers in Antarctica, living in tents and sleeping bags on the icecap. His work was in Marie Byrd Land, Ellsworth Land, and the McMurdo Dry Valleys. On one occasion he survived a helicopter crash. He also took astronomic observations before the advent of the global positioning system, to determine movements of the ten-thousand-foot-thick ice at the South Pole. The National Science Foundation needed this information for planning a South Pole scientific station.

In Saudi Arabia Morrison conducted surveys funded by the Saudi kingdom to find mineral resources in the eastern part of the country. In Yemen he worked on an AID project for providing much-needed water resources to the nation.

After retirement in 1984, Morrison became a volunteer guide at the Geological Survey's headquarters in Reston, Virginia. He took school groups and other visitors on tours of the building and explained the agency's earth science mission. He also was a docent at the National Air and Space Museum, and a volunteer for Meals on Wheels.

He was a member of various polar organizations, including the Antarctican Society and the Old Antarctic Explorers Association. The U.S. Board of Geographic Names named Morrison Bluff in Marie Byrd Land in his honor. He also was an active member of the USGS Topographic Retirees.

Louis W. Schatz (1912–2001)

After receiving a B.S. in forestry (1934) and a dual degree in business administration at Penn State, Louis Schatz earned a master's degree from the University of California (1939) at Berkeley and conducted doctoral studies at the University of Michigan. He was awarded an honorary doctoral degree in science from Humboldt State University. He had worked as a land appraiser for the U.S. Forest Service in Texas, as a forester in Minnesota, and as an executive assistant with the West Fork Timber Company in Washington before founding a company that made him wealthy. Looking back, Schatz wrote, "I am sincerely grateful for the education in studies and lifestyle I obtained in the School of Forest Resources. Without this start I never would have achieved the many successes in my life."

Louis Schatz was the owner and president of General Plastics Manufacturing Company, Tacoma, Washington. He founded the company in 1941 with $400 from the sale of his car. His inventive mind found various ways of applying knowledge he had gained in Michigan while using plastics to weld wood particles. During the early 1940s and into the early 1950s, General Plastics made preservative coatings for wood and other organic materials, later gradually expanding into fabricating phenolic-resin-impregnated composites for aircraft and commercial uses. The demand for light, strong, versatile plastics was growing, and General Plastics developed many innovative products.

The company grew into fabricating transparent acrylics (Plexiglas) for aircraft components and for consumer products, such as backyard greenhouses and commercial signage. Schatz also sought to take advantage of new polymer technologies created during World War II. One of the most useful and innovative materials to come out of the war was a family of plastics called polyurethanes. Ongoing research and development programs kept General Plastics ahead of market needs. The company experienced steadily growing demand for its products in the aerospace, defense, nuclear, construction, and marine industries. The company was cited by industry and governmental agencies for its contributions to the NASA space shuttle and navy submarine programs.

His gift of $5.6 million in 1998 created the Schatz Center for Tree Molecular Genetics in the School of Forest Resources. This endowment supports facilities, research, and education of students and faculty at Penn State and Mont Alto. During the 1980s he had given gifts to the School to support professional travel by students and faculty. He received the Achievement Award from the School of Forest Resources in 1982 during its seventy-fifth anniversary celebration. When he visited Penn State for three days in 1985 as a College of Agriculture alumni fellow he stated, "For a superlative general education, I could not recommend anything more valuable than a forestry education." In 2004 he was named an alumni centennial fellow by Penn State Mont Alto.

John T. Steimer (b. 1924)

John T. Steimer earned the B.S. degree in forestry at Penn State in 1949. He was employed for five years as a forester for the Pennsylvania Department of Highways, and on weekends worked as a forestry consultant. In 1955 he decided to help the family business, the Penn Glenn Oil Company, after his father-in-law died. He thought he would go back to forestry, but business was so successful that he founded a sister company, Industrial Terminal Systems, that packaged petroleum products and chemicals. By the time he retired as president in 1990, the number of employees had risen from twenty to 120, and he passed the presidency on to his son.

Although Steimer was so busy in those days that he had to hire a forester to manage his own land, he never lost his passion for the woods and streams, or for his alma mater. So he and his wife created the John and Nancy Steimer Scholarship Fund in the School of Forest Resources, and also the Nancy and John Steimer Professorship in Agricultural Sciences in

1989. The first Steimer Professor was Eva Pell, who later became dean of the graduate school; and the second was Marc Abrams, professor of forest ecology and physiology. The Steimers also supported the Sarni Tennis Facility, featuring a center court named for them, and the Bryce Jordan Center. Subsequently they gave more than $1.1 million to the School of Forest Resources for planning and constructing its new building.

Penn State named John Steimer a distinguished alumnus in 1992, the highest honor it can bestow on its graduates. He has served on fund-raising committees of the College of Agricultural Sciences and of the university. John is a life member of the Penn State Alumni Association and belongs to the President's Club, the Nittany Lion Club, the Mount Nittany Society, and the Laurel Society.

Steimer says as a student he had no goals to save the world or even to save every tree. "Still, the moment I got involved in forestry, I saw how important it was to manage our timber lands. Before I retired, I traveled all over the world and when I came back home, I was always impressed with the wealth of natural resources our state has to offer. Mother Nature did a good job in Pennsylvania—but we need to help her keep up the good work."

PROFESSIONAL IMPACTS OF THE SCHOOL OF FOREST RESOURCES

Looking back over the past hundred years of the School of Forest Resources, what can be said about how the School has influenced its several professional interests in Pennsylvania and in the nation? That is a straightforward question, but getting to the somewhat elusive answer is complicated. For it is the knowledge and applications of knowledge by people, rather than the School itself, that have made professional impacts. Accordingly, one can gain insight by examining the trail of knowledge, starting from the educational institution, where it is organized by the faculty, some of it created by their research but most derived from other sources, and transmitted to students in classes and more widely through publications and outreach. Alumni and professional colleagues then apply that knowledge through their employers and the projects they undertake. The success of alumni, faculty, and colleagues in applying their knowledge is subject to their own ingenuity and to economic conditions, biological realities, political considerations, and societal attitudes—all dynamic and changing. So when their work and careers are successful, how much of the credit should be attributed to their educational institution?

Clearly, quantified conclusions about impacts of the School of Forest Resources cannot be easily ascertained. But there is much evidence in previous chapters that the School has indeed been influential, in some cases quite significantly. Penn State has affected educational practices and programs, managerial practices, and forest resources, directly or indirectly, through applications of the teaching, research, and outreach of faculty and students, and by accomplishments of alumni that were enabled by their forestry education.

The three principal ways in which Penn State has influenced advances in forestry are: (1) through the effects of teaching, research, and outreach on educational programs and on professional organizations; (2) through impacts on forestry practices and accomplishments of industries, consultants, governmental agencies, and private owners of forestlands; and (3) through influences on the forest resources themselves, including vegetation, water, wildlife, and wood products.

Educational Programs

The educational influence of Penn State's Department of Forestry, expressed within the college and also at other institutions, was evident practically from its beginnings. John Ferguson's participation in the first national conference on forestry education in 1909 undoubtedly contributed to the ensuing report by Graves et al. (1912, cited in Dana and Johnson 1963, 45–46). Presumably Ferguson's ideas influenced the conclusions of the Graves report, for John Ferguson was well aware of differences in the curricula at some twenty other institutions, and he held strong convictions about the best way to educate forestry students. A principal conclusion of that report was that "Teaching in forest schools should first of all aim to stimulate the capacity for logical thinking and train and discipline the analytical faculties rather than merely test the assimilative capacity and memory of students. . . . Full weight must be given to the practical field work, but such work must serve a definite purpose; it is not an end in itself. . . . Graduates will be judged by what they know and by their trained capacity to apply their knowledge."

At the 1991 summit on forestry education, it was reiterated that curricula should "emphasize critical thinking and problem-solving skills." Was this an echo from the past, or simply the recognition of an enduring requisite in the forestry profession that also should be important for all college students?

The committee's 1912 report indicated that practical training in matters such as tree felling and horseback riding should be supplemental to the regular curriculum, not part of it. At that time the curricula at Mont Alto and at Penn State differed in the amount of emphasis given to conceptual and analytical thinking versus practical training, though both thinking and training received substantial attention in each program. And practical training has remained an important constituent since then, here and also at other institutions, but of course the subject matter has been modernized with the times.

School of Forest Resources faculty and administrators have met with their counterparts frequently at national professional meetings, and certainly they have spoken about academic matters in their discussions, particularly at meetings devoted to education. For more than fifty years Penn State's curricula included some forestry courses and practical experience in the first two years, so that students would better appreciate the relationship with basic courses when they took them. This was not typical in most other states, where students studied basic sciences and liberal arts courses before taking technical subjects in the last two or three years. It would be surprising if this philosophical difference had not come up in the intermural conversations. Evidence of interest in Penn State's ideas was particularly apparent at the national meetings in the 1990s, when our proposed curriculum in natural resources management was discussed.

But local circumstances and attitudes were probably the driving forces everywhere in most curricular matters, along with professional accreditation requirements. This certainly was true of our substantial revision of the Penn State curricula in 1963, when technical courses were moved to the junior and senior years, mainly to accommodate students who wanted to start at any of the Commonwealth Campuses of the university. If it is true that local considerations and professional accreditation guidelines generally have predominated, then Penn State's influence on the forestry curricula of other institutions probably has been modest, expressed mainly through stimulating ideas about curricula, courses, and teaching methods.

At the graduate level, advanced degrees and course offerings have kept pace with national professional developments, and the number of doctoral graduates has increased in the past two decades. Two recently established programs are forward looking in the context of contemporary natural resource management education. The interdisciplinary option in watershed

stewardship established in 1998 offered graduate students in forest resources, wildlife and fisheries science, and landscape architecture experience in watershed management with the depth of real-world community
engagement and the attendant benefits to practical applied learning. A
joint degree program with the Dickinson School of Law, approved in
2003, enables students to receive a law degree together with a graduate
degree in forest science or wildlife and fisheries science.

Extension and outreach activities of the faculty also have been under
way since the School's founding, even before such work was formally organized. Through educational meetings and technical advice, faculty and
colleagues in the counties have helped forest landowners to improve their
management practices and wood-using industries to increase their productivity and quality of products. The research and outreach on private woodland management has had some impact at the state and national levels,
and yet in Pennsylvania it has been very difficult to reach most of the half-
million owners of private forestlands. Extension foresters played a key role
in the founding and development of the Christmas tree industry and tree
nurseries in Pennsylvania. More recently they have made significant contributions to residential water supplies, municipal wastewater usage, management of deer herds, and municipal shade tree programs. The improved
academic planning process has brought about better focus on the more
important issues, and greater collaboration and coordination with partner
groups.

The biographies of our alumni include examples of especially significant contributions to academic institutions and professional organizations.
Many of them have displayed leadership both at universities and in professional organizations, exemplified by the biographies of "Pennsylvania's Pioneers," plus those of alumni and faculty.

When these people were students, who could have imagined how influential they and others like them would become in their careers, nationally and internationally? They certainly made good use of their education
in forestry and their innate talents! They improved educational programs
at their various institutions, and by extending their knowledge to organizations in other states and nations they have multiplied the benefits derived
from forests for their owners and the good of mankind.

Government Agencies, Industries, Consultants, and Communities

Initially almost all of the Mont Alto Academy graduates became managers
of Pennsylvania's Forest Reserves, protecting them against fire and initiat-

ing management practices. They planted seedlings, built and maintained roads and trails, marked boundaries, inventoried trees and marked them for harvest, and accommodated the interests of hikers, campers, hunters, fishermen, and others who used forests for a wide variety of purposes. These foresters deserve credit for developing an exemplary system of state forests of some 2 million acres, as do the chief executives of the Bureau of Forestry. Most of Pennsylvania's state foresters, and also many of the district foresters who implemented policies and programs, have been graduates of Mont Alto or Penn State.

In the first few decades Penn State's graduates found employment mainly with state and federal forestry agencies and wood-using companies; many of them advanced to state foresters, company executives, or other positions of prominence. In more recent times alumni have availed themselves of more diverse opportunities, including a greater array of agencies and companies, specialized university positions, and consulting services. Throughout the nation's forests they have practiced forestry and developed forest policies; conducted research on forests, wood products, wildlife, water, and outdoor recreation; and advised industrial and private forest landowners. Along with their colleagues educated elsewhere, they have increased the acreage of forests in the United States and made them more productive. Through improved and new manufacturing methods, they have elevated the quality and utility of wood products, and facilitated global marketing. Greater knowledge has been developed through research for other uses of forests and parks—water, wildlife, recreation, and urban landscapes—so that these benefits can be managed more effectively. These accomplishments of Penn State alumni have been realized mainly in Pennsylvania, where 53 percent of the School's graduates currently reside. Yet they extend also to every state of the nation and to more than twenty-five nations.

Specific contributions of our alumni and faculty are represented by numerous biographical examples of those whose careers have benefited state forestry and parks agencies, federal agencies, clients of forestry consultants, wood-using companies, wildlife organizations, and the water supplies and landscape trees of communities.

Hundreds of our alumni have been gainfully employed in managing Pennsylvania's state forests and state parks, and many more in the natural resource agencies of other states. The millions of people who camp, hike, boat, fish, ski, or engage in other forms of recreation in state parks are the beneficiaries of the professional work of these men and others like them.

A large proportion of our alumni have pursued careers with the U.S. Forest Service or other federal agencies responsible for managing forested lands and related research. Federal employees, through their managerial duties and research, have made significant contributions to the conservation, management, and products of the nation's forests.

Opportunities for forestry consultants have grown dramatically in Pennsylvania in the past fifty years, as cutover forests matured in size and value. Consultants form a vital link between forest owners and the wood industries and help to educate landowners about defining their multiple goals, managing their resources, and harvesting timber when the time is right. Whatever the individual goals of forest owners, consultants can help in making their forests sustainable, more profitable, and more enjoyable.

Some forestry graduates found employment in the forest industries years before it was possible to major in a wood utilization curriculum. That was the case with three forestry graduates who headed straight to the Pacific Northwest, all three of whom gained strong professional reputations. Meanwhile, back in Pennsylvania, eleven Penn State foresters worked to make the Glatfelter Pulp Wood Company an exemplary success in promoting good forestry and industrial operations, starting in 1935. Research on wood and wood products, manufacturing processes, and marketing methods has assisted wood industries in becoming more competitive and profitable. Throughout the nation and especially in Pennsylvania, graduates and faculty of the School have contributed in many ways to the success of forest industries, the sustainability of their forests, the quality of their products, and employment opportunities for many people.

Although wildlife has always interested forestry students, possibilities for majoring in this subject and for professional employment more than fifty years ago were quite limited. But two of our alumni do go back that far, both of whom registered significant achievements in western North America. Especially during the 1960s and 1970s faculty and alumni helped to formulate national policies about the environment, endangered species, pollution, and pesticides. In Pennsylvania and other states they influenced public opinion, wildlife management regulations, and restoration of threatened species. Even nationally, they have contributed significantly to educating people about wildlife, developing knowledge about wildlife biology, and implementing measures for protection and management.

The role of Penn Staters in assuring that communities have good supplies of pure water, effective sanitary systems, and protection against flooding has become increasingly important in the last few decades. Research in watershed management, recycling of municipal wastewater, development of the "living filter" concept, and reclaiming lands disturbed by mining and pollution has addressed serious environmental problems in Pennsylvania. Results have also helped to develop national analytical and monitoring systems and environmental legislation. Alumni have used their knowledge of hydrology and ecology to reduce flooding of streams and rivers, and to manage the nation's water resources. Pure water supplies flowing from forested watersheds are very important to communities, and so are the manifold benefits of landscape trees.

Planting and tending of trees in communities in communities has been going on for centuries, but the discipline of urban forestry began emerging just forty years ago, and became an important responsibility of the Forest Service just fifteen years ago. Alumni who pursued careers in urban forestry and arboriculture helped tree expert companies to improve scientific tree care services and utility companies to improve tree-pruning practices that assure reliable electrical services. Faculty and alumni pioneered the right tree–right place concept of planting low-growing trees under wires, thus removing unsightly street trees from communities. They have been involved in designing and installing many prestigious landscape architecture projects and in creating tree varieties that have genetically improved resistance to diseases and urban stresses. Scientists and professional practitioners such as these have made our communities safer, more attractive, and more prosperous places to live.

Forest Resources

Our forests and parks themselves have benefited from knowledge applied by the School's alumni and faculty. The 17 million acres of forests in the Commonwealth, covering nearly 60 percent of the land area, now furnish scenic beauty, protect vast watersheds and twenty-five thousand miles of waterways, provide a variety of wildlife habitats, supply raw materials for a dynamic wood products industry with a hundred thousand employees, and sustain a nature-based recreation and tourism industry. A century ago, in stark contrast, the cutover forests were in a disastrous state. They provided few benefits and collectively represented an economic liability and a natural tragedy. Their recovery was due to the natural resilience of eastern temperate forests, supplemented by forest management measures applied to much of the area. Forest management started with protection against fire and soil erosion and progressed to the application of scientific knowledge and methods, not only to forests but to industrial processes and the natural resources that affect communities and their residents.

The School of Forest Resources served as more than a catalyst in enhancing the value of natural resources. The School's faculty, staff, and students have generated scientific and practical knowledge that its alumni and clientele groups have used in a broad array of applications. They have helped to improve the many benefits of forests, including the beauty of landscapes, timber productivity, the supply of pure water, the habitats of wildlife, restoration of blighted and polluted landscapes, and opportunities for many kinds of recreation. Timber harvests in the northeastern United States generate $20 billion annually, employ more than half a million people, and provide raw materials for a $117 billion wood products industry. Trying to place a precise value on the School's impact may be futile. Yet, clearly, its educational input has been vital.

15

LOOKING AHEAD: STRATEGIC PLAN
FOR THE FUTURE

Planning for the future has become more systematic and comprehensive than it was even in the recent past. The School of Forest Resources began revising and updating its strategic plan in late 2004, as the College of Agricultural Sciences went to work on its plan for 2005–8. The college's plan was organized for the first time around three dominant and interrelated systems: the food and fiber system, the ecosystem, and the socioeconomic system. The School's strategic plan considers how its teaching, research, and extension/outreach activities can help to achieve the faculty's aspirations for the future; it addresses issues within all three of the systems identified in the college's plan.

The School's advisory board and the alumni group were consulted, and both provided sound advice. The resulting plan is the culmination of this effort. The faculty of the School of Forest Resources approved the plan in 2005. The following summary gives an overview of the rather lengthy plan, which does contain some interesting details.

The mission of our School is

to provide educational opportunities and science-based information and knowledge to protect, manage, and use natural resources for sustained benefits. This is accomplished through education, research, and service programs in forestry, wildlife and fisheries, water, wood products, and related areas.

Our vision for the future is in concert with our mission.

We are committed to enhancing the value and condition of forest resources and ecosystems. Because of that commitment, we seek to be the preferred source in the state and region for objective, high-quality, and up-to-date information about the use, management, and conservation of these forest resources and ecosystems. Our graduates will be recognized nationally and regionally for their competence, their ability to integrate information and think critically, and their skill in using the latest science and technology applicable to their fields. Through our research, we will produce and disseminate high-quality and authoritative information that helps decision makers cope with complex ecological, engineering, business, and societal issues.

We will accomplish this vision by creating an environment that assures the individual success of each School member—faculty, staff, and student—and that encourages sharing our individual capabilities through a collaborative, multidisciplinary approach to education, research, and service.

We will address our mission through the following goals:

1. We will be a premier provider of quality natural resources professionals at all degree levels for academia, nongovernmental organizations, governments, industries, and businesses.
2. We will discover and disseminate authoritative scientific, technical, and professional information about environmental and natural resources issues confronting the state, the region, and the world.
3. We will be the preferred regional source for objective, timely, and comprehensive information and knowledge to support professionals, leaders, and citizens in their understanding, decisions, and practices concerning forestry, wildlife, fisheries, water, and wood products.
4. We will create a working environment in which all faculty, staff, and students can perform their roles at the highest level of quality and professional fulfillment.

Strategies for attaining the following goals are detailed in the strategic plan, and implementation was well under way in 2005:

- Maintain the strength of our core undergraduate and graduate professional programs by maintaining and redirecting faculty strengths to ensure that we sustain the capacity to address the full breadth of our disciplines and to focus on key natural resources issues.
- Enhance the identity of our School, both within the university and to external stakeholders, as a key provider of educational, research, and outreach programs addressing the full range of environmental issues related to the conservation and management of ecosystems and the renewable natural resources they provide.
- Increase the number, quality, and diversity of our enrollments through a proactive marketing strategy based on (1) providing personal interaction with potential students and their parents, (2) providing high-quality advising and placement services for enrolled students, and (3) more effectively using various marketing ap-

proaches and media, including the internet, printed material, closer coordination with the university's Division of Undergraduate Studies advisors, continued cooperation with related two-year programs at Mont Alto, Dubois, and Penn College, and other targeted face-to-face recruiting activities.

- Strengthen, renew, and expand our relationships with the School's stakeholders, including public natural resources agencies, nongovernment organizations, industry, natural resource professionals, forest landowners, community leaders, graduates of the School, and the public.
- Complete a smooth transition into the new Forest Resources Building and capitalize on this opportunity to strengthen, expand, and integrate our programs in a modern and more functional facility.

The future of Penn State's School of Forest Resources is full of promise, despite challenges that arise from time to time. Our students are bright, self-confidant, and brimming with enthusiasm. Our talented faculty and staff are among the best in the nation. The programs of instruction, research, and outreach are well conceived, skillfully directed, and functioning smoothly. Facilities in the new building are adorned with the warmth and beauty of native hardwoods and furnished with state-of-the-art equipment. Various kinds of outdoor laboratories are readily accessible. College and university administrators have been increasingly supportive in recent years and have gained a greater appreciation of our fields of endeavor.

Among the accomplishments of our alumni are some that are truly amazing, and more are on the way. Donors have greatly enhanced the new Forest Resources Building and our educational programs. Helpful critiques and advice from our alumni group and the School's advisory board should keep us on the right track. So it is not unrealistic to have great expectations for the future of our School and alumni, hopefully exceeding even the achievements of the past. Surely they will keep us Penn State proud!

APPENDICES

Appendix A-1. Faculty of the Department of Forestry (1907–1954), School of Forestry (1954–1965), and School of Forest Resources (1965–present) at Penn State. (Adjunct faculty are not included; some, such as members of the fish and wildlife research unit, have been very active in the School, whereas others have been less involved. Nor are faculty in other departments, such as entomology and plant pathology, who traditionally have taught some of the required professional courses, included here.)

Faculty	Professorial Titles	Years Employed
Marc D. Abrams	Forest Ecology and Physiology	1987–present
Roy D. Adams	Wood Products	1995–1999
C. R. Anderson	Forestry	1914–1922
Robert G. Anthony	Wildlife Management	1972–1977
Hugh P. Baker	Forestry	1907–1912
Henry I. Baldwin	Forestry	1932–1933
Robert C. Baldwin	Wood Science and Technology	1968–1995
Ronald A. Bartoo	Forestry Research, Forestry	1937–1968
Melvin J. Baughman	Forest Resources Extension	1981–1982
Francis C. Beall	Wood Science and Technology	1968–1975
Rudolph W. Becking	Forestry	1957–1958
Victor A. Beede	Forest Management	1931–1952
J. B. Berry	Forestry	1911–1913
Lowell Besley	Forestry	1934–1936
James Bethel	Forestry	1939–1941
Paul R. Blankenhorn	Wood Technology	1975–present
Robert S. Bond	Forest Sciences	1977–1987
F. Yates Borden	Forestry	1963–1977
Todd W. Bowersox	Silviculture	1968–2004
William C. Bramble	Forestry	1937–1958
Margaret Brittingham	Wildlife Resources	1988–present
Robert P. Brooks	Wildlife Technology, Wildlife and Wetlands	1980–2003

Faculty	Professorial Titles	Years Employed
Nicole Robitaille Brown	Wood Chemistry	2003–present
William R. Byrnes	Forestry	1950–1962
Richard J. Campana	Forestry	1947–1947
Robert H. Carey	Forest Mapping	1936–1937
John Carlson	Molecular Genetics	1997–present
Hunter Carrick	Aquatic Biology	2001–present
R. R. Chaffee	Forestry	1911–1914
Henry H. Chisman	Forestry	1935–1976
W. D. Clark	Forestry	1909–1912
H. Norton Cope	Forestry	1929–1959
John R. Daugherty	Environmental Resources Management	1976–1982
Oscar M. Davenport	Forestry	1933–1935
Arthur A. Davis	Forestry and Environmental Resource Conservation	1984–1987
Paul B. Davis	Forestry	1930–1931
Joshua L. Deen	Silviculture	1933–1938
Dwight B. Demeritt	Forestry	1928–1931
Max Dercum	Forestry	1935–1942
David R. DeWalle	Forest Hydrology	1969–present
Peter E. Dress	Forestry and Statistics	1958–1972
W. G. Edwards	Botany and Forestry, Lumbering	1914–1948
Tage L. Elers	Wood Utilization	1964–1968
William F. Elmendorf	Urban and Community Forestry	1991–present
Stephen E. Fairweather	Forest Resources Management	1984–1993
Edward P. Farrand	Forest Resources Extension	1951–1978
John A. Ferguson	Forestry	1908–1911, 1913–1938
Bernhard Eduard Fernow	Forestry	1906–1907
C. Paola Ferreri	Fisheries Management	1995–present
James C. Finley	Forest Resources Extension	1975–present
Peter W. Fletcher	Forestry	1959–1977

.Faculty	Professorial Titles	Years Employed
Walter U. Garstka	Forestry	1930–1933
Charles G. Geltz	Forestry	1929–1930
John L. George	Wildlife Management	1963–1981
Henry D. Gerhold	Forestry, Forest Genetics	1956–present
Samuel F. Gingrich	Forestry	1951–1957
Caren E. Glotfelty	Forestry and Environmental Resource Conservation	1995–2000
Maurice K. Goddard	Forestry	1935–1955
James R. Grace	Forest Resources Extension	1983–1987
George R. Green	Forestry, Wood Utilization	1912–1924
Richard S. Grippo	Environmental Resource Management	1994–1995
P. J. Haler	Forestry	1921–1922
Betty J. Harper	Natural Resources	1999–2004
George W. Harvey	Forestry	1935–1938
Merwin W. Humphrey	Forestry	1937–1964
Russell J. Hutnik	Forestry, Forest Ecology	1956–1986
Alan L. Irwin	Forestry	1938–1939
Michael Jacobson	Forest Resources	1999–present
Lee M. James	Forestry	1937–1938
Rudolph J. Janecek	Forestry	1937–1938
John J. Janowiak	Forest Products, Wood Products Engineering	1989–present
Benjamin A. Jayne	Forestry and Environmental Resource Conservation	1988–1991
Walter W. Johnson	Forest Resources Extension	1973–1992
Stephen B. Jones	Forest Resources	1988–1997
Richard N. Jorgensen	Wood Technology	1949–1961
Margot Wilkinson Kaye	Forest Resources	2005–present
George M. Kelly	Wildlife Ecology	1976–1983
Brian M. Kent	Forestry	1969–1975
Paul C. Kersavage	Wood Science and Technology	1965–1991
Ludwig V. Kline	Forestry	1929–1931
Peter Labosky	Wood Science and Technology	1979–2002
Richard Lee	Forest Hydrology	1966–1968

Faculty	Professorial Titles	Years Employed
L. M. Lindenmuth	Forestry	1922–1923
Harold J. Lutz	Forestry	1929–1933
James A. Lynch	Forest Hydrology	1977–2005
Warren B. Mac-Millan	Forestry	1924–1928
R.S. Maddox	Forestry	1913–1914
Ellen A. Manno	Forest Resources	1990–present
Eldred R. Martell	Forestry	1933–1935
Thomas H. Martin	Aquatic Ecology	1996–2001
Karl R. Mayer	Forestry	1931–1932
Frank J. Mazzotti	Environmental Resource Management	1982–1987
Larry H. McCormick	Forestry, Forest Resources	1969–2004
Marc E. McDill	Forest Resource Management	1993–1994, 1997–present
Arthur C. McIntyre	Forest Research	1927–1936
Robert E. McDer-mott	Forestry	1959–1983
Robert B. McKinstry	Forestry and Environmental Resource Conservation	2001–present
Rex E. Melton	Forestry	1947–1988
H. Arthur Meyer	Forestry	1937–1955
Judd H. Michael	Wood Products Business Management	2000–present
Bruce Michie	Forest Resources	1980–1986
Paul Mohai	Forest Biometrics	1979–1983
Raymond R. Moore	Forest Research	1936–1937
John Muench Jr.	Forestry	1956–1965
Wayne K. Murphey	Wood Utilization, Wood Technology	1960–1978
Jamie A. Murphy	Coordinator for Undergraduate Programs	2006–present
Wayne L. Myers	Forest Resources, Forest Biometrics	1978–present
William T. Nearn	Forestry, Wood Utilization	1947–1960
Harold S. Newins	Wood Utilization	1924–1929
Larry A. Nielsen	Natural Resources	1994–2001

Faculty	Professorial Titles	Years Employed
Newell A. Norton	Forest Products, Wood Utilization	1941–1968
Jack M. Payne	Forest Resources	1983–1985
Theodore R. Pickus	Forestry	1946–1947
Paul W. Post	Forestry	1956–1959
James R. Pratt	Aquatic Ecology	1987–1994
Joseph T. Radel	Forest Research	1936–1937
Terry D. Rader	Forest Resources Extension	1973–1988
Charles D. Ray	Wood Products Operations	2002–present
Jerry H. Reyburn	Forest Resources Extension, 4-H	1977–1981
Jack P. Royer	Natural Resources Policy	1987–1997
G. F. Rupp	Forestry	1922–1927
Gary San Julian	Wildlife Resources	1995–present
Sanford D. Schemnitz	Wildlife Management	1960–1962
Orvel A. Schmidt	Forestry	1948–1974
James W. Schneider	Natural Resources	1997–1999
William C. Sechrist	Forestry	1932–1934
John F. Senft	Wood Technology	1957–1959
William E. Sharpe	Forest Resources Extension, Forest Hydrology	1972–present
Robert D. Shipman	Forestry, Forest Ecology	1963–1990
Frederick C. Simmons	Forestry	1931–1932
Lawrence W. Smith	Forestry	1920–1921
Lloyd F. Smith	Forestry	1934–1935
Paul M. Smith	Forest Products Marketing	1991–present
Sanford Smith	Forest Resources	2001–present
William E. Sopper	Forestry, Forest Hydrology	1955–1994
Gilbert P. Spangler	Forestry	1938–1940
Thurman J. Starker	Forestry	1931–1932
Jay R. Stauffer Jr.	Fishery Science, Ichthyology	1984–present
Kim C. Steiner	Forest Resources, Forest Genetics, Forest Biology	1974–present
Donald D. Stevenson	Forestry, Forest Research	1935–1945
Gerald L. Storm	Wildlife Management	1972–1997

Faculty	Professorial Titles	Years Employed
Charles H. Strauss	Wood Products Extension, Forest Economics	1961–present
Alfred D. Sullivan	Forestry	1988–1993
Claude E. Sutton	Forestry	1927–1928
Kenneth J. Swisher	Forestry	1964–1991
Steven G. Thorne	Forestry and Environmental Resource Conservation	1991–1994
George T. Tsoumis	Wood Technology	1961–1965
Brian J. Turner	Forest Management	1969–1984
Ben W. Twight	Forest Recreation	1978–1995
Walter M. Tzilkowski	Wildlife Science	1978–present
James Wakeley	Wildlife Ecology	1976–1986
Grace A. Wang	Natural Resource Policy	1998–2002
Wilber W. Ward	Forestry, Silviculture	1948–1980
Richard F. Watt	Forestry	1947–1948
Wallace E. White	Botany, Wood Utilization	1929–1964
Harry V. Wiant	Forest Resource Management	2002–present
Robert G. Wingard	Wildlife Management Extension	1952–1983
Boyd M. Witherow	Forestry	1948–1954
Gene W. Wood	Wildlife Ecology	1967–1974
David P. Worley	Forestry	1947–1957
Richard H. Yahner	Wildlife Management, Wildlife Conservation	1981–present
Eric K. Zenner	Silviculture	2006–present
R. Kurt Ziebarth	Forestry	1931–1935
Edwin A. Ziegler	Forestry	1907–1908

Appendix A-2. Forestry Faculty at Mont Alto Associated with the School of Forest Resources (asterisks indicate faculty who were also employed at University Park or DuBois).

Faculty	Professorial Titles	Years Employed
G. Andrew Bartholomay*	Forestry	1997–1999
Elizabeth A. Brantley	Forestry	1997–present

Faculty	Professorial Titles	Years Employed
Henry H. Chisman*	Forestry	1935–1976
H. Norton Cope*	Forestry	1929–1959
Phillip J. Craul	Forestry	1959–1960
Robert W. Douglass	Forestry	1963–1975
James A. Hale	Forest Resources	1974–1996
Craig T. Houghton	Forestry	1993–present
Nick B. Hunter	Forestry	1974–1985
Robert W. Lang	Forestry	1955–1962
Peter Linehan	Forestry	2000–present
B. John Losensky	Forestry	1960–1961
Rex E. Melton*	Forestry	1947–1988
Harry L. Mosher	Forestry	1963–1988
John Muench Jr.*	Forestry	1956–1965
William H. Pfeiffer	Forestry	1929–1966
Otto W. Pflueger	Forestry	1929–1951
Paul Rung	Forestry	1974–1983
Sanford D. Schemnitz*	Forestry	1960–1961
William E. Sopper*	Forestry	1955–1994
Kenneth J. Swisher	Forestry	1964–1997
Wilber W. Ward*	Forestry	1948–1980

Appendix A-3. Wildlife Faculty at DuBois Associated with the School of Forest Resources (asterisks denote faculty who were also employed at Mont Alto or University Park).

Faculty	Professorial Titles	Years Employed
Timothy R. Baker	Forestry	1996–2003
G. Andrew Bartholomay*	Forestry	2002–present
William Bauer	Wildlife Technology	1978–1982
Robert P. Brooks*	Wildlife Technology, Wildlife and Wetlands (at University Park)	1980–2003
J. Christopher Haney	Wildlife Technology	1992–1995
H. Glenn Hughes	Wildlife Technology	1982–1995
Joseph W. Hummer	Wildlife Technology	1974–present
Michael J. Lacki	Wildlife Technology	1986–1990

Faculty	Professorial Titles	Years Employed
Keely Tolley Roen	Wildlife Technology	2001–present
Charles P. Schaadt	Wildlife Technology	1990–present
John Skeen	Wildlife Technology	1974–1979
H. Lee Stribling	Wildlife Technology	1983–1985
Sherwood S. Stutz	Wildlife Technology	1970–1988
Arthur Lee Tibbs	Wildlife Technology	1971–1974
David D. Wanless	Wildlife Technology	1972–1976
Gary W. Witmer	Wildlife Technology	1988–1990

Appendix B-1. Undergraduate Degrees Granted Annually (some of the data are uncertain, as discrepancies, particularly in the two-year graduates, could not be verified).

Pennsylvania State University

	Associate Degrees				Baccalaureate Degrees		
	Mont Alto Academy		For.	Wildl.	Forestry/	Wood Ut./	Wildl./
Year	Forestry	Vocational	Tech.	Tech.	For. Sci.	Sci./Prod.	Fisheres
1906	7						
1907	4						
1908	7						
1909	13				4		
1910	8				7		
1911	6				10		
1912	10				23		
1913	10				28		
1914	10				23		
1915	4				15		
1916	12				11		
1917	8				9		
1918	5				6		
1919	7				4		
1920	6				8		
1921	13				5		
1922	10	5			5		
1923	0				19		

	Associate Degrees				Baccalaureate Degrees		
	Mont Alto Academy		For.	Wildl.	Forestry/	Wood Ut./	Wildl./
Year	Forestry	Vocational	Tech.	Tech.	For. Sci.	Sci./Prod.	Fisheres
1924	10				7		
1925	15	3			19		
1926	17	3			16		
1927	20				4		
1928	28	1			29		
1929	13				17		
1930		4			14		
1931		5			19		
1932		9			23		
1933		9			27		
1934		14			22		
1935		12			20		
1936		12			34		
1937		9			59		
1938		11			85		
1939		11			91		
1940		14			89		
1941		4			73		
1942		8			75		
1943		4			29		
1944					6		
1945					3		
1946					13		
1947					26		
1948					45	9	
1949					64	5	
1950					105	16	
1951					81	13	
1952					62	12	
1953					67	1	
1954					51	3	
1955					48	2	
1956					39	6	
1957					38	5	
1958					60	8	

	Associate Degrees				Baccalaureate Degrees		
	Mont Alto Academy		For.	Wildl.	Forestry/	Wood Ut./	Wildl./
Year	Forestry	Vocational	Tech.	Tech.	For. Sci.	Sci./Prod.	Fisheres
1959					49	11	
1960					65	2	
1961					70	9	
1962					53	5	
1963					54	8	
1964					64	2	
1965			15		52	9	
1966			9		43	7	
1967			18		58	8	
1968			39		52	3	
1969			36		80	3	
1970			33		58	7	
1971			38		64	3	
1972			57	17	61	13	
1973			55	24	77	8	
1974			39	20	79	8	
1975			51	39	99	6	
1976			40	46	89	11	
1977			43	46	137	15	
1978			34	33	119	28	
1979			42	41	104	26	
1980			29	38	95	30	
1981			32	32	49	19	
1982			35	45	78	31	
1983			53	31	43	18	2
1984			12	23	42	11	5
1985			4	14	22	14	17
1986			6	3	32	7	27
1987			1	0	17	6	32
1988			6	24	20	8	28
1989			6	14	16	5	27
1990			16	19	16	5	32
1991			14	12	15	5	26
1992			10	19	28	7	30
1993			15	23	15	2	44

	Associate Degrees				Baccalaureate Degrees		
	Mont Alto Academy		For.	Wildl.	Forestry/	Wood Ut./	Wildl./
Year	Forestry	Vocational	Tech.	Tech.	For. Sci.	Sci./Prod.	Fisheres
1994			23	2	25	4	42
1995			21	23	30	6	42
1996			19	25	19	3	51
1997			21	21	37	15	55
1998			15	25	28	16	54
1999			27	30	46	15	52
2000			17	16	39	15	71
2001			14	24	47	12	59
2002			19	29	46	7	43
2003			22	26	43	8	49
2004			16	25	33	13	31
2005			20	27	30	9	42

Appendix B-2. Graduate Degrees Granted in Forestry, Forest Resources, Wildlife Management, and Wildlife and Fisheries Science

Year	M.S.	M.F.	M.F.R.	M.Agr.	Ph.D.
1913	2				
1917	1				
1929	2				
1931	2				
1933	2				
1939	1				
1941	2				
1942	2				
1943	1				
1945		1			
1946		3			
1947		4			
1948	2	6			
1949	3	2			
1950	1	4			
1951	6	7			

Year	M.S.	M.F.	M.F.R.	M.Agr.	Ph.D.
1952	6	4			
1953	1	2			
1954	3	4			
1955	2	3			
1956	1	6			
1957	3	1			
1958	1	2			
1959	6	5			
1960	5	3			
1961	11	1			
1962	11	1			
1963	2	1			
1964	12	4			
1965	5	3			
1966	7	1			
1967	8	2			
1968	14	1			
1969	16	4			
1970	9	2			
1971	11				
1972	15	2			
1973	13				1
1974	17				1
1975	12				2
1976	12	1	1		5
1977	11				2
1978	19				5
1979	20		1		1
1980	7		2	1	2
1981	15		1		1
1982	19		1		2
1983	17		1		2
1984	18		1		5
1985	16		1		1
1986	9		1		2
1987	16				5
1988	10		2		1

Year	M.S.	M.F.	M.F.R.	M.Agr.	Ph.D.
1989	7				2
1990	8				5
1991	7		3		
1992	4		1		3
1993	12		2		3
1994	9				3
1995	14		2		8
1996	12		1		5
1997	14		1		4
1998	6		1	1	
1999	6		1		5
2000	18				4
2001	8		3		4
2002	9		3		4
2003	13		2		4
2004	11				4
2005	14		2		5

REFERENCES

Anderson, C. R. 1931. Ten years' forestry extension work in Pennsylvania. *Journal of Forestry* 29 (1): 100–104.

Aughanbaugh, J. E. 1953. Forty years research progress in education. *Pennsylvania Forests* 38 (4): 102–4.

Bartoo, R. A. 1967. Accomplishments of the past decade. *Pennsylvania Forests* 57 (2): 30–34.

Beede, V. A. 1937. Proposed forestry building for the Penna. State College. *Forest Leaves* 27 (4): 3, 16.

———. 1941. The Pennsylvania State Forest School. *Forest Leaves* 31 (5): 3, 12–14.

Bezilla, M. 1987. *The College of Agriculture at Penn State.* University Park: Pennsylvania State University Press.

Bramble, W. C. 1953. Landmarks in forestry research at Penn State. *Pennsylvania Forests* 38 (4): 100–101.

———. 1957. Fiftieth anniversary of Penn State–Mont Alto Forestry School feted. *Pennsylvania Forests* 37 (3): 66–69, 76.

Clepper, H. 1953. The Pennsylvania State Forest School. *Pennsylvania Forests* 38 (2): 28–31, 33–40.

———. 1954. The Pennsylvania State Forest School. *The Sylvan,* 7–12. University Park: Pennsylvania State University, Sylvan Department of Forestry.

———, ed. 1957. *Forestry education in Pennsylvania.* University Park: Pennsylvania State University, Mont Alto Forestry Alumni Association.

———. 1969. The Penn State–Mont Alto Forestry Alumni Association—An historical summary of its first three decades. *Pennsylvania Forests* 59 (2): 47–51.

Cope, H. N. 1954. The Pennsylvania State Forest School from 1929 to 1943. *Pennsylvania Forests* 38 (4): 98, 111.

Dana, S. T., and E. W. Johnson. 1963. *Forestry education in America today and tomorrow.* Washington, D.C.: Society of American Foresters.

DeCoster, L. A. 1995. *The legacy of Penn's Woods—A history of the Pennsylvania Bureau of Forestry.* Harrisburg: Pennsylvania Historical and

Museum Commission and the Pennsylvania Department of Conservation and Natural Resources.

Dercum, M. 1942. Forestry goes skiing. *Forest Leaves* 32 (4): 5–7.

Edwards, W. G. 1963. Professor John Arden Ferguson, Penn State's "Fergie," dies at 90. *Pennsylvania Forests* 53 (4): 54.

Farrand, E. P. 1964. Pennsylvania forestry extension. *Pennsylvania Forests* 54 (4): 76, 80.

Ferguson, J. A. 1914. A forest arboretum for the Pennsylvania State College. *Forest Leaves* 14 (7): 99.

———. 1931. Plan of forestry education in the Pennsylvania State Forest School. *Forest Leaves* 23 (4): 57–58.

———. 1937. Development of the Pennsylvania State Forest School at State College. *Forest Leaves* 27 (1): 5–6.

———. 1952. Forestry education at Penn State. University Park: Pennsylvania State University, Paterno Library, Special Collections.

Fernow, B. E. 1913. A brief history of forestry in Europe, the United States, and other countries. 3d ed. Toronto: Toronto University Press, and Washington, D.C.: American Forestry Association.

Finley, J. C. 1998. Extension's role: Ensuring sustainable forestry on private forests in the northeastern United States. In *Extension forestry: Bridging the gap between research and application*, ed. J. E. Johnson, 145–58. Blacksburg: Virginia Polytechnic Institute and State University, College of Forestry and Wildlife Resources.

Finley, J. C., and K. C. Steiner, eds. 1996. *Proceedings of the first biennial conference on university education in natural resources.* Bethesda, Md.: Society of American Foresters.

Fletcher, S. W. 1955. *Pennsylvania agriculture and country life: 1840–1940.* Harrisburg: Pennsylvania Historical and Museum Commission.

Forestry Organization Consolidation Operation. 1930–35. University Park: Pennsylvania State University Archives, Paterno Library, Special Collections, AX/PSUA/04812.

Goddard, M. K. 1953. The teaching of forestry at Penn State. *Pennsylvania Forests* 38 (4): 92–94, 114.

Graves, H. S., et al. 1912. Standardization of instruction in forestry, Report of the Committee of the Conference of Forest Schools. *Forestry Quarterly* 10: 341–94.

Hocking, J. M., ed. 2003. *Centennial voices, the spirit of Mont Alto, a continuing story.* Mont Alto: Penn State–Mont Alto.

Illick, J. S. 1925. *Pennsylvania trees*. Bulletin 11, 5th ed. Harrisburg: Pennsylvania Department of Forests and Waters.

———. 1953. I remember. *Pennsylvania Forests* 38 (2): 46.

Lickel, C. R. 1950. Integrated problems of recreation and education in Pennsylvania State Parks. Master's thesis, Pennsylvania State University, Horticulture Department.

Linehan, P. E. 2005. Strategies for forestry success: Examples from the early years of the Pennsylvania Forestry Association. *Journal of Forestry* 103 (5): 224–29.

Luttringer, L. A., Jr. 1938. The "last raft." *Forest Leaves* 28 (4): 7–12, 16.

Maass, E. A. 2003. *Forestry pioneer: The life of Joseph Trimble Rothrock*. Mechanicsburg: Pennsylvania Forestry Association.

MacCleery, D. W. 2002. *American forests: A history of resiliency and recovery*. Durham, N.C.: Forest History Society.

Manno, E. A., K. C. Steiner, and R. A. Day. 2002. Ralph E. Brock and the State Forest Academy at Mont Alto, Pennsylvania. *Forest History Today* (fall): 12–19.

Mickalitis, A. B. 1968. The state foresters of Pennsylvania. *Pennsylvania Forests* 58 (1): 31–32.

Morrison, E. 2000. *A walk on the downhill side of the log: The life of Maurice K. Goddard*. Mechanicsburg: Pennsylvania Forestry Association.

Morton, J. N. 1957. Memorials dedicated at Penn State. *Pennsylvania Forests* 37 (4): 84–85, 95.

Murphey, F. T. 1936. Forestry teaching by the Agricultural Extension Service. *Forest Leaves* 26 (3): 7–8, 16.

1930. Pennsylvania Forest Research Institute. *Forest Leaves* 22 (10): 152–53.

1925. Portable sawmill school at State College, Pa. *Forest Leaves* 20 (3): 34–35.

Rodgers, A. A., III. 1968. *Bernhard Eduard Fernow: A story of North American forestry*. New York: Hafner Publishing.

Rowland, H. B. 1946. A veteran forester retires. *Pennsylvania Forests and Waters* 1 (2): 30, 45.

Schnur, G. L. 1944. Lumber production in Pennsylvania. *Forest Leaves* 34 (4–5): 12–13.

1967. School of Forest Resources celebrates 60th anniversary. *Pennsylvania Forests* 57 (3): 89–92.

Simonds, W. W. 1953. The forestry extension program in Pennsylvania. *Pennsylvania Forests* 38 (4): 105–6.

Spector, R. 1990. *Family trees, Simpson's centennial story.* Seattle: Documentary Book Publishers.

Steiner, K. C., and T. W. Bowersox. 1987. Setting educational objectives for forestry curricula: What should forestry graduates know? *Journal of Forestry* 85 (12): 38–40.

Strauss, C. H., and E. A. Manno. 2000. Employment of Forest Resources baccalaureate graduates from Penn State: A 25-year review. Paper presented at the Third Biennial Conference on University Education in Natural Resources, University of Missouri at Columbia, March 25–28.

Thomas, E. H. 1985. *A history of the Pennsylvania State Forest School, 1903–1929.* Mont Alto: Pennsylvania State University, Pennsylvania State Forest Academy/School Founders Society.

Thorpe, R. R. 1997. *The crown jewel of Pennsylvania: The state forest system.* Harrisburg: Pennsylvania Department of Conservation and Natural Resources.

Ward, W. W. 1982. Forestry education at Penn State: 75th anniversary. *Pennsylvania Forests* 72 (4): 6–11.

Welch, B. G. 1900. A suggestion for a school of forestry. *Forest Leaves* 7 (11): 164–65.

Wirt, G. H. 1906. Pennsylvania's Forest Academy. *Forest Leaves* 10 (10): 153–57.

———. 1935. History of forestry education in Pennsylvania. *The Sylvan,* 14–20. University Park: Pennsylvania State University, Sylvan Department of Forestry.

———. 1953. The State Forest Academy. *Pennsylvania Forests* 38 (2): 43–45, 54, 57.

Zeigler, E. A. 1935. Practical forest research in Pennsylvania. *Forest Leaves* 25 (1): 52.

———. 1953. Mont Alto in early forestry education, 1903–1929. *Pennsylvania Forests* 38 (4): 95–97, 114–16.

INDEX

Gilbane Building Company, 67
Gipple, O. Ben, 164
Glatfelter Pulp Wood Company, 183, 243
Glattfelder, Calvin H., 163, 183–85
Glotfelty, Caren E., 56
Gnage, David C., 35
Goddard Chair. *See* Maurice K. Goddard
 Chair in Forestry and Environmental
 Resource Conservation
Goddard Forum. *See* Maurice K. Goddard
 Forums
Goddard, Maurice K., 32, 33, 35, 36–38, 43,
 62, 105, 108, 119, 176, 187, 191–94,
 215
Goddard Scholarship. *See* Maurice K. and
 Ethel C. Goddard Scholarship in For-
 estry
Goldenberg, David, 35
Good, John C., 70, 163, 215–16
Grace, James R., 145–46, 164
graduate assistantships and fellowships, 97
Graduate Center for Watershed Steward-
 ship, 123
graduate degrees, 36, 74, 75, 92, 93–95
graduate programs, multidisciplinary, 94
graduate student theses, 110–11
graduation rates. *See* School of Forest Re-
 sources, graduation rates
Graves, Henry S., 24, 239, 240
Gray, Asa, 11
Gray, John L., 163, 222–23
Green Acres Nursery, 71
Green, George R., 56, 91, 141
Greenbelt, 17
Greene Countrie Towne, 7
Gregersen, Hans M., 223–25
Griffith, Amy, 100

Haig, Irvine T., 31, 163
Hales, Donald C., 135
Hall, Albert G., 163
Hamilton College, 24
Haney, Glenn, 160
Harding, Joseph A., 64
Harrison, Terry, 160
Harvard University, 11, 78, 155, 186, 214,
 215, 234
Heintzleman, B. Frank, 163, 168–69
Hemlock Hall. *See* Forestry Building, orig-
 inal
Henning Building, Penn State, 67
Hess, Durell E., 163, 184, 185

Hetzel, Ralph Dorn, 30, 31, 32
Hill, Emily, 52
Hocking, Joan M., 59
Hofmann, Julius V., 6, 30
Honeywell Corporation, 129
Horst, Miles, 30
Hosler, Charles L., 72
Hough, B. F., 1
Howard Heinz Endowment, 94
Humboldt State University, 231, 236
Humphrey, Merwin W., 66, 102, 118, 217
Hutnik, Russell J., xv, 55, 57, 113

Ibberson Chair. *See* Joseph E. Ibberson
 Chair in Forest Resources Manage-
 ment, *and* Joseph E. Ibberson Chair in
 Urban and Community Forestry
Ibberson Conservation Area. *See* Joseph E.
 Ibberson Conservation Area
Ibberson Forestry Forum, 154, 156, 231
Ibberson, Joseph E., 37, 57, 108, 155, 156,
 163, 165, 169–70, 183, 193, 207, 227
Illick, Joseph S., 10, 20–22, 30, 34, 107, 164,
 221
Indiana Department of Natural Resources,
 38
Industrial Terminal Systems, 237
Institutes for the Environment, Penn State,
 54, 110
Integrative Biosciences graduate major, 94
InterAmerican Development Bank, 224
International Association of Fish and Wild-
 life Agencies, 213
International Association of Wood Anato-
 mists, 189
International Society of Arboriculture, 39,
 216, 219
International Standards Organization, 204
International Union for the Conservation of
 Nature and Natural Resources, 209,
 211
International Union of Forestry Research
 Organizations, 229
Iowa State College or University, 22, 77, 78,
 183
Irwin, Barb, 52

Jackson, Lyman, 31, 108
Jacobson, Michael, 112, 147–48
James, Lee M., 225–26
Janowiak, John J., 55, 127
Jarrett, Harold, 215

Masonite Corporation, 188
Massachusetts Department of Natural Resources, 44
Massachusetts Division of Fisheries and Wildlife, 213
Massachusetts Forestry Association, 35
Massachusetts Horticultural Society, 219
Massachusetts State College, 23
Master of Agriculture degree, 75
Master of Forest Resources degree, 74, 75, 92, 260–61
Master of Forestry degree, 36, 74, 92, 259–60
Master of Science degree, 74, 92, 259–61
Mastro, Victor C., 174–75
Maurice K. and Ethel C. Goddard Scholarship in Forestry, 215
Maurice K. Goddard Chair in Forestry and Environmental Resource Conservation, 44, 54, 56, 71, 95, 154, 155, 184, 185, 193, 223
Maurice K. Goddard Forums, 154, 155
MeadWestvaco, 179
Mell-Davies Lumber Company, 181
Melton, Rex E., xv, 33, 40, 42–44, 57, 64, 66, 154, 215
merger of Pennsylvania State Forest School with Pennsylvania State College, 2, 6, 26, 28, 29, 30, 31, 83
Merkle Laboratory, Penn State, 67
Metropolitan Tree Improvement Alliance, 120, 219
Meyer, H. Arthur, 64, 115–16, 189, 226–27
Michael, Judd H., 56, 127, 129–30
Michaux, André, 11
Michaux Forestry Lectures, 1, 11
Michigan Agricultural College, 26
Michigan State College or University, 2, 22, 47, 48, 87, 126, 200, 218, 225, 229
Michigan Technological University, 129, 210
Millington, Wayne, 137
Mississippi Forest Products Laboratory, 187
Mississippi State University, 46, 47
Missouri State Game Commission, 212
Mont Alto Academy, Mont Alto State Forest Academy. See Pennsylvania State Forest Academy
Mont Alto Alumni Association, 30
Mont Alto Arboretum, 44
Mont Alto campus. See Penn State Mont Alto campus

Montana Game and Fish Department, 209
Moore, Raymond R., 108
Morrison, Charles E., 235–36
Morrison, Ernest, 36
Mount Nittany, 2
Muench, John, Jr., 118
Municipal Tree Restoration Program, 137–38, 218
Murphey, Frank T., 142
Murphey, Wayne K., 32, 105, 118, 126, 227–28
Murphy, Jamie A., 55
Myers, Wayne L., 112, 117

Nagy and Webb, 177
Nancy and John Steimer Professor of Agricultural Sciences, 57, 115, 237
National Air and Space Administration, 117, 237
National Arbor Day Foundation, 46
National Association of Forestry Students' Wives, 105
National Association of Professional Forestry Schools and Colleges, 21, 45, 46, 87, 229
National Association of State Foresters, 176
National Association of State Universities and Land-Grant Colleges, 46
National Association of University Fisheries and Wildlife Programs, 6
National Atmospheric Deposition Program, 123
National Audubon Society, 212
National Department of Forestry, Mexico, 226
National Forest Products Association, 118
National Lumber Manufacturers Association, 183
National Park Service. See U.S. National Park Service
National Parks and Conservation Association, 208
National Research Council, 199
National Rifle Association, 176
National Science Foundation, 229, 236
Natural Resources Council, 221
Natural Resources Graduate Student Organization, 106
Natural Resources Management major, 87–88
Nature Conservancy, 110, 170, 176

Nearn, William T., 89, 125–26, 181, 186–88, 188
Nelson, James C., 146, 164
New Mexico Institute of Mining and Technology, 129
New York Forestry Association, 35
New York State College of Environmental Science and Forestry, 21, 23, 31, 44, 186, 214, 230
New York State College of Forestry, Cornell, 22
Newins, Harold S., 20, 103
Newins–Ziegler Hall, 20
Nielsen, Larry A., 33, 47–48, 55
Nittany Lion, 2, 157–58
Nittany Lion Inn, 2
Nixon, Richard, 192
North American Wildlife Technology Association, 77
North Carolina Forestry Association, 229
North Carolina State College or University, 6, 30, 46, 47, 48, 87, 189, 222, 229
Northeast Forestry Research Advisory Council, 42
Northeastern Forest Experiment Station. See USDA Northeastern Forest Experiment Station
Northeastern Loggers Association, 184
Northern Arizona University, 47, 87
Norton, Gale, 213
Norton, Newell A., 32, 56, 89, 118, 126, 127, 181, 188, 190
nurseries, 2, 61, 167, 188
Nutter & Associates, 201
Nutter, Wade L., 199–201

Office for Naval Research, 129
Office for Remote Sensing and Spatial Information Resources, 117
Office for Remote Sensing of Earth Resources, 117
Office of Remote Sensing and Ecological Research, 116
Ohio Agricultural Experiment Station, 227
Old Antarctic Explorers Association, 236
Old Botany, 2
Old Green Shack, See Forestry Building, original
Old Main, Penn State, 2, 5
Oliver, John, 139
Omicron Delta Epsilon, 50
Operations Research graduate major, 94

Oplinger, Arthur J., 183, 184, 185
Oregon Small Woodlands Association, 171
Oregon State University, 103, 186
Organization for Economic Cooperation and Development, 224
Outstanding Alumni Award, 39, 167, 170, 171, 172, 197, 216, 218, 219, 229
Outstanding Forestry Senior Award, 103
Outstanding Recent Alumni Award, 210
Outstanding Service to Forestry Award, 167
Ozanne, Lucie K., 100

P. H. Glatfelter Company, 183, 184
Pacific Logging Congress, 183
Palpant, Edgar H., 51
Paterno, Joe, 165
Pattee Library, Penn State, 15, 53
Pea-green Shack. See Forestry Building, original
Pell, Eva, 238
Penn Glenn Oil Company, 237
Penn Nursery, 61, 188
Penn State Alumni Association, 30, 100, 160, 172, 177, 204, 205, 238
Penn State Alumni Fellow, 173, 206
Penn State DuBois campus, 34, 54, 59, 67, 77, 92
Penn State Forester, 102
Penn State Forestry Society, 49
Penn State Mont Alto campus, 34, 35, 36, 41, 54, 59, 67, 74, 77
Penn State Mont Alto Centennial Fellows Award. See Centennial Fellows Award of Penn State Mont Alto
Penn State Mont Alto Constituent Society, 215
Penn State Mont Alto Executive Officers, 35
Penn State–Mont Alto Forestry Alumni Association, 31, 38, 159, 160, 220. See also School of Forest Resources Alumni Group
Penn, William, 7
Penn-York Lumbermen's Club, 71, 180
Pennsylvania Acid Deposition Network, 123
Pennsylvania Agricultural College, 11
Pennsylvania Association of Conservation District Directors, 218
Pennsylvania Council of Professional Foresters, 172, 177
Pennsylvania Department of Agriculture, 26, 129
Pennsylvania Department of Highways, 237

ABOUT THE AUTHOR

Henry D. Gerhold, Professor of Forest Genetics, has been a faculty member in the School of Forest Resources since 1956. He has produced a large number of scientific and popular articles, many of them written jointly with his graduate students. He is best known for his books *Breeding Pest-Resistant Trees* (1966), *Landscape Tree Factsheets* (2001), and *Our Heritage of Community Trees* (2002), and for two chapters in *Handbook of Urban and Community Forestry in the Northeast* (2006).